HERNANDO DE SOTO AND PROPERTY IN A MARKET ECONOMY

Law, Property and Society

Series Editor:
Robin Paul Malloy

The Law, Property and Society series examines property in terms of its ability to foster democratic forms of governance, and to advance social justice. The series explores the legal infrastructure of property in broad terms, encompassing concerns for real, personal, intangible, intellectual and cultural property, as well as looking at property related financial markets. The series is edited by Robin Paul Malloy, and book proposals are welcome from all interested authors.

Robin Paul Malloy is E.I. White Chair and Distinguished Professor of Law at Syracuse University College of Law, USA. He is Director of the Center on Property, Citizenship, and Social Entrepreneurism. He is also Professor of Economics (by courtesy appointment) in the Maxwell School of Citizenship and Public Affairs, Syracuse University. Professor Malloy writes extensively on law and market theory and on real estate transactions and development. He has authored six books (one now in its third edition and another in its second edition), and edited five additional books. He has also written more than 25 scholarly articles, and contributed to 12 other books. His recent books include: Law and Market Economy (2000, in English and translated into Spanish and Chinese); Law in a Market Context (2004); and Real Estate Transactions 3rd (with James C. Smith, 2007).

Hernando de Soto and Property in a Market Economy

Edited by

D. BENJAMIN BARROS
Widener University School of Law, USA

ASHGATE

Published by
Ashgate Publishing Limited
Wey Court East
Union Road
Farnham
Surrey, GU9 7PT
England

Ashgate Publishing Company
Suite 420
101 Cherry Street
Burlington
VT 05401-4405
USA

www.ashgate.com

British Library Cataloguing in Publication Data
Hernando de Soto and property in a market economy. -- (Law, property and society)
1. Soto, Hernando de, 1941- 2. Capitalism. 3. Property.
4. Right of property--Economic aspects. 5. Law and economics.
I. Series II. Barros, D. Benjamin.
346'.04-dc22

Library of Congress Cataloging-in-Publication Data
Hernando de Soto and property in a market economy / edited by D. Benjamin Barros.
p. cm. -- (Law, property and society)
Includes bibliographical references and index.
ISBN 978-0-7546-7705-5 -- ISBN 978-0-7546-9410-6
1. Right of property. 2. Law and economic development. 3. Land titles--Economic aspects. 4. Soto, Hernando de, 1941- I. Barros, D. Benjamin.

K721.5.H485 2009
346.04--dc22

2009042942

ISBN 9780754677055 (hbk)
ISBN 9780754694106 (ebk)

Mixed Sources
Product group from well-managed forests and other controlled sources
www.fsc.org Cert no. SGS-COC-2482
© 1996 Forest Stewardship Council
FSC

Printed and bound in Great Britain by
TJ International Ltd, Padstow, Cornwall

Contents

Notes on the Contributors

Gregory S. Alexander is the A. Robert Noll Professor of Law at Cornell Law School. His books include *The Global Debate Over Constitutional Property: Lessons For American Takings Jurisprudence* (The University of Chicago Press, 2006), *Commodity & Propriety: The Competing Visions Of Property In American Legal Thought* (The University of Chicago Press, 1997), and *A Fourth Way? Privatization, Property, And The Emergence Of New Market Economies* (with Grazyna Skapska) (Routledge, 1993).

D. Benjamin Barros is Associate Professor of Law at the Widener University School of Law. He writes principally on property law and theory, and is past-Chair of the Property Section of the Association of American Law Schools.

Denis J. Brion is Professor of Law at the Washington & Lee University School of Law. He writes on a wide-range of subjects, including property, law and economics, and land use regulation. He is the author of *Essential Industry and the NIMBY Phenomenon* (Quorum Books, 1991).

Alfred L. Brophy is the Reef C. Ivey II professor of law at the University of North Carolina. He is the author of *Reconstructing the Dreamland: The Tulsa Riot of 1921* (Oxford University Press, 2002) and *Reparations Pro and Con* (Oxford University Press, 2006) and he is completing a study of jurisprudence in the old South, tentatively titled *University, Court, and Slave.*

Nestor M. Davidson is Associate Professor of Law at the University of Colorado School of Law. His scholarship focuses on property, land use, affordable housing, local government law, and sustainability. He is the co-editor (with Robin Paul Malloy) of *Affordable Housing and Public-Private Partnerships* (Ashgate, 2009).

Rashmi Dyal-Chand is Professor of Law at Northeastern University School of Law. She writes on issues including property, microcredit, and financial markets. She is the editor of the *Human Rights and the Global Economy Journal* on the Social Science Research Network.

Nicole Stelle Garnett is Professor of Law at the University of Notre Dame. Her primary research interests include property, land use, local government law, and education reform. Her work, prior to joining the Notre Dame faculty, on behalf of low-income entrepreneurs as a public interest attorney is reflected in her contribution to this book. She is the author of *Ordering the City: Land Use, Policing and the Restoration of Urban America* (Yale University Press, 2009).

Larissa Katz is Assistant Professor in the Faculty of Law at Queen's University in Ontario. She has published widely on property theory and related topics.

Juliet M. Moringiello is Professor of Law at Widener University School of Law. She writes in the areas of bankruptcy, commercial law, electronic commerce, and property. She is a member of the Editorial Board of *The Business Lawyer* and *Business Law Today*, and is editor of *The Business Lawyer*'s annual survey of Cyberspace Law.

Eduardo M. Peñalver is Professor of Law at Cornell Law School. His research interests include property and land use. He is the co-author (with Sonia Katyal) of *Property Outlaws* (Yale University Press, 2010).

Carol M. Rose is the Lohse Chair in Water and Natural Resources at the University of Arizona James E. Rogers College of Law and G.B. Tweedy Professor of Law and Organization (emeritus) at Yale University. Her scholarly interests include property, natural resources, and environmental law. She is the author of *Property and Persuasion: Essays on the History, Theory, and Rhetoric of Ownership* (Westview Press, 1994). Professor Rose is a member of the American Academy of Arts and Sciences.

Ezra Rosser is Associate Professor of Law at the American University Washington College of Law. He teaches and writes in housing law, American Indian law, property, and poverty law. He is Chair of the Association of American Law School's Poverty Law Section.

In Memoriam
Barbara L. Barros
1950–2009

Introduction

D. Benjamin Barros

The Peruvian economist Hernando de Soto is one of the world's leading public intellectuals. His books *The Mystery of Capital* and *The Other Path* have been tremendously influential in shaping discussions about development economics and related fields throughout the world. He has been included on *Time*'s list of the 100 most influential people in the world, and has received praise from politicians from across the political spectrum. His work also has been controversial, and some of his arguments have received sustained criticism.

In his work in general, and in *The Mystery of Capital* in particular, de Soto makes two related arguments about property. First, he argues that the institution of property is necessary to the proper functioning of a market economy. De Soto's argument is supported by a detailed analysis of the role that property serves in making a capitalist economy work. In Chapter 3 of *The Mystery of Capital*, de Soto identifies six tasks that a formal system of property performs: (1) property fixes the economic potential of assets; (2) it integrates dispersed information into one system; (3) it makes people accountable; (4) it makes assets fungible; (5) it networks people; and (6) it protects transactions.

Second, de Soto argues that bringing the assets held by the world's poor into formal property systems will lead to a radical improvement in their wealth and wellbeing. De Soto observes that the poor often have assets—for example, the land they farm, the shanties they live in—but these assets are held informally. Because they are held outside of a formal property system, these assets are dead capital—they cannot easily be sold or used as security for a loan. Formalizing the poor's ownership of these assets, de Soto argues, will transform the assets into living capital that can be used to bring great improvement to their owners' lives. De Soto has acted on his theories, working through his Institute for Liberty and Democracy to pursue land titling programs.

Criticism of de Soto's work often centers on his apparent assertion that land titling is some sort of magic bullet for poverty. The results of empirical studies on the impact of land titling has been mixed, with some studies showing that formal ownership brings tangible, though modest, improvement in the owner's standard of living and access to capital.[1] In fairness to de Soto's critics, *The Mystery of*

1 *See, e.g.*, Sebastian Galiani & Ernesto Schargrodsky, *Property Rights for the Poor: Effects of Land Titling*, available at http://www.utdt.edu/Upload/CIF_wp/wpcif-062005.pdf; Erica Field & Maximo Torero, *Do Property Titles Increase Credit Access Among the*

Capital can be read as suggesting that bringing informally-owned property through a titling program will by itself lead to a radical increase in the wealth of the poorest members of society. In fairness to de Soto, however, he appears to agree that land titling alone will not be sufficient to bring the benefits of a market economy to the poor in developing countries. In an interview, de Soto said:

> I'm not saying . . . that other reforms aren't necessary. I'm simply saying that a property rights system is a principal reform, without which other reforms are difficult to manage. It's quite clear that property law alone does not resolve the other problems. But to me, what is also quite clear is that without property law, you will never be able to accomplish other reforms in a sustainable manner.[2]

As these comments suggest, it is important to distinguish between the two types of arguments that de Soto makes about property. De Soto's arguments that formal property systems are *necessary* to the proper functioning of a market economy receive little, if any criticism. In contrast, de Soto's apparent argument (the above quotation notwithstanding) that property formalization is *sufficient* to bring the benefits of a market economy to the poor has received sustained criticism.

Property lies at the heart of de Soto's ideas, and many property scholars closely follow de Soto's work. I know from personal experience that de Soto's ideas are a frequent topic of discussion at gatherings of property scholars. De Soto's ideas, however, have been strangely absent in legal scholarship about property. To be sure, de Soto has been cited occasionally by property scholars, but the discussion of his work within the legal academy has been minimal compared to the sustained attention that it has received in other arenas such as development economics. There thus has been a mismatch between the impact of de Soto on property scholars' thought and the discussion of his ideas in the work that those scholars produce.

This volume brings together contributions from eleven property scholars from the United States and Canada, taking an initial step in remedying the relative neglect of de Soto in property scholarship. The power and scope of de Soto's ideas are reflected in the range of topics covered in the chapters of this book. These chapters fall into four general categories.

First, the initial four chapters contain general critical analyses of de Soto's ideas about property. In Chapter 1, Eduardo M. Peñalver draws progressive lessons from de Soto's ideas. While de Soto has received praise from political figures across the political spectrum, his market-friendly ideas make him most easily identifiable with the political right. Peñalver suggests that this association

---

Urban Poor? Evidence from a Nationwide Titling Program, available at http://www.rwj.harvard.edu/papers/field/Field%20Do%20Property%20Titles%20Increase%20Credit....pdf.

2 Jeremy Clift, *Hearing the Dogs Bark*, Finance & Development, December 2003, at 11.

is misplaced by arguing that de Soto's positions should lead to a commitment to relative equality in resource distribution. Peñalver notes that de Soto has been critical of government policies that redistribute property from one interest group to another, but he argues that de Soto "by and large endorses the progressive notion that the state may properly redistribute wealth from the rich to the poor in order to assure that their basic needs (however defined) are satisfied."[3] This type of wealth redistribution, Peñalver argues, is necessary to maintain the stability and utility of formal property systems in both mature and developing market economies.

In Chapter 2, Carol M. Rose raises two groups of questions about de Soto's emphasis on land titling and property formalization. The first group of questions involves conflicts between title formalization, which often ratifies land invasions, and efforts to preserve land and other finite resources. The second group of questions asks whether de Soto's proposals about land titling would apply universally in all contexts. Rose suggests that de Soto's work, heavily influenced by the experiences of internal migrants in Peru, does not adequately engage in issues of resource preservation and might not easily translate out of its original Peruvian context. Rose also argues that consideration of these two groups of questions suggests important lessons for developed economies. One of these lessons is that the conflict between formalization and resource preservation highlights the need to protect a society's total wealth, not just the wealth reflected in private property rights.

In Chapter 3, Gregory S. Alexander argues that de Soto's account of why capitalism has worked in some countries but not others is incomplete because it neglects the role of culture in a country's economic performance. As Alexander notes, this neglect is intentional—de Soto has specifically rejected cultural explanations for economic differences between countries. Alexander argues that de Soto is wrong to reject the role of culture, and argues that capitalism has succeeded in countries with relatively egalitarian cultures but failed in countries with relatively hierarchical cultures. Many less-developed countries have what Alexander calls a culture of hierarchy, with high disparities of wealth and income, a small or non-existent middle class, limited social mobility, and customary systems of land ownership. The more-developed countries where capitalism has flourished have what Alexander calls a culture of propriety, where there is a robust middle class, a high degree of social mobility, a property ownership system that facilitates innovation and entrepreneurship, and a generally egalitarian political ideology. Simply expanding the reach of a formal property system in a country with a culture of hierarchy, Alexander suggests, will not be enough to allow capitalism to flourish.

De Soto devotes Chapter 5 of *The Mystery of Capital* to lessons to be learned from United States history. Alfred L. Brophy analyzes de Soto's use of U.S. history in Chapter 4 of this book. Brophy argues that de Soto is correct that the institution of property played an important role in the development of the United States, but that the lessons to be learned from U.S. history are far more complex than de

3 *Infra* at 14.

Soto suggests. Like Alexander, Brophy suggests that culture was as, or perhaps more, important than law in allowing capitalism to flourish in the United States. Drawing in part on reflections of property in American art and fiction, Brophy argues that the United States had, and has, a fundamentally capitalist culture. As a result, "a more complete picture is that both our law and our national character are capitalist."[4]

Second, the next two chapters discuss the possible dangers of land titling and other sudden introductions of property rights. In Chapter 5, Ezra Rosser examines de Soto's ideas about property formalization through the history of allotment of tribal property to Native Americans in the late nineteenth and early twentieth centuries. The transfer of tribal property to individual ownership was accompanied by pro-property arguments that are remarkably similar to those that feature in de Soto's work. The outcome of the allotment policy was disastrous for both the individuals and communities involved. The example of allotment therefore presents a cautionary tale about what can go wrong in a land-titling effort. Rosser notes that contemporary land titling efforts might be able to avoid the problems that plagued allotment, but he argues that the risks illustrated by allotment should be considered and addressed by de Soto and other modern advocates for land titling.

In Chapter 6, Rashmi Dyal-Chand uses the current financial crisis to raise further questions about the desirability of property formalization. Dyal-Chand argues that certain troubling patterns tend to emerge when new forms of property are introduced or when certain property rights are extended to poor or unsophisticated people who previously did not have access to them. Because of information asymmetries, the recipients of these newly-introduced property rights are often ignorant of their value. These new forms of property also are often accompanied by bubbles (followed by busts) in property values. The result may be financial meltdown leading not only to individual losses but also to system-wide loss of wealth. Dyal-Chand suggests that regulatory strategies are needed to avoid having the poor hurt by property formalization projects intended to help them.

Third, the following two chapters apply de Soto's ideas to issues in property theory. In Chapter 7, Nestor M. Davidson analyzes de Soto's argument that one of the most important roles that a property system serves is to gather information about an asset and to transmit that information at a distance. At a general level, de Soto's argument is clearly correct—property systems do, indeed, collect and transmit information. Davidson argues, however, that two potential problems may arise in translating the facts on the ground about an asset into the more general language of a property system. One problem is that a property system can only contain a finite portion of the information available about an asset. This subset of information, in turn, may be misleading, and may exclude many of the most relevant facts about the asset. Another problem is that the systems for transmitting information about property are not self-generating—they are typically created by

4 *Infra* at 60.

a state. As a result, these systems may reflect certain government-imposed choices about the conditions of property ownership.

In Chapter 8, Larissa Katz uses de Soto's work on the costs of informality to critically analyze the concept of anticommons, a very influential idea in contemporary property theory most associated with the work of Michael Heller. At its broadest, the concept of anticommons could encompass any scenario in which too many people control the use or disposition of an asset, resulting in that asset's underuse. Drawing on de Soto's discussion of the red tape that faces entrepreneurs in developing economies, Katz makes a distinction between underuse problems that arise when there are too many owners of an asset and underuse problems that arise from having too many people who have a say in the use of an asset. In the former category, the problems arise from facts about ownership; in the later, the problems arise from facts about who controls use. The two categories are not congruent because many non-owners (for example, government regulators or contract counterparties) may have a say about the use of an asset. Katz argues that the concept of anticommons should be limited to the former category, where asset underuse is the result of the ownership characteristics. Katz then argues that most problems of asset underuse fall outside of this narrow anticommons category, and are caused by problems with the distribution of private and public authority over the asset, rather than problems with the ownership of that asset.

Finally, the last three chapters apply de Soto's ideas to specific legal issues. In Chapter 9, Nicole Stelle Garnett considers the role of informality in urban transportation and street vending. These two areas of economic activity are at the center of de Soto's discussion of the burdens facing entrepreneurs in *The Other Path*. On the surface, de Soto's concern with mercantilist policies that inhibit innovation in less developed economies would seem not to apply in mature market economies like the United States, which are generally seen as being very open to innovation. Through examples drawn from American cities, Garnett shows that many of the same issues that de Soto encountered in countries like Peru also appear in countries like the United States. Garnett argues that urban transportation and street vending are amenable to mercantilist regulation because entrepreneurs operate in the public commons, making simple property solutions like titling untenable, and because informal entrepreneurial enterprises conflict with elite aesthetic images of good city life. Garnett concludes by suggesting that the continued presence of illegal transport and vending businesses in many U.S. cities emphasizes the need to draw on one of de Soto's important insights and focus on the costs required to bring a business into the formal legal economy.

In Chapter 10, Juliet M. Moringiello uses de Soto's analysis to critique the U.S. legal system's treatment of intangible assets. As de Soto explains in Chapter 3 of *The Mystery of Capital*, one important role of a property system is to collect and transmit information about an asset. Moringiello argues that while the U.S. legal system serves this function well for tangible assets, it does so much less effectively for intangible assets. Article 9 of the Uniform Commercial Code governs one type of interest in intangible assets, security interests in personal property. Moringiello argues that Article 9 fails to fulfill two of the important tasks that de Soto identifies for a property system—integrating dispersed information into one system and making assets fungible. These deficiencies in the legal system's treatment of intangible assets will become increasingly problematic, Moringiello suggests, as intangible assets become ever more central to the functioning of a mature market economy.

In Chapter 11, Denis J. Brion draws on de Soto's insights to criticize the broad use of eminent domain to promote economic development. The use of eminent domain for this purpose has received a great deal of public comment since the United States Supreme Court's controversial decision in *Kelo v. City of New London*.[5] The use of eminent domain for land assembly and the informal ownership of land present similar issues. If a parcel of property is divided among many owners, or if the parcel is held informally, then it may not be put to its highest and best use. The broad use of eminent domain, then, would appear to be consistent with de Soto's ideas about turning assets like land into the capital that allows a market economy to thrive. Brion uses welfare economics to argue, however, that the broad use of eminent domain counterintuitively removes land from the realm of efficient market exchange, and therefore reduces that land's effectiveness as capital. The result is that the broad use of eminent domain is likely lead to a long-term reduction in aggregate social welfare, even if it will lead to a short-term increase in wealth.

5 545 U.S. 469 (2005).

Chapter 1
The Costs of Regulation or the Consequences of Poverty? Progressive Lessons from de Soto

Eduardo M. Peñalver[1]

Titling is a hot topic in contemporary development circles. The World Bank's 2006 World Development Report, for example, touts the "potentially large benefits" that would result from formalizing title in both rural and urban lands.[2] And, since the 1980s, the Bank, along with a number of the other major international development agencies, has poured billions of dollars into titling projects in the hopes of improving the lives of some of the world's poorest human beings.[3] A great deal of the credit (or, depending on one's assessment of the merits of these programs, blame) for the explosion of titling programs lies with Hernando de Soto, whose books *The Other Path* and *The Mystery of Capital* aggressively and eloquently made the case for titling as a development strategy. De Soto's diagnosis, in a nutshell, is that underdevelopment is a result of "informality," to use his preferred term. By informality, de Soto means extralegal economic conduct, whether in the operation of a business, the construction of a house, or the occupation of a parcel of land. Widespread informality occurs when large numbers of people are excluded from participating in the market system.

Why does de Soto think that informality leads to underdevelopment? After all, he takes great pains to point out that the poor inhabitants of underdeveloped nations are not as destitute as they seem. Even landless squatters, who are living in homes they have built on land (state or private) that they do not own, have a great deal of wealth. Indeed, de Soto's most dramatic claim in *The Mystery of Capital* is that squatters have at their disposal \$9.34 trillion in real estate wealth. The problem, de Soto says, is that they "have houses but not titles."[4] And without titles, he argues,

---

1 Thanks to Larissa Katz for helpful comments and suggestions.

2 The World Bank, World Development Report 2006: Equity and Development (2005), available at http://www-wds.worldbank.org/servlet/WDSContentServer/WDSP/IB/2005/09/20/000112742_20050920110826/Rendered/PDF/322040World0Development0Report02006.pdf.

3 *See* Bernadette Atuahene, *Legal Title to Land as an Intervention Against Urban Poverty in Developing Nations*, 36 G.W. Int'l L. Rev. 1109, 1111 (2004).

4 Hernando de Soto, The Mystery of Capital: Why Capitalism Triumphs in the West and Fails Everywhere Else, 7 (2000) [hereinafter Mystery of Capital].

informal owners cannot put their assets to work as capital. "It is the unavailability of these essential representations," he argues, "that explains why people who have adapted every other Western invention, from the paper clip to the nuclear reactor, have not been able to produce sufficient capital to make their domestic capitalism work."[5] Without title to their homes, squatters cannot easily sell those homes or access formal credit markets that would enable them to leverage the value of their homes as collateral for loans that they might, for example, use as seed money for small businesses. De Soto's prescription is simple: to liberate the latent wealth that already exists among the poor, we must bring those operating in the "informal" economy into the formal economic system by, for example, granting squatters legal title to the land they occupy.

De Soto's embrace of markets and private property rights as his principal development strategy has earned him a great deal of affection from the political right, both in Latin America and the United States. *The Other Path* featured a foreword by conservative Peruvian politician and novelist Mario Vargas Llosa as well as cover praise from the first President Bush, Richard Nixon, and neoconservative Catholic theologian Michael Novak. Similarly, *The Mystery of Capital* attracted fawning comments by such leading conservatives as Margaret Thatcher, Milton Friedman, Jeanne Kirkpatrick, and William F. Buckley, Jr. Conversely, de Soto has frequently been on the receiving end of attacks from thinkers on the political left.[6] On one level, this line-up of praise and criticism is not very surprising. As Ray Bromley explains it, "[d]e Soto's advocacy of market forces, free trade, and privatization fits a classic right-wing prescription, as does his emphasis on entrepreneurship, technological innovation, and the inherent dynamism of the unplanned economy."[7]

Against this apparent consensus, and even to a certain extent against the thrust of de Soto's own writing, I will argue in this short paper that the political implications of de Soto's core ideas are actually far more ambiguous than might initially seem to be the case, and perhaps more than de Soto himself realizes. In the next section, I will argue that, despite the widespread tendency to understand de Soto's work as favoring traditionally conservative economic policies, we can draw more progressive lessons from it as well. In the third section, I will argue that de Soto's basic diagnosis brings to center stage the state's obligation to combat excessive inequality. In the concluding section, I will point toward some lessons this progressive reading of de Soto has to offer, even for those of us living and working in the developed world. Although de Soto employs a number of examples, including cases drawn from the world of landownership, transport, and street-vending, my principal focus throughout will be on his discussions of land.

---

5 Mystery of Capital, *supra* note 4, at 6–7.

6 Ray Bromley, *A New Path to Development? The Significance and Impact of Hernando de Soto's Ideas on Underdevelopment, Production, and Reproduction*, 66 Econ. Geography 328, 331 (1990).

7 *Id.*

The Conservative de Soto

The conservative, and in many ways the most natural, reading of de Soto's work understands his fundamental insight to be a profound skepticism of state intervention in the market. Viewed from this perspective, de Soto assigns primary responsibility for informality, and the poverty it enshrines, to the costs of wasteful state regulation. As Vargas Llosa puts it in his foreword to *The Other Path*, "[b]lack-marketeering is the masses' response to the system … which invents laws to frustrate the legitimate desires of the people to hold jobs and have a roof over their heads."[8] And if regulation is the root of the problem, then the solution for informality is the withdrawal of the state from economic intervention.

There is no denying that this powerfully anti-statist message is a crucial part of de Soto's self-understanding. Part II of *The Other Path* centers around a sustained critique of what de Soto (somewhat confusingly) calls the "mercantile" state. The mercantile state is characterized, de Soto argues, by wasteful regulation, a bloated bureaucracy, and endless cycles of rent-seeking and interest-group politicking. Thus, in discussing barriers to landownership, for example, de Soto goes into great detail about the bureaucratic hurdles that stand in the way of the legal acquisition of vacant state land. "[T]his procedure," de Soto observes, "takes 43 months (3 years and 7 months) and involves up to six different state departments, including the president of the Republic. … [T]he 43 months that it takes for adjudication are the result of 207 bureaucratic steps involving 48 different government offices. Each step takes about one working week."[9]

In addition to the anti-regulatory bent of many of his arguments, de Soto frequently condemns state-sponsored redistribution. Chapter Six of *The Other Path*, for example, is dedicated to a blistering condemnation of "the redistributive tradition" in Latin America.[10] "There appears to be a tradition among our country's lawmakers," de Soto argues, "of using the law to redistribute wealth rather than to help create it."[11] This redistributive tradition, he writes, "has created in Peru a society where almost all the country's vital forces have organized in political and economic groups, one of whose main aims is to influence government in order to obtain a redistribution which favors them or their members."[12] To summarize, then, the conservative reading of de Soto emphasizes wasteful regulation as the source of informality and opposes state-sponsored redistribution of resources in favor of policies that emphasize wealth creation.

---

8 Mario Vargas Llosa, *Foreword* to HERNANDO DE SOTO, THE OTHER PATH: THE INVISIBLE REVOLUTION IN THE THIRD WORLD [hereinafter OTHER PATH], xiii, xviii (Alfred J. McAdam, trans., 1989).

9 *Id.* at 136.

10 *Id.* at 189.

11 *Id.* at 189.

12 *Id.* at 190.

Taking de Soto Left

This conservative reading glosses over important assumptions and qualifications that seem to be at work (albeit at times well below the surface) within de Soto's analysis of the informal economy. Moreover, it relies on a mischaracterization of the position de Soto argues against in his admittedly confusing discussion of redistribution. At the end of the day, both de Soto's critique of the state's role in causing informality and his proposal for legal reform leave ample space for, and at times even seem to demand, state activism and redistribution in a way that should cause at least some discomfort for his conservative admirers.

Take, first, de Soto's explanation of informality in land tenure. In discussing the cause of land invasions, de Soto places the blame squarely on the state. "When it takes seven years and several thousand dollars to obtain land for housing, most people, regardless of their skills, education, and attitudes, will invade land and acquire it informally."[13] Although at first glance this passage seems to confirm that de Soto blames red tape for land informality, the specific legal mechanism de Soto is criticizing is a mechanism by which landless urban migrants can become titled owners of state land without purchasing it at the market price. The inefficiency at work in this explanation is not the inefficiency that results from the government regulating what people can do with resources that are already theirs; it is inefficiency in redistributing to the poor the resources they need.

But before the state can frustrate someone's desires to obtain land by making the process of acquiring state land bureaucratically difficult, it must be the case that the person is for some reason unable to purchase land in the private land market. As de Soto acknowledges, red tape does not prevent the Peruvian rich from operating within what he calls the "bell jar" of capitalism. In another part of the book, de Soto discusses the ease with which the wealthy can establish businesses, notwithstanding the hurdles faced by poor Peruvians. "[E]very major law firm I consulted," he writes, "assured me that setting up a formal business to access capital would take only a few days. I knew this was true for me and my lawyers, but I had a hunch it was not true for the majority of Peruvians."[14] Similarly, in the case of land acquisition, the bureaucratic obstacles on which de Soto focuses so much ire present no serious obstacle for the wealthy, who do not need to rely on the state's transfers because they can purchase land on the open market. Before it can possibly make sense to blame the state for informality, de Soto must rule out the possibility that it is *the distributive consequences of the market* that have excluded the poor from obtaining land.

There are two ways in which it might make sense to blame the state for informality in the private market for land. First, the state may bear responsibility for landlessness because it has not done enough to respond to the reality of the poor's lack of purchasing power in the private market for land. In discussing

---

13 Other Path, *supra* note 8, at 185.

14 Mystery of Capital, *supra* note 4, at 190–191.

the inefficiency of the state's process for turning over land to squatters, de Soto focuses on this source of state responsibility. This is not, however, the sort of state (in)action with which conservatives tend to be concerned.[15] The other way the state can interfere with the poor's acquisition of land is by enforcing regulations that have the effect of driving up the price of land (or other resources). Discussions of the cause of informal settlements in Latin America have, for example, focused on laws making it difficult or illegal for private landowners to subdivide land on the urban periphery, thereby creating an artificial scarcity in developable urban land that drives prices higher.[16] A parallel discussion has gone on within the North American legal academy of the ways in which laws like housing and building codes can make housing more expensive, possibly putting it out of reach of the poorest market participants.[17] Although some commentators lay the blame for this sort of price-exclusion at the feet of regulation as such, it is *always* the case that, when a regulation drives up the price of a good, making the good unaffordable for those at the bottom of the wealth distribution, we can treat the resulting exclusion as either a cost of the regulation itself or, alternatively, as a consequence of the distribution of wealth that reduces the poor's purchasing power.

Take the example of building codes. We can understand them as a sort of consumer protection statute that ensures buyers in the housing market that the construction of their home meets certain minimum standards, something that can be difficult to assess after the walls are up. The codes might also operate as an effort to prevent people at low ends of the housing market from opting to stretch their housing dollars by living in poorly built housing, both for paternalistic reasons and because their choice might have negative consequences for people in their care or for public health and safety. Whatever their purpose, it is highly likely that one of the consequences of building codes is to increase the price of housing, particularly at the lower end of the market, where builders might be more prone to use substandard building materials and methods. Will this increase in price push some poor people out of the market? Yes; as long as there are people who are stretched so thin financially that they cannot reallocate money from some other expense to pay for the increased cost of housing. Is this a reason not to favor the implementation of a building code? Many commentators simply assume so, but it is actually a difficult question.

Continuing with the example of building codes, the impact of the price increase on the poorest participants in the housing market due to regulation can be avoided

---

15 Informality can also occur among those who are not poor when regulations interfere with land uses that are so important to owners that they are willing to risk violating the law in order to engage in them or when regulations are poorly enforced. Because de Soto's focus is on informality among the very poor, I will focus primarily on the price mechanism discussed in the main text.

16 Mike Davis, Planet of Slums, 37–42 (2006).

17 *See* Richard A. Posner, Economic Analysis of Law §16.6, at 514–518 (5th ed., 1998).

in either of two ways. First, it can be eliminated by rescinding the building code and permitting the construction of cheaper housing that does not meet the standards of the code. Second, the impact can be mitigated by keeping the regulation in place while simultaneously increasing the purchasing power of the poor. Which option we ought to pursue would seem to depend on some prior judgment about the proper goals of the building code and the value of its contribution toward the achievement of those goals.

We can go through the same analysis for *every* regulation that has an adverse impact on the poor because of its tendency to increase the price of acquiring a regulated good. We can always attribute that adverse impact either to the regulation or to the reality that the poor are, in fact, poor. The price impact of regulation, by itself, tells us nothing. What we need is a theory by which good regulations can been distinguished from bad or wasteful regulations. De Soto uses a utilitarian cost-benefit analysis as his measure of the goodness of a regulation.[18] Elsewhere, I have argued against the use of efficiency as the measure for marking off the boundary of "good" state regulation of land-use activities.[19] My purpose, within the confines of this short chapter, however, is not to advocate a particular conception of "good" or "wasteful" regulation. Rather, it is simply to emphasize that the exclusion of some poor customers when land (or housing, or some other essential good) becomes more expensive due to regulation, and the informality that often results, is not, without much more, a conclusive reason to classify the regulation in question as bad. Nor is it a reason to conclude that the regulation should be rescinded.

The question of what to do in the face of such costs is a difficult question of applied political theory.[20] We need a theory capable of comparing the operation of a regulation *coupled with* redistributive mechanisms (for offsetting the effects of regulation-induced costs on the poor) with three competing alternatives: (1) regulation in the absence of such redistributive measures; (2) rescission of the regulation in the absence of such redistributive measures; and (3) redistributive measures in the absence of the regulation.

With respect to this last option (i.e., redistribution without regulation), one influential line of argument has it that cash redistribution is always a more efficient way to help the poor than either regulation alone or regulation coupled with redistribution.[21] The basic idea is that it is better to simply give people money

---

18 A good regulation, he says, is one that "that guarantees and promotes … economic efficiency." THE OTHER PATH, *supra* note 8, at 132.

19 *See* Eduardo M. Peñalver, *Land Virtues*, 94 CORNELL L. REV. 821 (2009).

20 *See* Larissa Katz, *Red Tape and Gridlock*, Chapter 8 of this volume.

21 *See* Louis Kaplow and Steven Shavell, *Why the Legal System is Less Efficient than Income Tax in Redistributing Income*, 23 J. LEGAL. STUD. 667, 677 (1994) ("Redistribution is accomplished more efficiently through the income tax system than through the use of legal rules").

and let them choose what to do with it (e.g., by purchasing sub-standard housing, but more of some other good they value more) than to force them to consume a particular good (e.g., code-compliant housing) by prohibiting the alternative through the enforcement of a building code. There are some obvious problems with this tax-and-redistribute-only strategy. First, people's choices about what to do with their transfer payments may have adverse and irreversible impacts on those in their care, most obviously their children. Second, there might be other reasons for pursuing the redistribution-plus-regulation path, reasons having to do with the moral obligations we owe to our fellow citizens or political feasibility.[22] Finally, and relatedly, the argument in favor of the tax-and-redistribute mechanism implausibly assumes the fungibility of the resources people need in order to flourish, across both resource and temporal dimensions.[23] My purpose here is not to present a knock-down argument for one or another approach, however, but merely to identify the question to be asked and to highlight the necessary complexity of getting to an answer.

Applying our best normative theories for making the above comparison, the proper course of action for the state may not be to eliminate the regulation, but rather to keep the regulation in place while taking steps to alleviate the effects of poverty by redistributing wealth. The potential of de Soto's discussion to support such redistribution is largely neglected by his conservative commentators. De Soto's analysis of land informality proceeds on the assumption that people have certain needs, and that among these needs is a place to call home. If the market (supplemented by private charitable redistribution) does not satisfy the needs of the poor, then the state is obligated to help them. If the state does not make it possible for the poor to obtain land on which to build their home through legal mechanisms, however, they will (and will be entitled to) take matters into their own hands by engaging in extralegal actions, such as land invasions. "Extralegality," he argues, "is rarely antisocial in intent. The 'crimes' extralegals commit are designed to achieve such ordinary goals as building a house, providing a service, or developing a business. Far from being the cause of disarray, this system of extralegal law is the only way settlers have to regulate their lives and transactions."[24] In de Soto's view, the state's response to this violation of the law should not be to punish squatters, but rather to ratify their violation of the law by granting them title to the land they occupy.

The state's ratification of squatter invasions is a plainly redistributive act. Through titling programs, the state hands over to squatters land that once belonged to a private owner or, more frequently, to the state. It is true that de Soto frequently

22 *Cf.* Elizabeth S. Anderson, *What is the Point of Equality?*, 109 Ethics 287 (1999).

23 *See* Peñalver, *supra* note 19.

24 Mystery of Capital, *supra* note 4, at 88.

writes as if the principal problem solved by formalization is the *clarification* of property rights. But he clearly cannot mean this. The problem of squatting in the developing world is not the absence of title. Someone, either the state or a private landowner, owns the property on which squatters reside. At a minimum, the squatters, who occupy the land by virtue of an extralegal act of land invasion, know that it is not theirs. The problem that de Soto has identified is not murkiness of title, but rather the mismatch between formal ownership of a parcel of land and the identity of its actual users. And his preferred solution is not to eject the user, which would also clarify title (albeit in the name of the original owner, whoever it is), but to transfer formal title from its owner to its possessor.

De Soto's endorsement of these forced and redistributive transfers through titling programs is consistent with the notion, which he endorses, that redistribution toward the poor is one of the principal obligations of the state. "One of the state's primary responsibilities," he writes, "is to redistribute resources to the poorest and least fortunate members of the population."[25] In so doing, the state's aim, he says, should be to alter "legal institutions so that ownership of property becomes widespread."[26]

How do we square this endorsement of redistribution and dispersed ownership with de Soto's protracted critique of the "redistributive tradition" in *The Other Path*? Viewed within the broader context of his work, particularly within the context of a Latin American landscape that has been characterized by economic inequality that is persistently the highest in the world, de Soto's critique of a "redistributive tradition" should not be understood as referring to efforts to improve the situation of the poorest. Instead, we would do better to understand it as a criticism of the pervasive political corruption and elite rent-seeking he observes in Peru. In other words, while de Soto condemns the tendency for states in the developing world to act at the behest of one powerful interest group or another in order to transfer wealth to the (currently) well-connected, he by and large endorses the progressive notion that the state may properly redistribute wealth from the rich to the poor in order to assure that their basic needs (however defined) are satisfied. As with regulation, then, the crux of the problem for de Soto is not redistribution (or regulation) as such, but the wrong sorts of redistribution (or regulation). As de Soto says, the state is empowered and, indeed, obligated to transfer resources to the poor, but "this [power] must not be used as a pretext for granting privileges to a few and thwarting everyone else."[27]

A somewhat reconstructive reading of de Soto can be built around these fundamentally progressive insights, which are consistent with his basic approach but which operate below the surface of his discussions. The first is that the market's distribution of purchasing power, and not just the state, can be a crucial barrier to ownership by the poorest members of society. The second is that, when

25 Other Path, *supra* note 8, at 251.

26 *Id.*

27 *Id.*

the market's allocation of purchasing power excludes the poor, the state has an obligation to implement policies that will help the poor to overcome their poverty in order to obtain a stake in the formal system of property ownership, of which titling is his key example. On this view, de Soto's key critique of developing states is not that they have *exceeded* their proper limits by over-regulating, but that they have not implemented effective policies to bring ownership to the masses, at times by enacting "bad" or wasteful regulation, but also by neglecting their obligations to spread ownership through redistribution of purchasing power. Indeed, as I will explain in the next section, their failure to spread ownership may help to explain the pervasiveness of the very sorts of bad regulation that de Soto decries.

Linking Inequality with Political Dysfunction: Lessons for the United States

Inequality and Democratic Culture

De Soto spends a great deal of time lamenting the failure of the Peruvian government to act in the common interest. Rather than enact "good laws," the Peruvian government consistently enacts "laws [that] are predominantly bad because those who drafted them did not take into account their costs and the ways in which they stifled economic activity." De Soto's explanation for this tendency to make bad laws is, in part, a pervasive lack of transparency and accountability. "In Peru," de Soto complains, "99 percent of the central government's rules emanate from the executive branch, which adopts them without public consultation or control."[28]

The most obvious shortcoming in de Soto's work is his failure to peer behind this important phenomenon to ask why it is that transparent and (relatively) effective democratic governments were able to emerge in those areas of the world where capitalism has come to flourish. This is obviously a complex and difficult question, but de Soto's focus on titling, understood as an effort to spread redistribute wealth to the poorest, may not be far from the mark. A number of economic historians and social scientists have argued that skewed property distributions impair the emergence of democratic and transparent government and encourage the development of political cultures dominated by elite rent-seeking.

For example, trying to explain the puzzle of the divergent development paths taken by the United States and Canada, on the one hand, and Latin America, on the other, despite starting from situations of virtual parity in the eighteenth century, economic historians Stanley Engerman and Kenneth Sokoloff have argued that "the United States and Canada were relatively unusual among New World colonies, because their factor endowments (including climates, soils, and density of native populations) predisposed them toward paths with relatively equal distributions of wealth and income and corresponding institutions that favored the participation

28 Other Path, *supra* note 8, at 192.

of a broad range of the population in commercial activity."[29] Engerman and Sokoloff go on to argue that the widespread involvement in economic and political activity facilitated by relatively egalitarian property distributions were crucial in the economic transformation of the United States and Canada over the course of the nineteenth century from agrarian societies with standards of living roughly comparable (or even inferior) to Latin American societies into industrial economies with far higher standards of living. Other scholars have pointed toward the contrast between rapid growth among the more egalitarian "Asian tigers" and the stagnant growth among Latin America's racially and economically stratified societies.[30]

The mechanism that connects highly unequal property distributions with subsequent underdevelopment, according to Engerman and Sokoloff, is government policies aimed at maintaining elite privilege. "Greater equality in economic circumstance" they argue, led North Americans to develop "a legal framework that was conducive to private enterprise in both law and administration."[31] In the United States, lawmakers invested in the development of human capital among non-elites and made routine the process of corporate formation and the granting of patents, making incorporation and the protection of intellectual property available to virtually anyone with an idea and some start-up capital. In Mexico and Brazil (and, as de Soto has observed, Peru), however, where the operation of government reflected the inequality that pervaded the underlying society, investments in human capital lagged, and the right to incorporate or obtain patents was granted sparingly, and primarily to the wealthy or well-connected.[32]

Linking up this (admittedly contested) model of the relationship between inequality and development with de Soto's observations about the operation of the Peruvian government provides some qualified support for de Soto's prescriptions but at the same time challenges him to formulate an even more ambitious agenda for social reform. If excessive inequality contributes to the dysfunction of Peruvian law, which, in turn, contributes to persistent Peruvian underdevelopment, then redistributive titling may constitute a good first step toward remedying the problem. But it seems unlikely that the degree of redistribution that can be accomplished through the titling mechanism alone will be adequate to generate the sort of economic equality necessary to foster the democratic norms and institutions that will help Peru (and other underdeveloped countries) to overcome centuries of economic and political stagnation. Extensive land reform and redistribution of

29 Stanley L. Engerman and Kenneth L. Sokoloff, *Factor Endowments, Institutions, and Differential Paths of Growth Among New World Economies: A View from Economic Historians of the United States*, in How Latin America Fell Behind, 260, 271 (Stephen Haber, ed., 1997).

30 *See* William Easterly, *Inequality Does Cause Underdevelopment* 7 (Center for Global Dev., Working Paper No. 1, Jan. 2002), available at http://www.cgdev.org/content/publications/detail/2789.

31 *See* Engerman and Sokoloff, *supra* note 29, at 287.

32 *Id.* at 271; *see also* Easterly, *supra* note 30.

other forms of wealth may be necessary to generate the economic dynamism that de Soto seeks. Granting title to existing informal communities, however, would be an important first step in that process.

The impact of economic inequality on political culture is an insight that has a great deal of relevance to our own situation in the developed world. Increasing economic inequality has once again become a topic of conversation in the United States in the face of stagnating middle class wages and dramatic increases in wealth and income among the very richest Americans. Economic inequality in the United States has, since the 1970s, risen to levels not previously seen since the Gilded Age.[33] The United States' relatively egalitarian past, and the economic dynamism and democratic culture that egalitarianism fostered, does not ensure that the United States will enjoy an egalitarian, democratic, and economically dynamic future. A failure to take adequate steps to prevent the emergence in this country of a segmented society like the one that predominates in Latin America might be leading to the development of a legal and political culture that resembles de Soto's Peru, in which economic elites work to subvert democratic processes in order to protect their privileged position within the economic status quo. The Nobel Prize-winning economist Paul Krugman posed the question bluntly in a 2006 essay for *Rolling Stone*:

> Will the United States go down the path that Latin America followed—one that leads to ever-growing disparity in political power as well as in income? The United States doesn't have Third World levels of economic inequality—yet. But it is not hard to foresee, in the current state of our political and economic scene, the outline of a transformation into a permanently unequal society—one that locks in and perpetuates the drastic economic polarization that is already dangerously far advanced.[34]

Redistribution as Crucial to Property's Stability

De Soto vividly describes the social dysfunction that have followed in the wake of Peru's highly unequal system of property distribution. Without legal means of obtaining property, Peru's poor have resorted to various forms of illegal self-help, such as land invasions and the operation of unlicensed businesses. Mirroring the vast inequality in the distribution of economic power, the state in Peru has frequently functioned as little more than a field for rent-seeking among elite groups while simultaneously acting as a bulwark against substantive property reform.

---

33 For a general discussion of increasing inequality in the United States at the turn of the twenty-first century, *see* Edward N. Wolff, Top Heavy: The Increasing Inequality of Wealth in America and What Can Be Done About It (expanded ed., 2002).

34 *See* Paul Krugman, *The Great Wealth Transfer*, Rolling Stone, Nov. 30, 2006, available at http://www.rollingstone.com/politics/story/12699486/paul_krugman_on_the_great_wealth_transfer.

While egalitarian property distributions seem naturally to accompany certain economic systems of production (e.g., subsistence agriculture, or hunter-gathering), the potential to shift away from egalitarianism within sophisticated capitalist economies is ever-present. For Robert Nozick, this fact was a reason for disfavoring patterned theories of distributive justice. Such patterns, he argued, could not be maintained in a free society without constant state intervention in property allocations.[35] Rather than understanding this difficulty as a reason for rejecting patterned theories of distributive justice, however, we might instead treat it as a simple observation about the fragility of the egalitarian property regime on which democratic culture depends: it requires constant vigilance and institutional support for its stability. If the scholars I have been discussing are correct in their assessment of the cultural, political and economic costs of excessive inequality in the distribution of property, acknowledging this fragility need not constitute a persuasive reason for rejecting egalitarianism, any more than acknowledging the fragility of a priceless work of art constitutes a reason for refusing to spend the money to maintain it. It is simply a reminder of the need for an awareness of the destabilizing consequences of allowing inequality to get out of hand and a political willingness to take action to stop this from occurring.

North Americans were once acutely aware of the dangers of inequality and the need to shape state policy in order to combat it. In the aftermath of the American Revolution, broad segments of the population believed that unequal distribution of land constituted a grave threat to American democracy. According to my colleague, Greg Alexander, John Adams agreed with James Harrington that "power always follows property," and he "expressed the recurrent anxiety about the consequences for republican virtue in terms of a need to maintain a balance of property in order to maintain a balance of power."[36] Similarly, Thomas Jefferson believed that republican government required a rough equality of distribution in landownership. In 1785, he wrote that the consequences of "enormous inequality" in landownership were so pernicious that "legislators cannot invent too many devices for subdividing property."[37]

Participants in the various agrarian uprisings and movements in the decades after the American Revolution believed that "God had given the Earth to mankind in common and that human beings had the same right to the land as they had to air and water."[38] For these Americans, the Revolution was fought, at least in part, "to protect small producers from the moneyed men who did not live by their own labor, but, instead, preyed on the many who did."[39] They feared "prolonged

35 *See* Robert Nozick, Anarchy, State, and Utopia, 160–164 (1974).

36 Gregory S. Alexander, Commodity and Propriety: Competing Visions of Property in American Legal Thought, 1776–1970, 33–34 (1997).

37 *Id.* at 33.

38 *See* Donald J. Pisani, *The Squatter and Natural Law in Nineteenth-Century America*, 81 Agric. Hist. 443, 444 (2007).

39 *See* Alan Taylor, Liberty Men and Great Proprietors 6 (1990).

economic dependence as tenants or wageworkers as the path to 'slavery.'"[40] Contemporary property discourse in the United States seems to have lost the sense of a deep connection between state redistribution to protect against economic inequality and the democratic function of private ownership. Instead, it tends to view redistribution as an unmitigated threat to ownership, as something operating external to it.

We can see this clearly in conservative thinkers' misunderstanding of de Soto's anti-redistributionist rhetoric. Far from constituting a blanket condemnation of redistribution or regulation of property, de Soto's description of the political dysfunction that dominates Peruvian society (with the poor struggling to obtain the means of their survival and the rich jockeying for power in order to protect their privileged position vis-à-vis one another and, most importantly, vis-à-vis the poor) drives home the potential risks of failing to attend to the costs of inequality.

De Soto's ideas gesture toward the importance of redistribution to the stability and productivity of property and the value of matching formal title to actual possession. In *The Mystery of Capital*, de Soto laments that residents of the developed world have forgotten the secret of capital's productive power and the liberating potential of formal ownership. This may be true, but it will do little good to remind us of the power of formal title without also reminding us of the importance of egalitarian property distribution, both as a safeguard of democratic values and an engine of economic innovation.

---

40 *See* TAYLOR, *supra* note 39.

Chapter 2
Invasions, Innovation, Environment

Carol M. Rose

For property law scholars, Hernando de Soto's most important writing is probably *The Mystery of Capital* (2000).[1] But de Soto's earlier book, *The Other Path* (1989), is if anything more important for scholars of law and economic development. *The Other Path*'s title was a self-conscious reference to the Shining Path, Peru's Marxist revolutionary movement—and the book's content was an exuberant refutation of that movement. For development scholars, *The Other Path* powerfully revived the idea of law as a key to development, even in the face of what was then a certain jaded disillusion with law-and-development.[2]

The Other Path certainly had ambitions to speak to a global issue: it aimed to de-fang revolutionary movements by unleashing capitalist activity among the poor. But the book's great fountain of examples was not the world at large, but rather modern Lima. Its real subject was the city's vast internal migration of rural people: their extensive extra-legal settlement of land areas around the urban core, their establishment of great numbers of itinerant businesses and informal markets, their creation of entire alternative transportation systems.[3]

De Soto's *Other Path* showed great respect for these people and for their enormous and under-appreciated contributions to the national economy. The book's central argument, however, was that their economic efforts were limited in scale and complexity, for a very specific reason: their houses and businesses were established outside the law, and hence outside the security and potential for growth that legal recognition could bring. Once legalized, he argued, these informal efforts would be capable of expansion and much greater leverage for economic development.[4]

The key to economic development, then, would be to add legal protection to these migrants' efforts. Legality would make their entrepreneurial activities

1 Hernando de Soto, The Mystery of Capital: Why Capitalism Triumphs in the West and Fails Everywhere Else (2000) [hereinafter Mystery of Capital].

2 *See, e.g.*, Kevin E. Davis and Michael J. Trebilcock, *The Relationship Between Law and Development: Optimists versus Skeptics*, 56 Am. J. Comp. L. 895, 902–903, 915–917 (2008) (describing De Soto's The Other Path as one of the well-known optimistic departures from several decades of skepticism about law's influence on development).

3 Hernando de Soto, The Other Path: The Economic Answer to Terrorism (1989) [hereinafter Other Path].

4 *See* Other Path, *supra* note 3, at 177–182 (summarizing beneficial effects of secure property, contract enforcement, and extra-contractual liability).

not only more secure, but also more capable of raising capital, creating joint enterprises, acquiring insurance, and enforcing contracts—all the elements that would allow for a new "wealth of nations."

For property law scholars, de Soto's second book, *The Mystery of Capital*, looms larger, for very good reasons. *Mystery* not only expands the geographic canvas from Lima to the entire developing world (including even the United States in its nineteenth century development stage), but even more important for property scholars, this book sharpens the development prescription, honing legalization of the informal economy in general down to property rights in particular, and especially to formal property rights in informally settled land.

Although *Mystery* too took up many other topics, it was especially striking for proclaiming that with formal title, barrio settlers can bring "dead capital" to life. In de Soto's presentation, formal title to land can leverage an interrelated nexus of other capacities: titling enables owners to divide interests (e.g., security interests, rentals, partnerships); to alienate whole or partial interests to anyone in the world; and most especially, to attract investment for entrepreneurial activities. Once again, the key to economic development is law, but now the central project is to assure formal property title to previously informally held landed assets. Formal title can turn those "dead" assets into living capital—assets with the capacity to produce more goods and services, to the greater well-being of all.[5]

These claims about formal land title have proved to be at once influential[6] and controversial,[7] but those questions will not be of central interest in this article. Instead, I want to take up two other issues that were not so evident in *The Other Path*, but that are brought into the open in *Mystery*. These two other issues are especially revealing about de Soto's views on the forces that move or impede economic development.

The first I will call the "scarce resource" issue. *Mystery*'s new attentiveness to land titles and propertization, as opposed to a more general program of legalization in the earlier *Other Path*, entails a cluster of unanswered questions about invasions of and conflicts over finite resources. By comparison, many examples of legalization in the earlier book involved micro-businesses, where resource conflicts are not at issue. If a small, informal business is made legal, no particular resources are

5 MYSTERY OF CAPITAL, *supra* note 1, at 7.

6 *See, e.g.*, Elizabeth Daley and Mary Hobley, U.K. Dept. for Int'l Development, *Land: Changing Contexts, Changing Relationships, Changing Rights* 12 (2005), available at http://www.oxfam.org.uk/what_we_do/issues/livelihoods/landrights/downloads/land_changing_contexts_relationships_rights.rtf (describing influence of De Soto's ideas on World Bank programs).

7 *See, e.g.*, Karol C. Boudreaux, *The Legal Empowerment of the Poor: Titling and Poverty Alleviation in Post-Apartheid South Africa*, 5 HASTINGS RACE & POVERTY L.J. 309, 313, 328–337 (2008) (arguing that titling programs have encouraged South African residents to improve their housing, but not to use houses as collateral for business loans); Jonathan Manders, *Sequencing Property Rights in the Context of Development*, 37 CORNELL INT'L L.J. 177, 182–190 (2004) (arguing that de Soto's thesis about property rights ignores other factors and sequencing issues central to economic development).

threatened; there may be questions about the character of the informal business (as is evident, for example, in discussions of legalizing gambling or narcotics), but generally speaking, bringing an informal business into the fold of legality simply means expanding the economy. Older firms may be subject to competition, but they are always free to become more competitive themselves.

But with *Mystery*'s narrowing of the legalization project to property rights, things look somewhat different. Land is a finite resource. To grant formal title to informal land settlers, effectively ratifying an invasion post hoc, means to dispossess some other claimant to the land, either a private owner or the public at large. It also means that the newly-legalized claimants may face further invasions and threats of dispossession by future claimants. Hence *Mystery*'s focus on land titling raises questions—sometimes disturbing ones—about the ways that ever-expanding titling programs might clash with efforts to avoid resource conflict and to protect and preserve both privately and publicly held resources. A mystery within *Mystery* is why de Soto devoted so little attention to this array of scarce resource problems. My hypothesis on this point is that much of the answer can be found in his celebration of the heroes of his first book, *The Other Path*—the internal migrants to Lima.

A second cluster of questions, which I will call the "universalizing issue," accompanies the extremely wide-ranging assertions about propertization and land titling that emerge so clearly in *Mystery*. Again by way of contrast, the informal land claims at issue in the earlier *Other Path* were generally claims made by relative newcomers, that is, internal migrants moving from rural to more urban areas, as exemplified in the areas around modern Lima. *Mystery*, on the other hand, proposed to formalize informal land claims in all kinds of land contexts, throughout the world, including informal claims in long-settled communities.[8] One might well suppose, however, that informal land claims in some traditional communities could be quite different in character from informal claims asserted by new migrants settling around modern urban areas, and by the same token, the impact of formalizing previously informal traditional claims might be quite different—and considerably more disruptive.

Mystery's insistence on granting formal title to all kinds of informal property claims is a second mystery within *Mystery*. I will argue, or at least suggest, that the example of Lima's new settlers again drives the supposedly universal land titling prescription of *Mystery*, even at the cost of a more nuanced set of approaches to property in the developing world. Subtleties may be swept away in an effort to get at a quite specific set of targets: the clubby elites in less developed countries (hereinafter LDCs) who heretofore have enjoyed formal rights, but in a system closed to outsiders—a system that de Soto, borrowing from the early modern European historian Fernand Braudel, labels the "bell jar."[9] When one analyzes this universalizing assertion, what is of most interest theoretically is the picture that

---

8 Mystery of Capital, *supra* note 1, at 180–182.

9 Mystery of Capital, *supra* note 1, at 1 (quoting Fernand Braudel, 2 Civilization and Capitalism: The Wheels of Commerce (Sian Reynolds, trans., 1982)).

emerges of the meaning of universalized formal property rights. In de Soto's work, it seems easy to extend formal title to all kinds of property claims, but in practice formalization can act as another invasion, indeed a revolutionary challenge to all kinds of closed or semi-closed traditional property regimes.

I will conclude with some observations about how these two issues—the scarce resource issue and the universalizing issue—play out in the context of more developed economies that already have reasonably workable property regimes. An important lesson is that new versions of the "bell jar" may emerge even in developed economies, where existing stakeholders attempt to exclude others from some aspects of the formal property regime. But in more developed economies, invasions of scarce resources, as well as invasions of established property conventions, can more sharply illustrate other kinds of concerns. Notable among those are concerns about environmental damage on the one hand and expressive backlash on the other.

The Scarce Resources Issue, or Speaking of Invasion …

De Soto himself has claimed that the developed nations have already solved the "mystery of capital" through functioning formal systems of property rights,[10] and one might ask whether there is really any demand for titling informal property claims in developed countries. But a moment's reflection reveals that there are plenty of informal property-like claims in developed countries, and that some of the relevant actors have already achieved a certain degree of legal toleration, perhaps even taking tentative steps toward formal legality. The Netherlands has a robust tradition of urban squatting—indeed, so robust that property owners hire "anti-squatters" to occupy houses or commercial buildings, pre-empting squatters who might move in during temporary vacancies.[11] In the United States, a small thought experiment would reveal numerous informal claimants who might have something to gain if they were to receive formal title to spaces that they have occupied or claimed extralegally—groups that are in some ways comparable to de Soto's enterprising migrant groups on the outskirts of Lima. Obvious candidates are urban squatters in unoccupied residential buildings, some of whom have benefitted from "sweat equity" titling programs.[12] Some degree of legal toleration goes to immigrant sidewalk vendors in New York and other large cities,[13] as is also

---

10 Mystery of Capital, *supra* note 1, at 10.

11 G. Pascale Zachary, *Amsterdam Finds Booming Business in Anti-Squatters*, The Globe and Mail (Canada), Mar. 26, 1999, at A4.

12 *See* Christine L. Wilson, Note, *Urban Homesteading: A Compromise Between Squatters and the Law*, 35 N.Y.L. Sch. L. Rev. 709, 718–720 (1990) (describing possibility for squatters to become "homesteaders" in New York).

13 *See* Gregg W. Kettles, *Formal Versus Informal Allocation of Land in a Commons: The Case of the MacArthur Park Sidewalk Vendors*, 16 S. Cal. Interdisc. L. J. 49, 52–53,

the case with longstanding uses of the resources on the federal public lands in the West.[14] Then too, there are the urban panhandlers and bench-sleepers who have regular spots that they claim as a kind of informal property.[15] Still other informal claimants might be cybersquatters and file-sharers on the Internet, although to date, their claims to legality have been at least partially stymied.[16]

While some informal property claimants—notably some urban squatters—have certainly received sympathetic commentary,[17] these and others still rouse a certain unease. The reason for unease, I would suggest, revolves around a feature that de Soto recognizes and to a very considerable degree applauds: invasion. When informal settlers arrive on some piece of land, they are dispossessing either other private owners or the public at large. Those private and public owners are likely to have other uses in mind for the land, even if those are merely passive uses, like scenery or wildlife habitat.

De Soto explicitly brought forth the topic of invasion in the *Other Path*, where he stressed not only the enterprise, courage, and inventiveness of Lima's new migrants, but also their conscious and premeditated plans to begin by invading areas and businesses legally held by others.[18] These included planned invasion of public and private lands for residences, invasion of streets for illegal business activities, and invasion of transportation routes claimed by formal licensees.[19] Later on, *Mystery* rather downplayed the rhetoric of invasion. Nevertheless, even in *Mystery*, de Soto wrote approvingly and at length of massively invasive actions during the settlement of the continental United States, notably by the illegal squatters, who preceded formal surveys as the frontier moved west,[20] and

---

55–56, 60–62 (2006) (describing prevalence of sidewalk vendors as well as one program of legalized sidewalk vending; the author argues, however, that illegal vendors have established better rules for allocating spaces).

14 Sally K. Fairfax, et al., *The Federal Forests Are Not What They Seem: Formal and Informal Claims to Federal Lands*, 25 Ecology L.Q. 630, 636–639 (1999) (describing a number of informal claims to use public lands for dune-buggying, mushroom hunting, wood gathering and other uses).

15 Brandt J. Goldstein, *Panhandlers at Yale: A Case Study in the Limits of Law*, 27 Ind. L. Rev. 295, 313–314, 328–331 (1993) (describing spot-claiming by panhandlers).

16 Cybersquatting is now illegal under the Anticybersquatting Consumer Protection Act, 15 U.S.C. 1125(d) (1999). File sharing was curtailed by making a major Internet service provider liable in *A&M Records, Inc. v. Napster, Inc.*, 239 F.3d 1004 (2001); for more recent developments, see Niva Elkin-Koren, *Making Technology Visible: Liability of Internet Service Providers for Peer-to-Peer Traffic*, 9 N.Y.U. J. Legis. & Pub. Pol'y 15 (2005–2006).

17 Wilson, *supra* note 12, at 713–727; *see also* Eduardo Moises Peñalver and Sonia Katyal, *Property Outlaws* 155 U. Pa. L. Rev. 1095, 1123–1128 (2007) (applauding urban squatters, among other informal property claimants).

18 Other Path, *supra* note 3, at 19–24.

19 Other Path, *supra* note 3, at 19–24 (residential invasions); 59–62 (trade); 93–98 (transportation).

20 Mystery of Capital, *supra* note 1, at 113–140.

by the Gold Rush miners, who established their own informal claim system while flagrantly trespassing on U.S. lands.[21]

What is largely missing in this picture is any discussion of the most problematic aspect of invasion, and of land invasions in particular: invasions will confront finite resources, and finite resources can get used up—hence there is competition for them. Competing uses and competitors for land get little attention in de Soto's books. With respect to the settlement of the United States, the ouster of native Americans receives only the most fleeting mention,[22] and the Gold Rush miners' trashing of the environment receives none at all. *Mystery* notes in passing that most land claims in the Brazilian Amazon are extralegal,[23] but the book passes over the violence and environmental degradation that has attended land invasions in that region.[24] The settlers around Lima would appear to be occupying lands that have no competing uses, for all one can see in *The Other Path*.

While de Soto's books are not entirely silent on the issues of resource limits and potential externalities of invasion, they are oddly indifferent to them. Commentators have been considerably more voluble. Some have noted that informal residential settlements—including those near Lima—often spring up in areas that are dangerous or environmentally sensitive, like floodplains, steep slopes, or areas subject to landslides.[25] These factors, of course, are among the reasons why such areas have not been settled formally. Moreover, commentators note that granting legal title is very likely to encourage more incursions into even more marginal areas.[26] In an undeveloped condition, such areas are by no means useless wastelands; far from it, they may perform important ecological services like erosion prevention or wildlife habitat—that is to say, there are public purposes for keeping some areas unsettled. In that respect, informal residential settlements in LDCs share a characteristic with the uneasy-making examples from more developed countries—informal claims by sidewalk vendors, for example, or public lands trespassers: the public also has a claim on these large and small pieces of real estate. Granting formal title to informal users might not only gobble up sensitive locations, but encourage others to come in and gobble up more.

---

21 Mystery of Capital, *supra* note 1, at 140–147.

22 Mystery of Capital, *supra* note 1, at 123 (noting that President Washington removed squatters cabins located on lands owned by Indians).

23 Mystery of Capital, *supra* note 1, at 85.

24 Lee J. Alston, Gary D. Libecap, and Bernardo Mueller, Titles, Conflict and Land Use: The Development of Property Rights and Land Reform on the Brazilian Amazon Frontier, 153–158 (1999).

25 Winter King, *Illegal Settlements and the Impact of Titling Programs*, 44 Harv. Int'l L.J. 433, 441 (2003) (noting these problems, including Lima outskirts' very steep hills).

26 King, *supra* note 25, at 445; *see* Bernadette Atuahene, *Legal Title to Land as an Intervention Against Urban Poverty in Developing Nations*, 36 Geo. Wash. Int'l L. Rev. 1109, 1130 (2004); *see also* Kenneth A. Manaster, *The Problem of Urban Squatters in Developing Countries: Peru*, 1968 Wis. L. Rev. 23, 46.

There is nothing very hidden or elusive about the general issue of resource scarcity and the competition that lurks behind granting title to land invaders, and certainly an economist would notice it. Why, then, are *The Other Path* and *Mystery* so seemingly indifferent to the finiteness of resources? Why in particular does *Mystery* show such a striking approbation of titling programs for invasive land settlement? Only the author would know, but a reader can speculate on some possible reasons. What follows is a non-exhaustive list of some that might be offered by a spokesperson for de Soto's ideas, though none of these reasons quite answers the problem.

Possible reason No. 1: Invasion does not really matter. De Soto mentions several times that land invasions occur with the tacit consent of public bodies, on lands that were presumably slated for settlement anyway;[27] the chief obstacle to formalizing settlers' title is simply the snail's pace of the bureaucracies.[28] The same might be said of the frontier settlers in the United States in the nineteenth century; even if the land offices could not keep up, the intent of public authorities was to have the land settled all along.[29] One might say that the modern urban squatters, like their nineteenth century frontier counterparts in the United States, have simply gotten out ahead of public bureaucracies, entering lands that have been in the public interest to settle sooner or later. One must issue a caveat to this answer, however: this line of reasoning implies some sunset on invasions, because at some point the lands recognized as appropriate for development will necessarily give out.

Possible reason No. 2: Invasion does matter, but the cost is worth paying. This answer would concede that land appropriate for development is finite, and that at some point further development runs into more valuable competing uses. It might even concede that some undeveloped land may be more valuable for environmental uses than for settlement, and/or that such land may be dangerous for settlement. But public health dangers and loss of environmentally sensitive land are simply the price of an "integrated" property system—that is, a land market that is unified rather than fragmented, that anyone can understand and enter, and that serves entire LDC populations and stimulates genuine economic growth.[30] According to this reasoning, internal migrants are the LDCs' shock troops in the acquisition of

27 MYSTERY OF CAPITAL, *supra* note 1, at 175, 217 (citing tacit official acceptance of informal squatter settlements).

28 MYSTERY OF CAPITAL, *supra* note 1, at 167 (noting delays in Peru of up to 20 years in recording titles); MYSTERY OF CAPITAL, at 192–193 (charting legal delays in acquiring formal title); *see also* OTHER PATH, *supra* note 3, at 140–141 (charting bureaucratic hurdles to adjudicating state-owned land). De Soto also asserts that in the Latin American context, ideological opposition of individual landownership has slowed the settlement process; MYSTERY OF CAPITAL, *supra* note 1, at 167–169; OTHER PATH, *supra* note 3, at 50–51 (noting bureaucratic preference for communal property in land reform).

29 *See, e.g.*, VERNON ROSCO CARSTENSEN, *Introduction* to THE PUBLIC LANDS: STUDIES IN THE HISTORY OF THE PUBLIC DOMAIN, xxiii–xxv (1963) (noting the learning process and administrative difficulties in U.S. land surveys and sales).

30 MYSTERY OF CAPITAL, *supra* note 1, at 52–54, 62–63, 218–219.

an integrated, growth-oriented economy. They need encouragement to pick up stakes from the countryside and undertake the risk of resettling. The prospect of formal title incentivizes migrants to come to the city in the first place, where their entrepreneurial character is unleashed and where they shake up the closed system of old elites. It may well be true that the lands that they settle are environmentally important and/or possibly risky to the migrants themselves, but titling is the only available lure in a poor country. There is no viable alternative until some higher level of economic development is achieved. But with this reasoning, too, the earlier caveat applies: there must be some sunset on invasion, among other reasons because at some point, environmental or public health losses at the margin may outweigh the gains of incremental economic development from settlement.

Possible Reason No. 3: Invasion is a positive good. Critics have complained that titling will favor those who arrive early enough or who are pushy enough to claim the best lands on the outskirts of town.[31] But on this argument, pushiness is a good thing. Pushy people should be applauded, not condemned. Successful reform projects generally entail rewards to those who excel in initiative and energy—e.g., the Stolypin land reforms in early twentieth century Czarist Russia, which that reforming minister described as a "wager on the strong" within the peasant population.[32] Stalin's later decimation of successful peasants as "Kulaks" was of a piece with the destruction of Russian agriculture and the demolition of a dynamic market economy.[33] Internal migrants are "the strong" of the modern LDCs; they, too, are pushy people, with the same kind of drive and willingness to innovate. Once again, they are agents of change, and their invasions deserve to be rewarded. But here comes the caveat again: rewards to the early and pushy suggest some kind of decline in invasion over time as the less pushy arrive.

Possible Reason No. 4: Yes, encouraging invasions does bump into issues of finite resources, but a growing capitalism will solve the problem. On this account, if the strong, early urban squatters can gain formal title to the areas they colonize, they can leverage their property into capital to start businesses. In turn, their early entrepreneurial activities will make it unnecessary to grant title willy-nilly to all who follow. To be sure, latecomers will be at a disadvantage if they cannot acquire title through land invasion, but offsetting that disadvantage is an enormous advantage that they have in entering an already-established market economy, where their labor is worth much more.

---

31 *Cf.* Bernadette Atuahene, *Land Titling: A Mode of Privatization With the Potential to Deepen Democracy*, 50 St. Louis U. L.J. 761, 767–770 (2006) (noting that titling to current occupants may reward the "most aggressive and cunning," but favoring the policy as best of the alternatives).

32 Stephen F. Williams, Liberal Reform in an Illiberal Regime: The Creation of Private Property in Russia, 1906–1915, 186–187 (2006) (describing the idea of the reforms, and arguing that the "strong" were sometimes wrongly associated with peasants who were merely wealthy as opposed to enterprising).

33 *Id.* at 1–2 (recounting fate of a supposed Kulak after the Russian Revolution).

Incidentally, this possible reason is very close to one modern explanation of John Locke's justification of the original acquisition of landed property from the commons. Locke famously required that the first takers leave "as much and as good" to latecomers; but given that land is a finite good, this prescription could not possibly be followed literally. An alternative, however, is that the latecomers can get "as much and as good" simply by virtue of entering an established economy in which others bid much more for their labor.[34] Hence, latecomers do not need to acquire land through invasion; instead, they will be able to earn wages, to save, and to buy whatever land they need in a system of established rights.

What is more, with economic growth, environmentalists too will be able to compete for sensitive lands. This is because, at least according to the conventional wisdom, environmental goods are in some measures luxury items; while environmental quality may decline early in economic development, environmental protection grows in relative importance as people have more wealth.[35] At the outset of development, poor people have to make use of whatever comes to hand. Richer people, on the other hand, can afford to fund parks and butterfly habitats. The early migrant poor, with titles in hand, can help everyone become rich—that is, they act as the engine of the economic growth that renders future land invasions unnecessary and encourages greater attention to the environment.

The heroes of this reasoning are those most adventurous of newcomers, the early migrants and first creators of informal residential communities. Through their efforts, the problem of finite resources is merely transitional, to be drowned in a sea of rising wealth.

In all these lines of argument, then, the back story is that invasion is merely a transitional stage on the way to a stable, well-defined, and wealth-producing system of uniform and universal property rights. As Nicole Garnett has astutely commented about "property outlaws," invaders are most likely to appear where property is not well-defined or well-defended; through their actions on the ground, invaders are attempting to position themselves to be the most prominent candidates for ownership in a follow-up regime of settled and uninvaded property.[36] Modern developed countries, with their stable property rights—including stable public property rights—thus need not permit land invasions, much less grant title to

---

34 Geoffrey P. Miller, Comment, *Economic Efficiency and the Lockean Proviso*, 10 Harv. J.L. & Pub. Pol'y 401, 406–408 (1987); *see also* Carol M. Rose, *"Enough and as Good" of What?* 81 Nw. U. L. Rev. 417, 424–431 (1987) (explaining implicit compensation in a property regime).

35 *See, e.g.*, Jonathan Adler, *When Is Two a Crowd? The Impact of Federal Action on State Environmental Regulation*, 31 Harv. Envtl. L. Rev. 67, 74–75 (2007) (reviewing the theory of a "Kuznets curve" in which environmental protection first declines and then increases with economic development); *see also id.* at 75 n. 28 (reviewing recent favorable and unfavorable accounts of Kuznets curve theory).

36 Nicole Stelle Garnett, *Property In-Laws*, 156 U. Pa. L. Rev. Pennumbra 279, 281–284 (2007) available at http://www.pennumbra.com/responses/12-2007/Garnett.pdf.

invaders. Their economies are sufficiently open and transparent to let anyone who wishes purchase scarce goods with money.

The Universalizing Issue, or Big Rights/Little Rights

When we look at the problem of scarce resources in de Soto's work, we find a very important set of characters on the path to development—the early newcomers, the informal entrepreneurs whose nerve and verve can set the development train in motion. When we look to a second issue, that of the universal applicability of titling as a key to development, we find those same characters, but some others as well.

In *Mystery of Capital*, de Soto insists that migrant settlers should be able to transform their informal property claims into what he calls "formal" property rights. His interest in formal rights dovetails with an important strand of recent property scholarship. This line of thinking argues that property consists of relatively simple, standardized rights, a *numerus clausus* or closed number of standard property forms.[37] Most importantly, simple and standardized property forms make property legible to anyone in the world, and thus available for trade near and far.[38] Moreover, standardization allows property to be divided into smaller standard pieces that can be mixed and matched, contracted and recorded.[39] The *numerus clausus* delineates a form of property rights that I have called modernist,[40] and that de Soto calls formal, but whatever the preferred appellation, these rights are the building blocks of an integrated modern economy. Formal or standardized or modernist property can lead what de Soto calls an alternative life—even as the owner keeps the property for his or her own use, it has a shadow life as a potential commodity, marketable to vast numbers of others. A matter of particular importance for de Soto is that marketability enables property to be pledged as security and thus transformed into a platform for raising capital.

As early as *The Other Path*, de Soto maintained that Latin American countries, along with most LDCs, actually have formal property regimes, but that those

37 Thomas W. Merrill and Henry E. Smith, *Optimal Standardization in the Law of Property: The* Numerus Clausus *Principle*, 110 Yale L.J. 1 (2000).

38 *Id.* at 31, 33; *see also* Carol M. Rose, *What Government Can Do for Property (and Vice Versa)*, *in* The Fundamental Interrelationships Between Government and Property, 209, 213–214 (Nicholas Mercuro and Warren J. Samuels, eds., 1999) (describing legislatively and judicially created "off the rack" property entitlements); Mystery of Capital, *supra* note 1, at 56–58 (describing formal property as creating easily legible "fungible" rights).

39 Merrill and Smith, *supra* note 37, at 35; *see also* Mystery of Capital, *supra* note 1, at 57–58 (noting that formal rights can be mixed and matched in many different combinations).

40 Carol M. Rose, *Big Roads, Big Rights: Varieties of Public Infrastructure and Their Impact on Environmental Resources*, 50 Ariz. L. Rev. 409, 423–425 (2008).

regimes only extend to an elite group with political connections and established wealth.[41] He further argued, especially in the later *Mystery*, that it would take little to extend the existing systems of formal rights to migrant settlements.[42] The latter, he writes, already have the basic elements of a formal property system, namely an efficient deployment of resources toward productive ends; more specifically, they have documents and record systems of who owns what, and who has transferred what to whom, often kept not only by the immediate parties in an informally held community but also in a central location, by the initiators of the initial invasion.[43] The only thing that is missing for these claimants is legal recognition, which will extend property claims far beyond the specific community in which they are recognized, and into the world at large, where infinite numbers of bidders await.

Thus in migrant communities, formal rights may indeed be relatively simple to establish; in those communities, the kinds of rights claimed informally are not qualitatively different from the formal claims to title elsewhere.[44] But in *Mystery*, de Soto takes an important step beyond migrant communities, asserting that *all* systems of informal property rights in land can be translated into formal property systems. When asked how, he answered with one of his most memorable directives: "Listen to the barking dogs," he said. The dogs know when intruders are crossing into "their" property.[45]

The barking dogs, however, show the kind of property rights de Soto has in mind. The rights at issue follow what Henry Smith has called an "exclusion" strategy,[46] and what Stuart Banner has called "geographic" rights: the property right extends to a given terrain, over which the owner has more or less free reign, most especially the right to exclude or permit entry by others.[47] Barking dogs are good guardians of this kind of property right; they let the owner know when strangers intrude upon the boundaries.

But dogs are not very helpful in guarding against overreaching *behavior*, as opposed to boundary violation.[48] There is much evidence that many traditional communities base property rights, roughly speaking, on something closer to behavior than to location. Banner's work on New Zealand argues that the Maori

---

41 *See, e.g.*, OTHER PATH, *supra* note 3, at 209–210; *see also* MYSTERY OF CAPITAL, *supra* note 1, at 67, 156.

42 MYSTERY OF CAPITAL, *supra* note 1, at 179–182.

43 MYSTERY OF CAPITAL, *supra* note 1, at 182–188.

44 Not that issues are lacking—e.g., the cost of title registration in many parts of the world, and the problem of actually extending state protection to property claims in informal communities. *See, e.g.*, Boudreaux, *supra* note 7, at 334 (describing high costs of titling in South Africa).

45 MYSTERY OF CAPITAL, *supra* note 1, at 163, 179.

46 Henry Smith, *Exclusion versus Governance: Two Strategies for Delineating Property Rights*, 31 J. LEGAL STUD. 453, 469 (2002).

47 Stuart Banner, *Two Properties, One Land: Law and Space in Nineteenth-Century New Zealand*, 24 LAW & SOC. INQUIRY 807, 810 (1999).

48 Robert C. Ellickson, *Property in Land*, 102 YALE L.J. 1315, 1329 (1993).

understood landed property as a set of varying rights of use rather than rights of location; thus different persons might lay claim to different parts of a single plant, with the plant and its location shared among them.[49] Similarly, some traditional fishing communities have allocated fishing rights to certain persons based on the kind of equipment that they use (e.g., certain kinds of nets);[50] others allocate fishing rights in complex rotations.[51] In medieval England, villagers held their agricultural plots "geographically" at some seasons, but in common with others at other seasons.[52]

Barking dogs would not be of much use for property rights with these complex mixtures. Hence it is no wonder that one source of criticism of de Soto's work concerns the application of titling programs to traditional communities.[53] In nineteenth century New Zealand, the introduction of European-style land titling disrupted community control over property claims, and seriously weakened indigenous clan governance.[54] More recently, in Niger, a substantial class of persons descends from former slaves; this group has worked land in a kind of compromise arrangement with the "nobles." But with titling, the "nobles" have claimed exclusive control over all these lands.[55] Some commentators have complained that formal titling programs dispossess women or other less powerful groups, disrupting formerly protective informal practices like consultation over property dispositions.[56]

Thus, traditional groups' customary property understandings may not be so easily assimilable to formal title after all, precisely because titling contemplates the introduction of a modernist exclusion strategy into a complicated set of

---

49 Banner, *supra* note 47, at 811.

50 James C. Carrier, *Marine Tenure and Conservation in Papua New Guinea: Problems in Interpretation*, *in* THE QUESTION OF THE COMMONS: THE CULTURE AND ECOLOGY OF COMMUNAL RESOURCES, 142, 147 (Bonnie J. McCay and James M. Acheson, eds., 1990).

51 ELINOR OSTROM, GOVERNING THE COMMONS: THE EVOLUTION OF INSTITUTIONS FOR COLLECTIVE ACTION, 149–152 (1990).

52 Henry E. Smith, *Semicommon Property Rights and Scattering in the Open Fields*, 29 J. LEGAL STUD. 131 (2000).

53 *See, e.g.*, Thomas Kelley, *Unintended Consequences of Legal Westernization in Niger: Harming Contemporary Slaves by Reconceptualizing Property*, 56 AM J. COMP. L. 999, 1021–1022 (2008) (describing adverse effects of titling on lower-status groups in rural Niger); Bosire Maragia, *The Indigenous Sustainability Paradox and the Quest for Sustainability in Post-Colonial Societies: Is Indigenous Knowledge All That Is Needed?*, 18 GEO. INT'L ENVTL L. REV. 197, 231–232 (2006) (describing disruptive effects of colonial titling project in traditional communities).

54 Banner, *supra* note 47, at 844–847.

55 Kelley, *supra* note 53, at 1011, 1030–1034.

56 *See, e.g.*, Atuahene, *supra* note 26, at 1126–1129 (arguing for joint title to couples rather than title to male head of household); *see also* Daley and Hobley, *supra* note 6, at 13–14, and sources cited therein (citing criticisms of land titling programs for ill-effects on traditional communities and women in Thailand and sub-Saharan Africa).

traditional, use-oriented relationships. Modernist property aims at simplicity, transparency, and trading possibilities that are open to the world. Traditional property arrangements, on the other hand, are often closed to outsiders, marked by much community involvement, and few transfers and trades.[57] Their very complexity has served to stifle trade and alienability, in what modern property scholarship would designate an "anticommons"—a resource in which rights are so numerous and varied that no consensus can be reached about altering use.[58] The introduction of a simple *numerus clausus* of exclusive rights is a very different form of property organization, and it is likely either to create new winners and losers, or to exacerbate the differences between winners and losers in traditional hierarchies. Anglo settlers were the new winners in nineteenth century New Zealand; the Kulaks were the new (though temporary) winners in early twentieth century Russia's turn to modernist property; the "nobles" are the new (or perhaps "renewed") winners in modern Niger's titling program.

As with de Soto's seeming indifference to the impact of settlers' invasions on scarce resources, it is useful to pause here to ask about his indifference to the impact of formal property on traditional communities, where formal titling in itself resembles a kind of figurative invasion—a modernist invasion of a traditionalist set of property arrangements. Here again, answers must be speculative, but one can imagine at least four:

Possible Answer No. 1: These rights invasions really do not matter. On this argument, there are not enough genuine traditional communities to count for much. Moreover, special arrangements can be made for groups with special status, particularly indigenous groups. As for the rest, they are likely to fade away in time anyway, as new roads makes exit from the countryside easier,[59] and as traditionalist rural people migrate to the cities and even to other countries where their life chances may be greater. Once they themselves become migrants, they will be beneficiaries when informal migrant communities get formal rights.

Possible Answer No. 2: Disruption of traditional communities' property arrangements is a good thing. This rationale would argue that traditional communities are often hierarchical in structure, dominated by local notables to the detriment of weaker members. Besides, their economies are static and poor. Because they lack modernist formal property rights, they cannot attract investment and the innovation that comes with investment. Formal rights can enhance the ability of the downtrodden to compete, and can make traditional communities as a whole more competitive in a global economy. All of this means that formal

57 *See, e.g.*, Banner, *supra* note 47, at 813–815 (describing pre-settlement Maori land ownership).

58 *See* Rose, *supra* note 40, at 424–425; Michael A. Heller, *The Tragedy of the Anticommons: Property in the Transition from Marx to Markets*, 111 Harv. L. Rev. 621, 667 (1998) (describing the "anticommons").

59 De Soto notes the importance of roads in Peruvian urbanization. *See* Other Path, *supra* note 3, at 8; Mystery of Capital, *supra* note 1, at 79–80 (noting the role of roads).

rights will increase overall wealth of traditional communities, even at the cost of temporary losses by some. Moreover, with care, the introduction of formal modernist rights need not be so ham-handed; even if not everyone gets title to a particular location, they can be compensated for any lost rights that they had.[60]

Possible Answer No. 3: The disruption of traditional communities is unfortunate, but it is unavoidable. Formal rights are one aspect of globalization, but another of the most important paths to globalization is already at the door of traditional communities: roads.[61] Roads turn villagers into migrants, and the introduction of formal rights is likely to do the same.[62] But then, whether they would willingly choose their role or not, the migrants are the change agents in LDCs: they are the ones who will challenge existing economic arrangements, compete with existing urban elites, and ultimately force them open. Which leads to:

Possible Answer No. 4: Any or all of the above answers may be correct, but the concern for traditional communities is misplaced. Here the argument is that the most prevalent and tenacious "traditional" communities are not peasant villages. They are actually the elites who hold a simulacrum of formal rights, but in a closed system that benefits only themselves; only they and their friends enjoy the "bell jar" of formal rights; only they and their friends have access to formal property, business law, and commercial credit.[63] This closed system is intertwined with the political authorities, who guard the system behind dense thickets of bureaucratic delay, and who give admission to outsiders only in exchange for bribes.[64] The formal rights of the elite are no more than a modern "mercantilism," a coalition in which political authorities assure themselves of income by granting monopoly powers to the economic elite.[65]

60 The distributional patterns appearing in other property rights transitions are not particularly encouraging for compensating weaker members of the community, however. Gary Libecap has argued extensively that shifts in property regimes entail paying off "winners" under former regimes; *see* Gary D. Libecap, Contracting for Property Rights, 5 (1989). Thomas Merrill, among others, has noted that modern systems of tradable environmental rights generally follow the route of "grandfathering" rights to major resource users; *see* Thomas W. Merrill, *Explaining Market Mechanisms*, 2000 U. Ill. L. Rev. 275, 284. For a practical example, see John Tierney, *A Tale of Two Fisheries*, NY Times Magazine, Aug. 27, 2000, §6, at 38 (describing allocation of fishing quota to some but not all fishermen in a community, with resulting bad blood); but see Katrina Miriam Wyman, *From Fur to Fish: Reconsidering the Evolution of Private Property*, 80 N.Y.U. L. Rev. 117, 161 (2005) (stating that distributional concerns over allocations of individual fishing quota can be alleviated through appropriate program design).

61 Other Path, *supra* note 3, at 8; Mystery of Capital, *supra* note 1, at 79–80.

62 *See* Rose, *supra* note 40, at 426–428.

63 Mystery of Capital, *supra* note 1, at 66–67, 156–157.

64 *See* Other Path, *supra* note 3, at 208–210 (describing traditional elites, intertwining of bureaucracy and politics); *id.* at 154 (describing bribes that informal entrepreneurs pay to engage in business).

65 *Id.* at 201–205.

Figure 2.1

	Informal	Formal
Closed	1) traditional	2) elite club (“bell jar”)
Open	3) migrant	4) capitalist

Notice that if there is anything to this fourth answer, the real target of de Soto’s formalization is a different kind of traditional group: the pseudo-modern but actually traditional elite. This elite effectively “owns” the older property and contract system as a club good. Extending formal rights to those in the informal economy upends the traditional elite. It is a good invasion, because it causes a revolutionary change in the character of the formal rights regime, by adding an essential ingredient: genuine openness, which means dissolving the old elites’ club good or “bell jar” of formal rights. Once the elites no longer own the formal rights system, they are subject to the competition of upstarts. If this means that the cherry orchard is lost to the grasping newcomers, so much the better. The cherry orchard is not worth preserving, nor are its current owners.

When one brings together all the questions that are raised by the project of universal titling, a kind of four-square of property systems becomes evident (see Figure 2.1), spread out on an axis of formal/informal and open/closed.

The property regimes of traditional groups and wealthy elites have more in common than it may seem—both are closed to outsiders. By the same token, migrants have at least as much in common with capitalists as with either the traditional communities that they leave behind or the closed urban elites they confront. Indeed, the migrants who are de Soto’s heroes are capitalists manqué. Once they are armed with formal title, not only do they become capitalists, but they also force the old elites to join them. They begin by invading land, they follow by invading the elites’ system of formal rights, and thenceforth, formal title equips them to keep on invading—no longer by trespass, but by the voluntary invasions of buying, selling, and competing.

Lessons for—and from—the Developed World

Are there implications of De Soto’s analysis for the law of developed countries, and specifically the United States? One might think not: in modern American law, formal title would seem to be readily available to everyone for everything. But for developed countries, one of de Soto’s most interesting implicit warnings is that nominally open formal property regimes can degenerate into closed clubs. This is the implicit lesson in his depiction of Peru’s traditional elite, where formal property regimes became the limited property of specific groups who can hide behind a maze of regulations to become as closed as the most traditional of informal regimes.

In the modern United States, as Nicole Garnett's contribution to this volume points out, some local regulations seem to have little purpose except to protect local merchants from competition from street vendors. On a larger scale, some would find an analogy to an elite's closed property regime in the suburban communities, where land use regulations, it is said, effectively exclude outsiders in favor of an insiders' "cartel."[66] Nevertheless, outsiders can also deploy formal property law to break up the club—notably in "takings" litigation under the Fifth Amendment to the U.S. Constitution.

But the experience of the United States also suggests a major caveat: land use and environmental regulations, so often the target of takings litigation, also serve to protect scarce resources.[67] As Henry Smith's work emphasizes, property regimes routinely include elements of both "exclusion" and "governance," owner sovereignty and the vindication of neighbor and public rights.[68] Entrepreneurial activity is a source of national wealth, but so are environmental uses. Indeed, this is true in less developed nations as well as developed ones. Sanitation, clean water and air, and even wilderness and scenery contribute to overall well-being everywhere. Regulation to protect those goods can indeed create winners and losers, but insofar this is the case, modern property thinking might well turn its attention to devising new methods for winners to compensate legitimate losers.[69] The solution is not necessarily to liberate property ownership from regulation altogether. Indeed, the ultimate object of development policy should not be simply to protect private property, but rather to create and protect *total* wealth, including private, neighborly, and public sources of that wealth.[70]

---

66 Robert C. Ellickson, *Suburban Growth Controls: An Economic and Legal Analysis*, 86 Yale L.J. 385 (1977) ("cartel" analysis); *see also* William A. Fischel, The Homevoter Hypothesis, 4 (2001) (arguing that homeowners attempt to maximize their own wealth through local governmental actions).

67 *See, e.g.*, Vicki Been, *Lucas v. The Green Machine: Using the Takings Clause to Promote More Efficient Regulation?*, *in* Property Stories, 299, 330–331 (2nd ed., 2009) (arguing that regulations limiting development have great benefits, though the latter are difficult to quantify, and that compensation requirement may lead to under-regulation).

68 Smith, *supra* note 46.

69 One such idea is benefit or "windfall" recapture; *see, e.g.*, Margaret H. Clune, *Government Could Hardly Go On: Oregon's Measure 37, Implications for Land Use Planning, and a More Rational Means of Compensation*, 38 Urb. Law. 275, 302–305 (2006) (reviewing major schemes for "windfall" recapture as a source of funds to compensate for losses due to land use regulation). A major earlier work on this theme was Windfalls for Wipeouts (Donald G. Hagman and Dean J. Misczynski, eds., 1978); *see also* Eric Kades, *Windfalls*, 108 Yale L.J. 1489 (1999) (justifying windfall recapture); Abraham Bell and Gideon Parchomovsky, *Givings*, 111 Yale L.J. 547 (2001) (revival of idea of windfall recapture). Another such idea would involve creative uses of tradable rights in environmental goods; for a recent example, *see, e.g.*, Jan Laitos, *The Problem with Wilderness*, 32 Harv. Envtl. L. Rev. 503, 554–568 (2008) (proposing the use of tradable rights in wilderness).

70 Carol M. Rose, *Property Rights and Responsibilities*, *in* Thinking Ecologically: The Next Generation of Environmental Policy 49, 57 (1997). It is interesting to note that

The experience of developed nations has another kind of warning for the use of formal rights to break up clubby, in-group property arrangements. There is much to be said for those invasions, but they can run afoul of backlash based on issues of expressiveness. Those who use formal rights to invade closed systems are not necessarily nice or polite. De Soto's work downplays the cutthroat character of at least some informal businesses and land settlement practices.[71] It is easy to do so; informal invaders often draw sympathy because they have seem to have no other options. When their activities are legalized, however, the rough edges of previously informal operators are likely to be much more noticeable, because legalized activities lose their shield of necessity at the same time that they expand into a much larger market. Take, for example, payday loans, the loans that firms make—often at high interest rates—in exchange for the next paycheck of the borrower. In the modern United States, payday loans are generally legal; more genteel lenders may not like them, but the payday lenders provide services to an under-served population that finds the more genteel bankers opaque, distant, and unusable.[72] To take another and even more controversial example, in the 1940s and 1950s and later in the United States, "blockbusting" real estate agents used legal purchase agreements to buy low from alarmed white homeowners and sell high to minorities. These realtors were considered the scum of the real estate world; professional realtors considered racial "steering" to be a requirement of professional ethics, and they routinely expelled the blockbusters from their professional organizations. But unpleasant and outrageous as they were, the blockbusters expanded the housing market for minority buyers, and some did so consciously.[73]

---

in the World Economic Forum's Global Competitiveness Index, the United States ranks first in the world in competitiveness, but only 26th in protection of property rights, immediately behind Mauritius (22), Jordan (23), Barbados (24), and Namibia (25). The United Kingdom ranks 36th, somewhat behind Cypress, Syria, and Tunisia. World Economic Forum, Global Competitiveness Report 2008–2009, at 8, 364, available at http://www.weforum.org/pdf/GCR08/GCR08.pdf.

71 *Cf.* George L. Priest, *The Ambiguous Moral Foundations of the Underground Economy*, 103 Yale L.J. 2259, 2282–2287 (1994) (noting morally reprehensible or ambiguous elements in generally favorable treatment of informal economic activity).

72 *See* Douglas McGray, *Check Cashers, Redeemed*, N.Y. Times Magazine, Nov. 9, 2008, at 36 (describing extensive services provided by payday loan firms).

73 *See* Carol M. Rose, *The Story of* Shelley v. Kraemer, *in* Property Stories 189, 209–210 (2nd ed., 2009) (describing Raphael Urciolo, a Washington, D.C., blockbusting realtor resisting racial covenants in the Washington, D.C., counterpart case to *Shelley v. Kraemer*). My view is that there is a doctoral dissertation waiting to be written on Urciolo, who appears to have been an unusually reflective businessman in a much-maligned enterprise. An obituary of Urciolo appeared in the Washington Post, Oct. 7, 1994, reporting that Urciolo was born in Sardinia; in addition to his real estate and law practices, he held advanced degrees from the University of Rome, Catholic University, and the University of Maryland, spoke nine languages aside from English, taught business law and French at two separate universities, and authored a dictionary of Haitian Creole as well as a three-volume treatise on the etymology of Sardinian words.

Blockbusting realtors and payday lenders are examples of entrepreneurs who use formal property rights to invade clubby property arrangements. One might expect resistance from the members of the club, but the club members are not the only objectors. In earlier decades, many citizens found blockbusting an outrage, and many now look upon payday lenders as little short of loan sharks. Given that pattern, the unattractiveness of these formally correct "invasions" may lead to their suppression. The Fair Housing Act of 1968 outlawed blockbusting,[74] and much current legislative activity looms to cut back payday loans.[75]

The "not-nice-ness" of invaders presents a constant issue: Is it better to allow not-nice but useful activities to flourish under legal recognition, even though these practices cause discomfort to the median voter; or is it preferable to make them illegal or impracticable through heavy regulation, and hence less prevalent and less serviceable to their underserved clientele? If illegalized, might they possibly morph into even less controlled underground forms? De Soto's work teaches that we need to be very careful before condemnation of entrepreneurial invasions, but his work, in lionizing the invading migrants and their informal economy, may not have sufficiently addressed the expressive issues that come to the fore in legalization. Legalization empowers invaders, but it can cause backlash, sometimes warranted and sometimes not. The experience of more developed countries suggests that legalizing informal practices may require some care—not because they are not useful, which they often are, but because they cause popular outrage in spite of their real service.

Conclusion

This chapter has explored two quite obvious but puzzling blank spots in de Soto's work, and especially *Mystery of Capital*: His indifference to the invasion of scarce resources, and his insistence on formal title as a universally desirable way to hold property. That exploration shows how much the globalizing *Mystery* rests on the Peruvian *Other Path*, revealing a set of conflicts with a particularly Latin American flavor: a striving barrio population confronting an entrenched social elite, where the extension of formal rights entails an almost revolutionary change in a closed-club economy.

There are answers that one can speculatively give to fill the gaps that this chapter explores. To the first, the silence about scarce resources, one might answer that whatever social and ecological effects may be caused by land titling *ab initio*, those effects will be cured through the economic progress that will follow. To the

74 Fair Housing Act, 42 U.S.C. §3604(d) (1988).

75 *See, e.g.*, *Qwik Payday Inc. v. Stork*, 549 F.3d 1302, 1312–1313 (10th Cir. 2008) (holding that Kansas licensing requirements for payday loans are not pre-empted by federal law); McGray, *supra* note 73, at 38 (noting increasing local, state and federal curbs on payday loans).

second, the disruptions caused by formal titling, one might answer that there may indeed be damage to traditional communities' social relations, but those impacts are dwarfed by the good that comes from demolishing the most pernicious of traditional privileges, the "ownership" of the supposedly formal property regime by mercantilist elites.

In both answers, the hero of the story is the internal migrant to the cities, the figure most strikingly depicted in de Soto's first book, *The Other Path*. The migrant takes part in land invasion, acquires a house, and with formal property may turn the house into expansive capital. He or she invades the previously cartelized property regime itself, destroying elite privilege, and turning a tightly closed simulacrum of formal property into an expansive and open regime in which all can participate, and whose openness invites competition, investment, and trade.

What is this hero's role in an already-advanced economy? Eduardo Peñalver and Sonia Katyal suggest that the "property outlaw" is still a heroic figure, even in the much-developed United States.[76] But it is one thing to be a property outlaw when the door is closed, and quite another when the door is open. In de Soto's own theory, the advanced economies are advanced precisely because their property regimes function well; they open the door and permit anyone to play at buying and selling and investing. If that is the case, then invasions even in LDCs should be no more than transitional, a step on the way to a stable and open property regime. Where a property regime already functions in a stable and open manner, invasions merely bypass the market, and they are likely to transfer resources from higher- to lower-value uses—and that goes for public and environmental resources, too. While a creeping cartelization may indeed affect relatively open economic systems, not all regulation reflects that pattern. The regulations that prevent invasion are not necessarily the trappings of elite cartels or wannabe monopolists; they may actually be important for protecting private and public resources—matters of concern to the poor as well as the rich. In more developed countries as well as less-developed ones, it is important to sort out the differences.

Then, too, economic activities have a different expressive content when the door is open. In a legalized world, activities that the migrant-invader hero once undertook from necessity now seem much more a matter of choice, and that factor of choice changes the moral climate. Many informal economic arrangements serve poor and marginal customers. Once legalized, these arrangements still serve the same customers, only more extensively, and possibly better and more cheaply. But there are still risks for those customers. In legal form, the hardboiled practices of low-end economic entrepreneurs can take on a connotation of gouging and mean-spiritedness. In turn, that reputation can lead to public backlash and to a rollback of legality—in some cases to the detriment of otherwise underserved classes. In such cases, modest public regulation or collective self-regulation might help to protect the entrepreneurs themselves, as well as the persons whom they serve.

76 Peñalver and Katyal, *supra* note 17.

Hernando de Soto's work is in some ways a very Latin American story, especially insofar as it centers on the legal empowerment of a non-elite, energetic, and underappreciated entrepreneurial class of urban migrants in LDCs. It is a mark of the force of his ideas that one can draw much not only from the things that he says, but from the things he leaves unsaid.

Chapter 3
Culture and Capitalism: A Comment on de Soto

Gregory S. Alexander

In *The Mystery of Capital*, Hernando de Soto provides a simple but bold explanation for why capitalism has worked in the West but not elsewhere. The explanation is that Western countries have formalized their systems of property rights, particularly land titles, while lesser-developed countries (LDCs) have not. Although de Soto's thesis has some traction, it is grossly incomplete. An equally, if not more, compelling factor in explaining why LDCs have not economically caught up with wealthier countries is culture. Specifically, what I will call the "culture of hierarchy," which has historically dominated LDCs but not (or at least to a much lesser extent) wealthy countries like the United States, has inhibited wealth development in poor countries around the world. By contrast, Western countries have developed socio-political cultures that envision the proper social order as egalitarian and non-hierarchical. This proprietarian culture has greatly facilitated innovation and wealth creation by a vibrant middle class.

Max Weber was right. In his famous book *The Protestant Ethic and the Spirit of Capitalism*,[1] Weber argued that Protestantism, specifically the Calvinist version of Protestantism that he knew from his native Germany, promoted the rise of modern capitalism. Protestantism did this by nurturing a social vision and a culture of daily behavior that was highly conducive to economic development. The conventional wisdom today is that Weber was wrong.[2] In this chapter I want to take a contrarian position and use Weber's thesis as the basis for showing what is wrong with, or at least missing from, de Soto's account of why capitalism has led to economic growth in some countries but not in others. It is not Weber's specific thesis, that Calvinist Protestantism led to the rise of capitalism, that I wish to endorse but Weber's more general theory, namely, that culture matters.

Culture is all but missing from de Soto's explanation for the rise of capitalism in the developed world. As Jeffrey Sachs has stated, "[t]he greatest

---

1 MAX WEBER, THE PROTESTANT ETHIC AND THE SPIRIT OF CAPITALISM (1930).

2 David Landes, *Culture Makes Almost All the Difference*, *in* CULTURE MATTERS: HOW VALUES SHAPE HUMAN PROGRESS, 2, 11–12 (Lawrence E. Harrison and Samuel P. Huntington, eds, 2000).

puzzle in economic development is why sustained economic growth is so hard to achieve."[3]

There is no silver bullet for economic development. Developmental economists, sociologists, and anthropologists have suggested multiple factors that explain why development has occurred in some places but not others. Among these are geography[4] (e.g., climate,[5] natural resources), social systems (e.g., post-colonial, post-socialist), religion, political systems (e.g., the association between capitalism and democracy, popularized by Milton Friedman, among others), hard work and frugality, and social capital/trust.[6]

What I want to do here is to contrast de Soto's formalist theory with that of Weber, with its stress on culture. Throughout much of the twentieth century, cultural explanations did not enjoy much respect. Economists, for example, have been generally skeptical of any link between culture and economic development.[7] More recently, however, there have been signs that culture is making a comeback as an explanation of different rates of economic growth. For example, in 1999, the Harvard Academy for International and Area Studies held a three-day conference on culture and economic development, resulting in an influential collection of essays descriptively entitled *Culture Matters*.

Culture is a notoriously difficult concept to pin down. Perhaps the most common meaning is one that includes strictly subjective factors, including the values and attitudes that guide society.[8] I shall use the term in a broader sense to include objective factors, such as social structures and practices which themselves reflect ideological systems that characterize societies, as well as subjective factors. In this broader sense, for example, the practice of rendering a wide array of resources as exchangeable commodities is a fundamental aspect of American culture, for that practice reflects a widely shared market ideology within American society.

---

3 Jeffrey Sachs, *Notes on a New Sociology of Economic Development*, *in* Culture Matters: How Values Shape Human Progress, 29 (Lawrence E. Harrison and Samuel P. Huntington, eds, 2000).

4 *See, e.g.*, Jared M. Diamond, Guns, Germs, and Steel: The Fates of Human Societies (1998); Sachs, *supra* note 3, at 31–33.

5 There is reason to be skeptical of this factor. The striking contrasts between northern and southern Italy and between Costa Rica, on the one hand, and Honduras, Guatemala, and El Salvador, on the other, suggest that geography (including climate) plays only a minor role in economic development. *See* Lawrence E. Harrison, *Introduction: Why Culture Matters*, to Culture Matters: How Values Shape Human Progress, at xvii, xxix (Lawrence E. Harrison and Samuel P. Huntington, eds, 2000).

6 *See, e.g.*, Robert Putnam, Making Democracy Work: Civic Traditions in Modern Italy (1993).

7 *See* Harrison, *supra* note 5, at xxiv.

8 David Landes, *Culture Makes Almost All the Difference*, *in* Culture Matters: How Values Shape Human Progress, 2 (Lawrence E. Harrison and Samuel P. Huntington, eds, 2000).

Using this broader conception of culture, I shall argue that an important reason why capitalism has made some societies wealthy while leaving others poor is the *culture of hierarchy*. By that term I mean the social institutions, structures, and practices that create or maintain a high degree of wealth and social status in the hands of a relatively small subset of a society's population and a low degree of actual social mobility and expectations of mobility in society. Some aspects of the culture of hierarchy contribute to poverty directly, while others do so indirectly. The aspects that contribute directly to low levels of social prosperity might be considered sociological or demographic rather than cultural, but I will treat them as cultural because their role cannot be fully appreciated except as part of a larger phenomenon.

A final introductory point: Culture is not an independent variable. To the contrary, culture is influenced by many factors including such materialist factors as climate, natural resources, institutions (including legal institutions), and the like. Indeed, culture is dependent on property. The distribution of resource holdings affects the culture that develops in a capitalist society. Culture cannot be ignored in explaining economic development.

Two Alternatives to Neo-classical Economic Explanations

De Soto's theory places him within the approach to economic development that is based on neo-classical economics, with its heavy emphasis on property rights. The neo-classical economic approach in turn developed in reaction to two other developmental theories applied to Third World countries—dependency theory and colonialist theory.

Dependency Theory

It bears emphasis that the focus on the culture of hierarchy does not signify endorsement of dependency theory. As Stephen Haber explains, "Dependency theory wed Marxist notions of class analysis to a structuralist critique of international trade theory, though dependency was neither structuralism nor Marxism. At the center of the theory was the notion that the terms of trade of Latin American countries deteriorated over time. …Economic exploitation … occurred through 'unequal exchange.'"[9] The focus in dependency theory is on a weak and dependent bourgeoisie.

Colonialist Theory

The other theory, focusing on the effects of colonialism, also has Marxist-Leninist overtones. It was Lenin, after all, who identified colonialism as a late stage of

9 Stephen Haber, *Introduction: Economic Growth and Latin American Economic Historiography*, to HOW LATIN AMERICA FELL BEHIND, 9 (Stephen Haber, ed., 1999).

capitalism made necessary by capitalism's need to find new markets as it became increasingly monopolistic. Colonialist theory explained the lack of economic progress in newly independent countries in the Third World on the basis of the residual effects of years of colonial domination. This was especially true of African nations, whose independence was much more recent than underdeveloped countries in Latin America.

Like dependency theory, colonialist theory has little currency today. It was not simply the demise of Marxist-Leninist ideology that caused its decline. An equally significant problem was that there were too many exceptions for the theory to have much credibility. How does one explain, for example, the phenomenal success of Hong Kong and Singapore, two former British colonies (not to mention South Korea and Taiwan, former Japanese colonies)? Perhaps colonialism has had some continuing effects in some countries, but it cannot provide a comprehensive explanation for why capitalism has failed to generate economic development.

Characteristics of the Culture of Hierarchy

Here I will briefly describe the main characteristics of a culture of hierarchy. I emphasize at the outset that none of the cultural characteristics I will describe necessarily inhibits economic growth. Here, as in any cultural account, the same cultural feature can have very different consequences for economic development.[10]

Disparities in Wealth and Income

The culture of hierarchy begins with hierarchy in wealth and income levels. Without exception, the countries that must be considered as capitalist failures on any reckoning exhibit pronounced polarization in the distribution of both wealth and income throughout their societies. Exact data for distribution of wealth around the world are difficult to come by, but some statistics will give us a clear picture of inequality of wealth distribution in several underdeveloped capitalist countries of the Third World. The most widely used metric for measuring wealth and income distributions is the Gini coefficient, which is defined as a ratio between 0 and 1. A lower Gini coefficient indicates a more equal distribution of wealth or income, as the case may be. Conversely, a high Gini coefficient indicates more unequal distribution. An April 2008 study listing Gini coefficients for distribution of household wealth among several countries indicates that the coefficient for

10 *See* Michael E. Porter, *Attitudes, Values, Beliefs, and the Microeconomics of Prosperity*, *in* CULTURE MATTERS: HOW VALUES SHAPE HUMAN PROGRESS, 14–15 (Lawrence E. Harrison and Samuel P. Huntington, eds, 2000).

Namibia is 0.847, compared with 0.547 for Japan. (Interestingly, the second highest Gini coefficient, after Namibia, is that of the United States—0.801.)[11]

In most underdeveloped capitalist societies, great disparities in wealth and income distribution are historically rooted. In many Latin American countries, for example, ownership of land historically has been highly concentrated, as is the distribution of income.[12] The long histories of land maldistribution have deeply affected popular attitudes and beliefs in ways that inhibit economic growth. Historical patterns of wealth inequality tend to reproduce themselves by contributing to attitudes, beliefs, and expectations that such patterns are inevitable.

The Missing Middle Class

The second characteristic grows out of the first. Within the societies of failed capitalist nations, the distributions of wealth and income are bipolar. A small percentage of the total population owns or controls a very large percentage of total social wealth while a large percentage of the population lives below or near poverty levels. In between the two levels, a relatively small middle class exists. (In Brazil, for example, the 20 percent of households in the middle of the income distribution hold less than 10 percent of Brazil's total income.)[13] The size of the middle class tends to be stagnant, and it wields little economic or political power. Power, in both senses, is concentrated in the hands of a small elite class.

Limited Social Mobility

Within failed capitalist societies, social mobility tends to be limited. Escaping poverty is extremely difficult, and there are few, if any, Horatio Alger stories. While some members of the middle class may gain sufficient wealth to place them among the elite, because the middle class is small and relatively stagnant, this is not a typical experience. Indeed, it is generally considered aberrational. As a result, there is a kind of feudal-like quality to these societies. People tend to be born into the socio-economic status that in large measure defines their identities for the remainder of their lives.[14]

---

11 *See* James B. Davies, Susanna Sandstrőm, Anthony Shorrocks, and Edward N. Wolff, *The Level and Distribution of Global Household Wealth* (Univ. of W. Ontario, RBC Fin. Group Econ. Policy Research Inst. Working Papers, Paper No. 20075, April 2008) available at http://ideas.repec.org/p/uwo/epuwoc/20075.html.

12 *See* Nancy Birdsall, *Rising Inequality in the New Global Economy*, 2 Wider Angle 1 (2005) available at http://www.cgdev.org/doc/commentary/birdsall/WIDERlecturefull.pdf.

13 Birdsall, *supra* note 12, at 2.

14 *See generally* Andrés Solimano, *The International Mobility of Talent: Determinants and Development Impact*, 2 Wider Angle 8 (2005) available at http://www.cgdev.org/doc/commentary/birdsall/WIDERlecturefull.pdf.

Lowered Expectations of Improvement

Related to limited social mobility is the existence of low expectations among non-elites regarding the prospect that their lives may be significantly improved through their own efforts. There is a pervasive perception that the fix is in and that while capitalism may work for others, it will not work for them. This perception inhibits a willingness to engage in innovative risk-taking that is the life blood of successful capitalist economies.[15]

Popular Resentment, Distrust, and Resignation

Due in large part to the lack of social mobility, high levels of resentment, cynicism, and resignation exist among non-elite members of society in capitalist Third World countries. Due in large measure to the great disparities in wealth and the lack of social mobility, the have-nots perceive no legitimacy in their social order. In this sense, their cultures are decidedly proprietarian, meaning that the culture is not grounded in some popular vision of the proper social order. Trust is in low supply, and risk-taking is minimal. At the same time, this resentment and distrust do not lead the disadvantaged to exercise either their voice or exit options. Rather, they suffer in silence, bitter but resigned to the status quo.

Accompanying this lack of trust and resentment is a popular belief that the basis for prosperity is not productivity but insider status. The perception is that those who hold favored positions within business and political circles, usually acquired through personal or family connections, are the persons who reap the benefits of capitalism. This creates incentive not to engage in risk-taking or other behaviors that might increase productivity but rent-seeking, as those on the outside (and who see themselves as such) try to gain advantage by expending resources trying to gain favor with elites.

Customary Land Ownership

In underdeveloped capitalist nations (or underdeveloped areas of developing nations), land is often owned according to a traditional or customary system. Customary land is characteristically managed by a group of elders or chiefs. Attempts to title such land often fail because locals view customary ownership as more stable and reliable than government-issued land titles.[16] Locals rely on their

---

15 *See* Lawrence E. Harrison, *Promoting Progressive Cultural Change, in* Culture Matters: How Values Shape Human Progress, 296, 306 (Lawrence E. Harrison and Samuel P. Huntington, eds, 2000).

16 *See* Donald E. Krueckeberg, *The Lessons of John Locke or Hernando de Soto: What If Your Dreams Come True?*, 15 Hous. Policy Debate 1, 4 (2004) available at http://www.mi.vt.edu/data/files/hpd%2015(1)/hpd%2015(1)_forum_krueckeberg.pdf.

families for financial assistance rather than using mainstream sources of capital.[17] Hence they stay outside of the "bell jar" of successful capitalist economies.

Landownership Not Highly Valued

Within underdeveloped capitalist countries, there tends not to be a widely shared preference for ownership of land. Renting is often preferred. Renting dominates not simply because people lack the financial ability to own their homes but because people positively prefer renting over ownership. A number of factors contribute to this preference. Seasonal migration of laborers is one factor. Another is that renting is viewed as a more secure form of housing than ownership (no mortgage or taxes for renters).[18]

The Culture of Propriety: Capitalism and Property in the American Republic

The culture of hierarchy contrasts strongly with the culture of propriety. The latter is characterized by a large and robust middle class, a high degree of social mobility, a widely shared attitude of optimism, a substantial degree of economic risk-taking, and a popular value system that celebrates innovation and entrepreneurship. The countries in which capitalism has worked, in de Soto's terms, all have such a culture, although some longer than others (Japan's and South Korea's, for example, postdate the Second World War). To a considerable extent, that culture took root in the very founding of the colonies that became the United States. But throughout American history that culture has been importantly nurtured by a variety of government programs at all levels. These programs include the following examples:

- *Early American land reforms and territorial acquisitions*: Much has been written about colonial elimination of the English institutions of primogeniture and the fee tail. Whatever the actual effects of these property reforms, they were grounded in a social vision that was at odds with the English aristocratic social order. More important, perhaps, was the Northwest Ordinance of 1787, which implemented a reformist Jeffersonian land policy.
- *The Homestead Acts*: The 1862 Act provided that citizens could acquire 160 acres of public land at no cost other than a modest filing fee. The grant was conditioned, however, on the grantee working the land for five years. The condition was aimed at avoiding use of the land for land speculation purposes, using it instead as the basis for self-sufficiency and stability.

17 Hous. Policy Debate 1, 4 (2004).

18 *See* Peter Marcuse, Comment on "*The Lessons of John Locke or Hernando de Soto: What If Your Dreams Come True?*, 15 Hous. Policy Debate 39, 40–41 (2004) available at http://www.mi.vt.edu/data/files/hpd%2015(1)/hpd%2015(1)_forum_marcuse.pdf.

- *The nineteenth century Land Grant Acts*: These acts endowed free-access institutions of higher learning. Significantly, Land Grant Acts were coupled with the Homestead Acts from the very outset. Land-spreading and the spreading of human capital were viewed as of a piece.[19]
- *Federal home finance legislation*: Fannie Mae, for example, was created during the Roosevelt administration in part to broaden homeownership. Whatever flaws that program has, as we now see, it is still important to remember what its democratizing mission was.

All of these programs, and others, were developed for the specific purpose of strengthening the middle class by spreading landownership. They helped to create a popular culture very different from the culture of hierarchy that characterizes under-developed capitalist countries.

The causal relationship between this culture and property runs in both directions. The culture of propriety has actually contributed to property-spreading (although, significantly, it has not prevented a gross disparity in wealth distribution). Simultaneously, property has contributed to the development of the culture itself. The existence of a substantial propertied (or at least modestly propertied) class predates the founding of the Republic, and it is this class from which the characteristics of the culture of propriety—a popular emphasis on the importance of owning property, emphasis on productivity, belief in opportunity, a belief in the possibility of social mobility, an attitude of confidence and, with it, risk-taking—developed.

Conclusion

If Weber was right about the role of culture in the success of capitalism, then what are the implications for economic development in the capitalist countries of the Third World? I will end on an ambiguous note, for it seems to me that there is both bad and good news. The bad news is that, contrary to de Soto's argument, there is no quick fix. Culture is very sticky and resists change. Moreover, it is not clear what the relevant unit of analysis is—the individual, the group, the society? As Robert Edgerton writes, there is one economy, but many cultures.[20] Added to this is the problem that, as efforts to change the thinking of business and political leaders in lesser-developed countries have indicated, these leaders have a strong tendency to fall into strategic and behavioral patterns that impede their ability to develop sources of advantage in an increasingly competitive global economy.[21]

---

19 I owe this point to Bob Hockett.

20 *See* Stace Lindsay, *Culture, Mental Models, and National Prosperity*, *in* CULTURE MATTERS: HOW VALUES SHAPE HUMAN PROGRESS, 296, 306 (Lawrence E. Harrison and Samuel P. Huntington, eds, 2000).

21 Lindsay, *supra* note 20, at 288.

The good news is that although culture is difficult to change, it *can* be changed. Developmental studies suggest that within nations there are multiple mental models. Efforts to change attitudes and practices that inhibit economic growth are most likely to succeed if policymakers focus on those mental models that inhibit the wealth-creation process and operate at the level of the individual or firm rather than at a macro-level.[22]

The final point is a normative one: *Should* culture change? Or is this another form of imperialism? I have no answer to that question, but it surely is a fundamental dilemma that policymakers need squarely to face.

---

22 Lindsay, *supra* note 20, at 294–295.

Chapter 4
Hernando de Soto and the Histories of Property Law

Alfred L. Brophy

Hernando de Soto is interested in big-picture history. He asks a huge question in his most famous book, *The Mystery of Capital*, and looks in many places and at many times to find the answer. The question is about why capitalism works so well in the United States and seems to work less well in other places, primarily Latin America. His search for an answer stretches across centuries and across continents. The question is an important one, which resonates with many people today. Indeed, one of the reasons he has attracted so much attention is that he asks a question many others want to answer: is there anything that can be done to bring the bounties of capitalism to more countries and more people? The subtitle of *The Mystery of Capital* presents the question that motivates his work: *Why Capitalism Triumphs in the West and Fails Everywhere Else*. Why, indeed?

De Soto's answer is grounded in the institution of property. His thesis is that when property rights are secure and when it is easy to identify owners and for owners to develop and transfer property, capitalism will flourish. He sees several things as critical here, including ease of transfer and clear recording of property rights. A key element of his thesis is the statement at the conclusion of the book that "what the poor are missing are the legally integrated property systems that can convert their work and savings into capital."[1] I applaud de Soto's efforts to make the benefits of property available to as many people as possible with a minimum of interference. And I look forward to the day when progress—economic, moral, technological—is facilitated in every way by the law.[2]

De Soto's world is built around the idea that "small is beautiful." He finds the vehicle of liberation in the protection of property rights of "little" people—and he sees magic in the property systems that allow the common people easy access to capital and to the transfer of capital. In one eye-opening chart, he depicts the hundreds of steps (more than 700 steps, actually) necessary for a peasant in Peru

---

1 Hernando de Soto, The Mystery of Capital: Why Capitalism Triumphs in the West and Fails Everywhere Else, 227 (2000) [hereinafter Mystery of Capital].

2 At some point, we should talk about the costs of some of this commodification—of the ease with which others can then come to own and possess property once it has been commodified. But those are issues for another time. Right now, I am concerned with making property law work for people at a minimum cost.

to secure title to land.[3] But there may also be something of a mythology (or maybe that's not quite the right word—"an undue focus" may be a better term) that arises to explain that magic. For de Soto advances a particular reading of U.S. history regarding property that gives more attention to informal property systems in the evolution of property rights in the United States than is warranted.

Questions about the Importance of the Recognition of Extra-Legal Property

De Soto notes in Chapter 5, "The Missing Lessons of U.S. History," that the United States was in the late eighteenth and early nineteenth centuries a developing country. And so he hopes that there may be lessons from the United States' development that are applicable to other developing nations today. De Soto posits that the United States recognized informal property rights—such as squatters' rights—and converted those informal rights into legal rights. He credits this recognition of informal rights as "a key element in the United States becoming the most important market economy and producer of capital in the world."[4] This is true, to some extent. What is not so clear is the *centrality* of that recognition to the development of a capitalist economy in the United States. First, there was fierce opposition in the nineteenth century to the recognition of squatters' rights. Even when the law accommodated squatters in Kentucky by giving them a right to compensation for improvements made in good faith on another's property, that law was reflecting a basic value of promoting development and of avoiding conflict by giving each side something—the "owners" got their land back and the squatters got the value of their improvements.[5] But property law in the United States was then—and continues today—to be primarily about the protection of vested rights. Occasionally, a statute gives the right to a company to purchase property through a private condemnation act—such as happened in the building of the Erie Canal—but even those statutes recognize the centrality of our nation's respect of—and love of—property.[6]

Squatters' rights—such as the claims by settlers to land in Kentucky—loom, perhaps, larger in *The Mystery of Capital* than they did in U.S. history. For when Daniel Boone and his fellow settlers passed through the Cumberland Gap in the early nineteenth century to settle Kentucky, they carried the law with them. It is not just nostalgia that when George Caleb Bingham painted *Daniel Boone Escorting*

3 Mystery of Capital, *supra* note 1, at 192–193.

4 Mystery of Capital, *supra* note 1, at 148.

5 *See*, *e.g.*, Theodore W. Ruger, *A Question Which Convulses the Nation: The Early Republic's Greatest Debate About the Judicial Review Power*, 117 Harv. L. Rev. 826, 840–845 (2004).

6 On private condemnation during the Erie Canal, see Leah Green, *The Erie Canal and the American Imagination: The Erie Canal's Effects on American Legal Development, 1817–1869*, 56 Ala. L. Rev. 1167, 1171–1174 (2005).

Settlers through the Cumberland Gap, he showed Boone and his company coming into nature with the tools of settlement: a gun, cattle, a dog, and a covered wagon, as well as people.[7] Those settlers brought with them ideas of law and property. And one can see this in other landscape art of the time, which frequently celebrated humans' triumph over nature. Thomas Cole's *Daniel Boone At His Cabin at Great Osage Lake* depicts Boone in Missouri with a house planted there—a sign of an outpost of civilization in the wilds of nature.[8]

Although the law sided mostly with vested rights, our nation wrestled with the conflict between squatters and "owners" of land. James Fenimore Cooper's novel *The Pioneers* depicts a conflict between Natty Bumppo, the frontier hero and scout, and "the law." Bumppo had hunted deer out of season and on land owned by Judge Marmaduke Temple. Yet Bumppo could not understand why he was being prosecuted, as he had hunted on this very land for many years. Cooper's novel depicts the conflicts in the American character of that age, yet it is tragically clear that the law is dominant here. There is little in the way of accommodation of the law to Bumppo's practices (though the judge later comes to appreciate Bumppo).[9] Law was one of the weapons frontier Americans had in their arsenal to conquer nature.[10] Those laws included registries of property rights, along with regulations that made it possible transfer land easily and to finance its purchase through mortgages.

De Soto presents a passionate call for protection of property, for making it possible to do what we take for granted in the United States: easily record ownership, figure out who owns property, transfer it, and mortgage it. This is a goal deeply rooted in the American dream that by decreasing the uncertainty of property ownership and in facilitating its transfer we will reduce the burdens of ownership and usage of property—that the law will, in the words of legal historian

---

7 *See* Mildred Lane Kemper Art Museum, Washington University in St. Louis, available at http://kemperartmuseum.wustl.edu/wu2171.html.

8 *See* Mead Art Museum, Amherst College, http://www3.amherst.edu/mead/collections/bassett/P-1939-7.html. I discuss Cole and other landscape painters of the antebellum era and their (sometimes) ambivalent embrace of the spirit of enterprise and economic progress in *Property and Progress: Antebellum Landscape Art and Property Law*, 40 McGeorge L. Rev. 602 (2009).

9 G. Edward White, The Marshall Court and Cultural Change, 1815–1835, 71–72 (1988) (discussing *The Pioneers*).

10 Claire Priest and Gregory Alexander both depict the multiple ways that property law promoted economic growth. *See* Claire Priest, *Creating an American Property Law: Alienability and its Limitations in American History*, 120 Harv. L. Rev. 385 (2006); Gregory S. Alexander, Commodity and Propriety: Competing Visions of Property in American Legal Thought, 1776–1970 (1999). *See also* Morton J. Horwitz, The Transformation of American Law, 1790–1860, 31–62 (1977); William W. Fisher, *The Law of the Land: An Intellectual History of American Property Law, 1776–1876* (Sept. 1991) (Ph.D. dissertation, Harvard University).

Willard Hurst, facilitate the "release of energy."[11] The goal here is to have law serve in the least intrusive manner possible and to facilitate the market economy. The more needlessly complicated property law is, the worse it performs that critical function.

Not only does de Soto give more credit to extralegal rights than I think is appropriate, I think he locates the origins of Americans' respect for property rights too late. It is not so much that property law becomes standardized in the late eighteenth and early nineteenth centuries. Instead, liberalism emerges as a dominant ideology out of the revolutions in technology, economy, and transportation of the late eighteenth and early nineteenth centuries. At one point, de Soto invokes Gordon Wood's article in the *New York Review of Books*, Inventing Capitalism, as evidence of the change in property rights.[12] But Wood is talking not so much about property rights as about the ideology of liberalism.[13] And one of the lessons of Wood's wide-ranging discussion of whether capitalism emerged in the aftermath of the Revolution—or whether it existed well before that in the minds and practices of colonial farmers who produced more than they needed and entered the market—is a sense that the debates about when America became capitalist are misplaced. They may be vestiges of an era when Marxist theory was popular. But we can now focus more on questions of the centrality of property to American thought, of Americans' love of property, of their respect for the beauty of real property and the bounties it produces, and of the ways that they struggle with competing claims to property. These questions of capitalism have proved particularly confusing to historians of the Old South (the southern United States in the years leading into the Civil War), when there has been substantial debate about whether slave-owners were capitalist or anti-capitalist. That debate may distract us from a central feature of Southern labor and economy: the law established a framework for an economy that produced labor at low cost and generated extraordinary wealth.

The capitalism of the late eighteenth and early nineteenth centuries emerged, so the consensus goes, from a series of factors—including technological developments and a sophisticated commercial law that supported such developments. That commercial law seems to have been the result of demands of the market; the law was the dependent, not the independent, variable. In short, I believe de Soto gives too much credit to the recognition of extralegal property rights (like squatters' rights) and too little to other factors.

My hypothesis is that from the origins of the United States in the English-speaking colonies in British North America, property rights were secure.[14] Our country's love affair with property was there from the beginning, as were methods

11 Willard Hurst, Law and the Conditions of Freedom in the Nineteenth-Century United States (1956).

12 Mystery of Capital, *supra* note 1, at 10, 148.

13 Gordon S. Wood, *Inventing American Capitalism*, N.Y. Rev. Books (June 9, 1994).

14 James W. Ely makes this point well in *The Guardian of Every Other Right: A Constitutional History of Property Rights* (3rd ed., 2008).

of recording ownership and surveying and mapping the landscape, and respect for the fundamental rights of property. Among the first legislation for colonial Pennsylvania, for instance, was an act that required recording of property transfers;[15] as the colony was being founded, William Penn ordered the production of a map listing the owners of each plot of land.[16] One of the first books printed in colonial Pennsylvania was William Penn's treatise on English liberties, which included talk of property rights.[17]

De Soto's institutional approach, which focuses on legal institutions and legal protections for property, is doubtless critical. People will have little incentive to invest if they will not reap the benefits of their labor. There are, of course, some exceptions to this. There are people who labor for the good of others—one might think of Wikipedia and shareware software. And going back in history, there were priests, nuns, ministers, sometimes academics and artists who worked for free, or for less than they could have made elsewhere. But those people are not the norm. In fact, moral philosophers from Adam Smith onward have all emphasized de Soto's story. William Paley, an early nineteenth century English moral philosopher whose work was widely read in the United States at the time, emphasized the need for protection of property. He acknowledged the seeming unfairness of property with a parable about birds collecting food and giving the food to their leader, who did no work:

> If you should see a flock of pigeons in a field of corn; and if (instead of each picking where and what it liked, taking just as much as it wanted, and no more) you should see ninety-nine of them gathering all they got into a heap; reserving nothing for themselves but the chaff and the refuse; keeping this heap for one, and that the weakest perhaps, and worst pigeon of the flock; sitting round and looking on all the winter, whilst this one was devouring, throwing about, and wasting it; and if a pigeon, more hardy or hungry than the rest, touched a grain of the hoard, all the others instantly flying upon it, and tearing it to pieces: if you should see this, you would see nothing more than what is every day practised and established among men. Among men, you see the ninety and nine toiling and scraping together a heap of superfluities for one; getting nothing for themselves

---

15 *The Frame of the Government of the Province of Pennsilvania in America: Together with certain Laws Agreed upon in England by the Governour and Divers Free-Men of the aforesaid Province*, Number 20 (1682), *reprinted in* WILLIAM PENN AND THE FOUNDING OF PENNSYLVANIA, 1680–1684, 130 (Jean R. Soderlund, ed., 1983) (requiring recording of deeds within six months).

16 IRMA CORCORAN, THOMAS HOLME, 1624–1695, SURVEYOR GENERAL OF PENNSYLVANIA, 257–282 (1992) (discussing Holme's A Map of the Improved Part of the Province of Pennsylvania in America). The map is available at http://www.pagenealogy.net/maps/PA%20-%20Thomas%20Holme%20-%201687.jpg.

17 WILLIAM PENN, THE EXCELLENT PRIVILEGE OF LIBERTY AND PROPERTY (1687); Alfred L. Brophy, *Ingenium est Fateri per quos profeceris: Francis Daniel Pastorius'* Young Country Clerks Collection *and Anglo-American Legal Literature, 1680–1716*, 3 U. CHI. L. SCH. ROUNDTABLE 637 (1996).

> all the while, but a little of the coarsest of the provision which their own labour produces (and this one, too, oftentimes the feeblest and worst of the whole set,—a child, a woman, a madman, or a fool); looking quietly on, while they see the fruits of all their labour spent or spoiled; and if one of them take or touch a particle of it, the others join against him, and hang him for the theft.[18]

But Paley found a justification for that seeming unfairness: property rights led to all sorts of benefits that outweighed their harms. The primary virtue of property in Paley's mind was that it promoted production. He concluded that, on balance, property was useful, even if it led to inequality. For that inequality was a by-product of the virtues of property—that it rewards industrious and talented people.[19]

Some criticized Paley's utilitarian calculations. When Henry David Thoreau sought to criticize the principle of utility in his address that we know as "Civil Disobedience," he referred to Paley. Thoreau offered to replace a consideration of morality for those of the utility of slavery. And there were people who eagerly sought to limit property rights in early America. One example comes from the 1830s, in New York State. Tenants on low-rent, long-term leases in the Hudson River Valley sought to abrogate their "landlords'" rights to the property (or to purchase the rights at a low cost). This led to discussion about the virtue of property rights; would other poor people be able to obtain credit to buy land? Novelist James Fenimore Cooper wrote a trilogy about the movement in which he developed the property-rights position that the anti-rent movement was destroying property and the hopes of further prosperity.[20]

Another attack on property took place through the judiciary, as courts narrowly interpreted corporate charters. This appeared most conspicuously in the 1837 case of *Charles River Bridge v. Warren Bridge*.[21] There, Chief Justice Roger B. Taney wrote a majority opinion that narrowly construed the Charles River Bridge's charter, against a vigorous dissent by Justice Joseph Story. Chancellor Kent took to the pages of the *New York Review* to raise the specter of Democratic jurists destroying the rights of property—and leading to financial ruin in the process.[22] Similar conflicts between Democratic modes of charter interpretation and Whig interpretation appeared in state courts at this time.[23] The point of this vignette is that not everyone agreed on the amount of protection of property.

---

18 William Paley, The Principles of Moral and Political Philosophy, 80–81 (1821).

19 *Id.* at 83.

20 James Fenimore Cooper's Littlepage trilogy, *Satanstoe* (1845), *The Chainbearer* (1845), and *The Redskins* (1846), deals with the anti-rent movement and the time leading up to the movement. *The Redskins* is the most explicit in engaging with the ideology of property and the likely consequences of the anti-rent attack on property rights.

21 *Charles River Bridge v. Warren Bridge*, 36 U.S. (11 Pet.) 420 (1837).

22 2 New York Review 372, 385 (1838).

23 *See* Alfred L. Brophy, *"Necessity Knows No Law": Vested Rights and the Styles of Reasoning in the Confederate Conscription Cases*, 69 Miss. L.J. 1123 (2000) (discussing the conflicting Democratic and Whig ideologies towards protection of government charters).

In another—most unexpected—place, this conflict over property and no-property appeared in debate in the Virginia House of Delegates in 1832, over the future direction of Virginia's course regarding slavery. The debate was set in motion by Nat Turner's August 1831 rebellion. By the spring of 1832, the House of Delegates was debating what to do about slavery; some delegates (mostly from the western part of the state, where enslaved people were few) wanted to abolish slavery and provide no compensation to the slave-owners. Charles Faulkner, a delegate from Martinsburg in western Virginia, advanced a theory based on nuisance: slave property was a nuisance to the state and could be abated without compensation.[24] This was said in the Virginia legislature's building, the same building where 30 years later the Confederate Congress met. While that position was heavily criticized, the majority thought slave property quite valuable, indeed indispensable to the state's prosperity, and there was a serious debate about the role of property. One of the leading proponents of slavery in Virginia in the wake of the 1832 debate was Thomas R. Dew, then a young professor at William and Mary. Dew wrote a long pamphlet about slavery's virtues. He concluded that slavery was "the principal means for impelling forward the civilization of mankind."[25]

All of these examples—the *Charles River Bridge* controversy, the anti-rent controversy, and Dew's writings on slavery and economy—remind us that Americans have thought a lot about the role that respect for property rights plays in development. Yet, even regimes in our country that are less protective of property than some would like still offer enough incentive to lead to a vigorous spirit of economic and technological progress. That is, there has been a diversity of opinions on relative protection to accord property rights in the United States, even as our country has tapped the bounties of capitalism.

Questions about de Soto's "Institutional" Story of Property and Capitalism

So while de Soto focuses on the emergence of American property law in the late eighteenth and early nineteenth centuries, much of what he advocates was already in place. But I think there was something else that was in place, beyond the law: an ideology of capitalism. We see some of this in Richard Pipes' *Property and Freedom*,[26] published at about the same time as *The Mystery of Capital*. Pipes runs on a parallel track to de Soto. He emphasizes the importance of a legal system's respect for property. However, Pipes and de Soto part company on the issue of the

24 *Charles Faulkner Speech*, Richmond Enquirer, Feb. 2, 1832, at 1.

25 Thomas Roderick Dew, *Professor Dew on Slavery*, *in* The Pro-slavery Argument, as Maintained by the Most Distinguished Writers of the Southern States—Containing the Several Essays on the Subject of Chancellor Harper, Governor Hammond, Dr. Simms, and Professor Dew, 287, 325 (Charleston, Walker, Richards & Co., 1852).

26 Richard Pipes, Property and Freedom (1999).

centrality of cultural explanations, for Pipes believes a long-term commitment to property is necessary to condition a people to respect freedom.

I ask why de Soto concentrates on the institutional perspective: why is there such a focus on the legal protection of property, without attention to the human spirit that runs parallel to (and, I would argue, ahead of) the legal regime that protects property? That is, there is something else necessary besides a legal regime that will protect the fruits of labor; there has to be a desire to produce the fruits of labor and to make money off that labor. Other people have observed the centrality of those ideas. Max Weber, writing about a century ago, referred to this as the "spirit of capitalism."[27] Second, and closely related, what is the relationship between the legal protection of property and the "spirit of capitalism?" Perhaps for de Soto it is obvious, indeed natural, that individuals have within them a spirit of capitalism—but it is far from clear to me that these ideas are universal. In fact, at lots of times and lots of places in human history, other ideas have predominated. De Soto is, of course, aware of the discussion that capitalism is partly cultural. Yet he brands those who advance a cultural explanation as Brahmins who live in bell jars—that is, within the capitalist system.[28] De Soto challenges those who advance a cultural explanation for capitalism to answer a question about Bill Gates.[29] How much wealth would he have created if there were no secure intellectual property rights? That, of course, leads to the question of why are there are not more Bill Gateses? There are now 300 million people in the United States, where there is a secure property regime. Even within the United States, many people are not in the market system, whether from personal choice or from limited opportunity.

De Soto further charges that the cultural theories about capitalism cannot be tested (and, I would add, can be easily falsified). Those are apt charges, to which I plead guilty. These kinds of meta-questions are difficult to analyze with any kind of precision. De Soto writes, "[A] great part of the research agenda needed to explain why capitalism fails outside the West remains mired in a mass of unexamined and largely untestable assumptions labeled 'culture,' whose main effect is to allow too many of those who live in the privileged enclaves of this world to enjoy feeling superior."[30] This presupposes that the people who employ cultural explanations think capitalism superior to its alternatives; I am not sure that they do. That is perhaps more likely de Soto's sense of how we should view capitalism: those who apply it successfully are superior to those who do not. But we should be careful about making charges that an explanation is untestable, because it is not all that easy to test any of these grand theories. How much does a secure land recording system contribute to the environment for capitalism? Probably a lot. But people have to want capitalism, too. Just as Bill Gates opted in and took advantage of the property regime, many others did not. To explain why some people succeed

---

27 Max Weber, The Protestant Ethic and the Spirit of Capitalism (1904).

28 Mystery of Capital, *supra* note 1, at 225.

29 *Id.* at 224.

30 *Id.* at 225.

and others do not requires a lot of searching, beyond the legal baseline. And just because something cannot easily be tested does not mean it is irrelevant.

There are more than a few people in Western history who sought to glorify God rather than mammon. And a lot of times their interpretation of the Bible was that it counseled against making money. Taking a page from the seventeenth century radical Protestants like the Quakers, one might recall that some have found capitalism mysterious—in that they sought a life freed from the concerns of accumulation of wealth. Yet the Quakers in the Americas were concerned with protection of individual rights, including property.[31] Certainly, that is hard to understand. But one may locate the American love of property in places like seventeenth and eighteenth century Pennsylvania, where property served as a way of securing limited independence, even as property owners were critical of acquisition.

People have been speculating on this for a long time. Daniel Webster's oration at Plymouth in 1820 linked widely distributed property with the United States' political stability. Widely dispersed property holdings gave many people a stake in the government and lent our country a stability unknown in much of Europe.[32] Nineteenth century Americans respected property, for they believed that it brought civilization in its wake. It is not some cold legal principle in an old book that brought capitalism to the shores of British-speaking North America in the seventeenth or eighteenth century. It is people who brought these ideas—along with a lot of other ideas—in their heads and in books with laws in them that confirmed these ideas. It is no surprise that the first legal treatise written in British North America was a form book that dealt largely with real-estate transactions, contracts, wills, trusts, and criminal prosecution—for all of those things were closely related.[33] When settlers arrived and began mapping their property, establishing boundaries, providing for common pasturage when that made sense and for private property when that made even more sense, they were writing in our national character a truth: we are a people concerned with utility. Those considerations of utility, of what will generate the most wealth, have been central to us from that day to this.[34]

31 Brophy, *Ingenium est Fateri per quos profeceris*, *supra* note 17 (discussing Quaker thought on law and the market).

32 Daniel Webster, A Discourse Delivered at Plymouth, December 22, 1820, *in* Commemoration of the First Settlement of New England (3rd ed., 1825), 54–59 (Webster's point is made especially well at 58–59).

33 *See* Brophy, *Ingenium est Fateri per quos profeceris*, *supra* note 17 (discussing Francis Daniel Pastorius' *Young Country Clerk's Collection*, the first legal treatise written in British North America).

34 Scholars as diverse in political orientation as Judge Richard Posner and Harvard Law Professor Morton Horwitz have agreed on this: we are a people who love utility and our law reflects that love. As Posner wrote recently, "[E]conomics is the deep structure of the common law, and the doctrines of that law are the surface structure. … [T]he common law establishes property rights, regulates their exchange, and protects them against unreasonable interference …" Richard A. Posner, Economic Analysis of Law, 249–250 (7th ed., 2007). Horwitz writes of the judges' "instrumental conception" of law, through

A return to the United States' history regarding property law suggests, I think, several things. First, that our legal system does, indeed, provide a robust protection of property rights. That is, de Soto's depiction of the United States' protection of property *is* critical to our development as a capitalist nation. However, it is not clear to me that it is the law that made us capitalist. There is a question here about how the arrows indicating direction of influence point. I think a more complete picture is that both our law and our national character are capitalist. Our legal system did much to promote this spirit: it established a sophisticated commercial law, including a system of mortgaging property; it limited liability for corporations; it limited injunctions against corporations; and it embodied a vigorous spirit of "progress." We see this even in our landscape art. Asher Brown Durand's 1853 canvas, *Progress*, contains all sorts of symbols of progress, all of them related to money: from the peddler to the farmer, the telegraphs, steamboats, and railroads. Painted for a railroad executive, *Progress* was about how capitalism came to America.[35] These symbols are what made America. In the United States, the law was king, as Tom Paine wrote in *Common Sense*; our nation's spirit of capitalism is what made the law.

---

which they modified common law doctrine to promote economic growth. *See* Horwitz, *supra* note 10, at 1–30.

35 *See* Asher Brown Durand's "Progress," available at http://cgfa.sunsite.dk/d/p-durand4.htm.

Chapter 5
Anticipating de Soto: Allotment of Indian Reservations and the Dangers of Land-Titling

Ezra Rosser

Hernando de Soto would have liked the symbolism: an Indian brave steps up before a crowd of government officials, lifts a bow, shoots an arrow into the sky, and with that act becomes a landowner.[1] Such ceremonies, marking the switch from savages to citizens and landowners, were the theatrical high point of one of the most devastating policies imposed on Native American tribes in our history. The official solution to the "Indian problem" from 1887 to 1934 was allotment, a forced breaking apart of Indian reservations into separate parcels owned by Indian individuals or families. Though allotment preceded Hernando de Soto's celebration of land-titling and legal formalization found in *The Mystery of Capital* by more than 100 years, the same thinking underpins both de Soto's ideas and the allotment policy. The allotment experience of Indian tribes suggests that unqualified faith in the transformative power of land-titling is misguided and highlights the particular dangers disadvantaged groups face when their land rights are formalized as individual ownership rights.

Allotment provides a lens for considering the ideas of Hernando de Soto, offering a way of thinking about de Soto's "new" ideas in a historical perspective. In Part I, the legal status of Indian tribes is briefly introduced. Part II focuses on the allotment policy and the prioritization of individual landownership by tribal members. The connection between allotment and Hernando de Soto's emphasis on formalized private property as a development tool is explored in Part III. Modern implementations of land-titling could perhaps avoid having today's disadvantaged groups experience the losses Indians suffered under allotment, but the land alienation risks ought to be considered before going forward with de Soto's property proposals.

---

1 N. Bruce Duthu, *Crow Dog and Oliphant Fistfight at the Tribal Casino: Political Power, Storytelling, and Games of Chance*, 29 Ariz. L. Rev. 171, 194–195 (1997).

Status of Indian Tribes

The classic and probably best single formulation of the status and legal powers of Indian tribes was written by a respected legal realist and Yale law professor, Felix Cohen. Under President Franklin Roosevelt, Cohen worked for the Department of the Interior and while there he took it upon himself to organize Indian law, taking assorted cases, treaties, and other sources of law and authoring the field's first treatise: *The Handbook of Federal Indian Law*.[2] Cohen's *Handbook* summary of the powers and limitations of Indian sovereignty is worth quoting at length:

> [T]hose powers which are lawfully vested in an Indian tribe are not, in general, delegated powers granted by express acts of Congress, but rather inherent powers of limited sovereignty which has never been extinguished. Each Indian tribe begins its relationship with the Federal Government as a sovereign power, recognized as such in treaty and legislation. The powers of sovereignty have been limited from time to time by special treaties and laws designed to take from the Indian tribes control of matters which, in the judgment of Congress, these tribes could no longer be safely permitted to handle. The statutes of Congress, then, must be examined to determine the limitations of tribal sovereignty rather than to determine its sources or its positive content. What is not expressly limited remains within the domain of tribal sovereignty.[3]

By emphasizing that the pre-existing nature of Indian sovereignty meant the assumption should be for, not against, tribes having authority over their territory and governance, Cohen helped establish the primacy of tribal policy-making. The passage also included the darker side of U.S. policy toward Indians: the conceit that Congress could unilaterally limit tribal sovereignty. Reconciling the enormous power Congress has over Indian tribes with tribal sovereignty is perhaps Indian law's biggest intellectual challenge.[4]

---

2 Felix S. Cohen, Handbook of Federal Indian Law (1945). The University of Oklahoma has made images of every page of the *Handbook* available at http://thorpe.ou.edu/cohen.html.

3 Cohen, *supra* note 2, at 122.

4 Justices and scholars have wondered and debated whether such reconciliation is advisable or even possible. Justice Thomas, in his concurrence in *United States v. Lara*, argued that reconciliation is not possible: "It seems to me that much of the confusion reflected in our precedent arises from two largely incompatible and doubtful assumptions. First, Congress (rather than some other part of the Federal Government) can regulate virtually every aspect of the tribes without rendering tribal sovereignty a nullity. Second, the Indian tribes retain inherent sovereignty. … In my view, the tribes either are or are not separate sovereigns, and our federal Indian law cases untenably hold both positions simultaneously" 541 U.S. 193, 214–215 (2004). The two academics to most passionately argue the reconciliation question in a series of articles are professors Robert A. Williams, Jr. and Robert Laurence. Their debate is best read sequentially: Robert A. Williams, Jr., *The Algebra of Federal Indian Law: The*

Cohen based his formulation of the rights of tribes in large part upon the writings of Chief Justice John Marshall, whose decisions in *Johnson v. M'Intosh, Cherokee Nation v. Georgia*, and *Worchester v. Georgia* are the foundational texts for the legal relationship between the United States and Indian tribes. In *Cherokee Nation v. Georgia*, Marshall first labeled tribes "domestic dependent nations," a term that stuck.[5] As these first cases make clear, tribal sovereignty has long been defined more by the land demands of the United States and whites than by justifiable distinctions between Indian nations and non-Indian nations. With the end goal, appropriation of Indian land, being largely fixed, the legal rationales advanced to deny Indian rights to their land end up being just that, rationalizations of policies and power rather than principled stands.[6]

Perhaps nowhere is the Supreme Court's use of legal theory in support of power for its own sake more evident than in *Johnson v. M'Intosh* (1823),[7] the first case in the leading property law casebooks.[8] In his decision, Marshall argued that upon contact with whites, Indians lost most of their rights to land through the "Doctrine of Discovery." Marshall explained that for Europeans entering the New World, "discovery gave title to the government, by whose subjects or by whose authority, it was made, against all other European governments."[9] He went on to say that though Indians "were admitted to be the rightful occupants of the soil … their rights to complete sovereignty, as independent nations were necessarily diminished."[10]

Hard Trail of Decolonizing and Americanizing the White Man's Indian Jurisprudence, 1986 Wis. L. Rev. 219; Robert Laurence, *Learning to Live with the Plenary Power of Congress over the Indian Nations: An Essay in Reaction to Professor Williams' Algebra*, 30 Ariz. L. Rev. 413 (1988); Robert A. Williams, Jr., *Learning Not to Live with Eurocentric Myopia: A Reply to Professor Laurence's Learning to Live with the Plenary Power of Congress over the Indian Nations*, 30 Ariz. L. Rev. 439 (1988); and Robert Laurence, *On Eurocentric Myopia, the Designated Hitter Rule and "The Actual State of Things,"* 30 Ariz. L. Rev. 459 (1988).

5 30 U.S. (5 Pet.) 1, 17 (1831).

6 Professor Ronald Trosper, one of the few Indian economics scholars, makes a similar point: "Academics studying Indians often tend to overlook simple explanations or simple issues, turning instead to complicated ones. The simplest fact about Indians is that their land was taken unfairly. The interesting questions accompanying the simple story should not obscure it" Ronald Trosper, *Who is Subsidizing Whom?*, *in* American Indian Policy: Self-Governance and Economic Development, 175, 186 (Lyman H. Legters and Fremont J. Lyden, eds, 1994).

7 21 U.S. (8 Wheat.), at 543 (1823).

8 *See* Jesse Dukeminier, James E. Krier, Gregory S. Alexander and Michael H. Schill, Property, 3–9 (6th ed., 2006); Joseph William Singer, Property, 4–15 (3rd ed., 2002). It is also the first case in most Indian law casebooks, see David H. Getches, Charles F. Wilkinson and Robert A. Williams, Jr., Federal Indian Law, 63–68 (5th ed., 2005); Robert T. Anderson, Bethany Berger, Philip P. Frickey and Sarah Krakoff, American Indian Law, 35–40 (2008); Robert N. Clinton, Carole E. Goldberg and Rebecca Tsosie, American Indian Law: Native Nations and the Federal System, 51–55 (5th ed., 2007).

9 21 U.S. (8 Wheat.), at 573.

10 21 U.S., at 574.

What is remarkable about *Johnson v. M'Intosh*, and some more recent Indian law decisions as well, is the lack of awareness of irony in the opinion.[11]

Indian rights to land ultimately were forced to give way to power and conquest. Courts, Marshall said, were powerless to reject a doctrine which "the property of the great mass of the community originates in" and upon which the country was founded.[12] Indians were different enough, lesser, in ways that made conquest more palatable according to the Court: "the character and religion" of Indians "afforded an apology for considering them as a people over whom the superior genius of Europe might claim an ascendency."[13] As Professor Robert A. Williams, Jr. argues powerfully in his work, the racism found in *Johnson v. M'Intosh* both reflects a history of racist understandings of "the other" in pre-contact Europe and can be found throughout the Indian-related decisions of the U.S. Supreme Court from 1823 to the present.[14] By 1832, although describing tribes as "numerous and warlike nations," Marshall in *Worchester v. Georgia* moved away from his earlier lengthy defense of the Doctrine of Discovery.[15] Without a nice legal theory on which to rely, Marshall had no choice but to acknowledge the primary basis—"power, war, conquest, give rights"—for his affirmation of legal superiority of the United States over Indian nations.[16]

---

11 Compare, for example, "Frequent and bloody wars, in which the whites were not always the aggressors," *Johnson v. M'Intosh*, 21 U.S. (8 Wheat.), at 543, 590 (1823), with "There were undoubtedly greed, cupidity, and other less-than-admirable tactics employed by the Government … but the Indians did not lack their share of villainy either," *United States v. Sioux Nation of Indians*, 448 U.S. 371, 435 (1980) (Rehnquist, J., dissenting).

12 21 U.S. (8 Wheat.), at 591.

13 21 U.S., at 573.

14 Professor Williams' publications trace the racist origins as well as the lasting effects and modern examples in Federal Indian Law of racist notions regarding Indians as savages or as lesser peoples. *See, e.g.,* Robert A. Williams, Jr., The American Indian in Western Legal Thought: The Discourses of Conquest (1990); Robert A. Williams, Jr., Like a Loaded Weapon: The Rehnquist Court, Indian Rights, and the Legal History of Racism in America (2005). Within the Indian law community, some scholars, while crediting Professor Williams for his in-depth research, argue against focusing too much on the racism in *Johnson v. M'Intosh* because they argue that the opinion provides a workable foundation for decisions supportive of Indian rights. *See, e.g.,* Robert T. Anderson, *supra* note 8, at 895–900 (describing the different intellectual camps within Indian law scholarship).

15 31 U.S. (6 Pet.), at 515, 517 (1832).

16 31 U.S., at 543. The focus on power in *Worchester v. Georgia* is striking considering how the events that followed the case highlighted the Court's own dependence on executive power. After the case, President Andrew Jackson openly defied the Court's holding that "the laws of Georgia can have no force" within the Cherokee nation. 31 U.S., at 561. As Justice Breyer has noted in multiple speeches, "President Andrew Jackson reportedly said, 'John Marshall has made his decision; now let him enforce it.'" *See, e.g.,* Commencement Address of Justice Stephen Breyer, Boston College Law School (May 23, 2003), available at http://www.supremecourtus.gov/publicinfo/speeches/sp_05-23-03.html; Commencement Address of Justice Stephen Breyer, University of Pennsylvania Law School (May 19, 2003), available at http://www.supremecourtus.gov/publicinfo/speeches/sp_05-19-03.html.

The primary goal of the United States' assertion of superiority over tribes has been acquisition of Indian land and control over the form in which Indians hold land. Unlike other Americans, Indians do not enjoy protections against uncompensated takings.[17] As recently as 2005, the Court, without any precedent or legislative support, denied Indians have the power to control land within their original reservation boundaries when those lands have been held in non-Indian hands for a long enough period of time.[18] Even where Indian land rights are acknowledged and reservation boundaries respected, the U.S. and state governments have too frequently acted in ways that limit the ability of tribes to govern themselves and to get the most from their land.[19] Throughout American history, the "superior genius" of Washington policy-makers has undermined tribal control over land—a requirement for both sovereignty and economic development—and never more so than during allotment.[20]

Allotment

Between 1887 and 1934, the official stance of the United States regarding Indian reservations was that they should be divided into individual parcels. This was quite consciously an effort to do away with Indian reservations; President Theodore

17 *Tee-Hit-Ton Indians v. United States*, 348 U.S. 272, 290 (1995) ("no other course would meet the problem of the growth of the United States except to make congressional contributions for Indian lands rather than to subject the government to an obligation to pay the value when taken"). *See also* Joseph William Singer, *Double Bind: Indian Nations v. The Supreme Court*, 119 Harv. L. Rev. F. 1, 3–6 (2005) ("Indians are routinely denied rights and powers they would be granted if they were non-Indians. … the Supreme Court would have protected the tribe's possessory rights if it had been a non-Indian corporation rather than a Native nation.").

18 *City of Sherrill v. Oneida Indian Nation of New York*, 544 U.S. 197 (2005). For more on the case, see Sarah Krakoff, *City of Sherrill v. Oneida Indian Nation of New York: A Regretful Postscript to the Taxation Chapter in Cohen's Handbook of Federal Indian Law*, 41 Tulsa L. Rev. 5 (2005). For more on non-Indian resistance to the land claims of the Oneida, see Ezra Rosser, *Protecting Non-Indians From Harm? The Property Consequences of Indians*, 87 Ore. L. Rev. 175, 198–209 (2008).

19 *See, e.g.,* David D. Haddock and Robert J. Miller, *Can a Sovereign Protect Investors from Itself? Tribal Institutions to Spur Reservation Investment*, 8 J. Small & Emerging Bus. L. 173, 213 (2004) (connecting the "glacial pace of BIA title searches" and the more than 100-year staff backlog on such requests with tribal economic development difficulties); *United States v. Navajo Nation*, 537 U.S. 488, 518–520 (2003) (J. Souter in dissent describing the *ex parte* communications that led the Secretary of the Interior to withhold information regarding the appropriate royalty rate for coal extraction from the Navajo Nation and to approve a lease with a lower rate).

20 *See, e.g.,* Stacy L. Leeds, *The Burning of Blackacre: A Step Toward Reclaiming Tribal Property Law*, 10 Kan. J.L. & Pub. Pol'y 491, 491 (2000) (describing allotment as the "most devastating blow to tribal land tenure").

Roosevelt called the authorizing legislation, the Dawes Act of 1887, "a mighty pulverizing engine to break up the tribal land mass," adding, "[i]t acts directly upon the family and the individual."[21] The title of the General Allotment Act—or Dawes Act, for its principal proponent in Congress, Henry A. Dawes—was An Act to Provide for the Allotment of Lands in Severalty to Indians on the Various Reservations.[22] By the time it ended under Franklin Delano Roosevelt, more than 60 percent of the 1887 tribal land base had been lost.[23] Moreover, though hailed as a way of lifting Indians out of the poverty and bad conditions found on reservations by providing them the "benefits" of individual landownership, Indians ended up being socially and economically worse off rather than better off as a result of allotment.

The goal and "expectation" of allotment was to turn savage Indians into noble farmers through individual landownership.[24] The Dawes Act was by no means the first Indian legislation passed, in the words of Chief Justice Marshall regarding a different policy in *Worchester v. Georgia*, with the hope of "civilizing and converting them from hunters into agriculturalists."[25] The Indian-to-farmer hope was the central element of allotment. Unfortunately, referencing tribal land loss and the number of Indians who were completely landless by the end of the period, the Supreme Court observed that "this goal of allotment proved to be a disastrous failure."[26]

Allotment first divided reservations among tribal members. On reservations selected for allotment by the president, Indian children received 40-acre parcels; 160-acre parcels went to each Indian head of households; and single adults were entitled to 80 acres.[27] The Act contemplated these parcels being in a protected

---

21 Charles F. Wilkinson, American Indians, Time, and The Law: Native Societies in a Modern Constitutional Democracy, 19 (1987). For more on the legislative and social history leading up to the Dawes Act, see Francis Paul Prucha, American Indian Policy in Crisis: Christian Reformers and the Indian, 1865–1900, 227–252 (1976).

22 The *full* title is: An Act to Provide for the Allotment of Lands in Severalty to Indians on the Various Reservations, and To Extend the Protection of the Laws of the United States and the Territories over the Indians, and for Other Purposes, Chap. 119, 24 Stat. 388 (Feb. 8, 1887).

23 L. Scott Gould, *The Consent Paradigm: Tribal Sovereignty at the Millennium*, 96 Colum. L. Rev. 809, 830 (1996) (Indian land holdings went from "138 million acres in 1887 to 52 million acres in 1934").

24 Institute for Government Administration, The Problem of Indian Administration 7 (Lewis Meriam et al. 1928) [hereinafter Meriam Report]. *See also* Judith V. Royster, *Of Surplus Lands and Landfills: The Case of the Yankton Sioux*, 43 S.D. L. Rev. 283, 284 (1998) (noting that allotment represented a shift from an earlier goal of isolating Indians to assimilating them as "Christianized yeoman farmers").

25 31 U.S. (6 Pet.) 515, 557 (1832).

26 *Hagan v. Utah*, 510 U.S. 399, 425 (1994).

27 Kenneth H. Bobroff, *Retelling Allotment: Indian Property Rights and the Myth of Common Ownership*, 54 Vand. L. Rev. 1559, 1564 (2001). As Vine Deloria, Jr. noted: "The formula used—160 acres for the head of the family, 80 acres for older children and wives, and 40 acres for minor children—did not look even five years down the road to the future of

status for 25 years, during which period the land was held in trust by the U.S. government and could not be alienated or encumbered. Behind this limitation was the thought that Indians needed time to "complete[] their intended transformation" and become successful farmers.[28] Ending the dependence of reservation Indians on annuities and other forms of government support was one of the goals of allotment, but it was thought that effecting such a change would require Indians to become self-sufficient farmers.[29] The United States recognized, based on prior allotment attempts, that simply providing fee simple title to allottees would not accomplish this goal because non-Indians would immediately obtain the land.[30] Non-Indians had more farming experience and greater access to capital; allottees were thus made owners of their land, but ordinarily had to wait 25 years for their ownership to convert into fee simple ownership.

The protective justification of U.S. trusteeship over allotted land meant that exceptions allowing for full fee simple ownership were made when protection was not required. Indians who could show that they were "competent" to manage their

---

the tribe. If an adult man were capable of supporting his family on 160 acres, did that mean that his 18-year-old son could do so on 80 acres, and a decade later his 12-year-old, now 22, on 40 acres?" Vine Deloria, Jr., *Reserving to Themselves: Treaties and the Powers of Indian Tribes*, 38 ARIZ. L. REV. 963, 978 (1996). *See also* Meriam Report, *supra* note 24, at 467 ("In the future unallotted lands should generally be reserved to the Indians themselves. The needs of most tribes must slowly but surely increase").

28 Jessica A. Shoemaker, *Like Snow in the Spring Time: Allotment, Fractionation, and the Indian Land Tenure Problem*, 2003 WIS. L. REV. 729, 737–738.

29 Given the role the United States played in creating Indian "dependence," such a description is misleading. Within Indian law, however, dependence plays a significant role in deciding whether something is Indian country, which is defined as: "(a) all land within the limits of any Indian reservation under the jurisdiction of the United States Government, notwithstanding the issuance of any patent, and, including rights-of-way running through the reservation; (b) all dependent Indian communities within the borders of the United States whether within the original or subsequently acquired territory thereof, and whether within or without the limits of a state; and (c) all Indian allotments, the Indian titles to which have not been extinguished, including rights-of-way running through the same" 18 USCS §1151 (LexisNexis 1949). Two Supreme Court cases on the relationship between "dependence" and "Indian country" stand out: *United States v. Sandoval*, 231 U.S. 28, 41 (1913) (holding that Pueblo tribes qualified as Indians over whom the Indian commerce clause governed because they are "dependent upon the fostering care and protection of the Government, like reservation Indians in general; that, although industrially superior, they are intellectually and morally inferior to many of them") and *Alaska v. Native Village of Venetie Tribal Government*, 522 U.S. 520, 527–534 (1998) (holding that the tribe's Alaska Native Claims Settlement Act lands do not satisfy the dependent Indian communities prong of the definition of Indian country). For a review of the Court's treatment of "dependent Indian community," as well as an alternative test, see Paul W. Shagen, *Comment: Indian Country: The Dependent Indian Community Concept and Tribal/Tribal Member Immunity from State Taxation*, 27 N.M. L. REV. 421 (1997).

30 Judith V. Royster, *The Legacy of Allotment*, 27 ARIZ. ST. L.J. 1, 10 (1995).

own affairs could get restrictions on their ownership removed. As a testament to the racism found throughout Indian-white relations, allottees with less than half Indian blood were presumptively competent.[31] So-called "competency hearings" were used, but as non-Indian demand for allotted land intensified, the standards of "competency" decreased and became more systematic in order to facilitate the Indian-to-white transfer of land.[32] Assimilation of Indians and their land led Congress to amend the law, with the Burke Act of 1906, so that the Secretary of the Interior could issue fee patents—ridding land of federal trusteeship—earlier than the General Allotment Act had first contemplated.[33] As Professor Judith Royster noted, "allottees who neither applied for nor wanted to accept them" were issued fee patents.[34] The U.S. government wanted Indians, or purchasers from Indians, to own in fee simple, and consequently, fee patents were "issued too freely."[35]

The results were predictable and tragic. Many Indians who received fee patents sold their land. Of those who either voluntarily or without their consent had their allotment converted into fee early, reports indicated that 90-plus percent "lost their lands."[36] Once Indians held land in fee, the land could be taxed, and many Indians lost their lands as a consequence through tax foreclosure.[37] The consequences were similar for those who waited out the 25-year period; all told, "two-thirds of the land allotted—approximately 27 million acres—had passed into non-Indian ownership."[38]

The problems did not end there. Allotments that were never sold to non-Indians still passed from generation to generation and became increasing fractionated among a multitude of owners, each with a very small interest in the original

---

31 Rose Cuison Villazor, *Blood Quantum Land Laws and the Race Versus Political Identity Dilemma*, 96 CALIF. L. REV. 801, 808 (2008) (discussing the one-half blood quantum line and the relationship of blood quantum to allotment). The one-half blood quantum definition of competency became policy in 1917. Royster, *The Legacy of Allotment*, *supra* note 30, at 12.

32 Royster, *The Legacy of Allotment*, *supra* note 30, at 12.

33 *Id.* at 11.

34 *Id.* at 11.

35 Meriam Report, *supra* note 24, at 100.

36 Royster, *The Legacy of Allotment*, *supra* note 30, at 11–12.

37 Robert J. Miller, *Economic Development in Indian Country: Will Capitalism or Socialism Succeed?*, 80 OR. L. REV. 757, 814 (2001). *See also* Angelique A. EagleWoman, *The Philosophy of Colonization Underlying Taxation Imposed Upon Tribal Nations Within the United States*, 43 TULSA L. REV. 43, 50–55 (2007) (discussing how allotment opened up tribal lands to taxation).

38 Royster, *The Legacy of Allotment*, *supra* note 30, at 12. A useful map for understanding the effect of allotment on an Indian reservation can be found in IMRE SUTTON, AMERICAN INDIAN TERRITORIALITY: ONLINE RESEARCH GUIDE 10 Fig. P. 4 (Oct. 17, 2003 ed.) available at http://thorpe.ou.edu/treatises/AIT%20hdr%20pdfs/Preface2.pdf (noting in the map's caption that "[f]or many reservations, because of allotment, a high percentage of holdings are in non-Indian hands").

allotment land.[39] Such fractionalization can make land-use decisions hard and can result in yet more land loss, something Professor Thomas Mitchell has explored in the context of black-owned farms, and which is equally true for Indians.[40] Even when Congress stepped in—through the Indian Lands Consolidation Act and an amended version of the Act—to turn tiny ownership interests back over to the tribe, the Supreme Court twice stepped in to block such a correction to the predictable long-run effects of allotment.[41] This reflects a general difficulty that Indian tribes have in getting back land that has been lost.[42] Tribes seeking to reacquire land have seen the United States place a series of roadblocks in their path: everything from policies that require monetary restitution rather than land restoration to opinions that Indian land rights should be time-barred by the judiciary.[43] There is little hope that tribes will be restored the land lost because of allotment.

Though allotment was sold as a way to get land out of tribal hands and into the hands of Indian families and individuals, the second stage of allotment was a more straightforward non-Indian land grab. Reservation land that remained after all tribal members had gotten their parcels was considered "surplus land," even though tribes had guarantees protecting the permanence of their reservation land base.[44] Surplus land would be sold, often at cut-rate prices, to non-Indian settlers.[45] Low populations coupled with relatively large tribal land holdings guaranteed that tribes subjected to allotment would see significant portions of their reservations alienated as surplus

---

39 *Hodel v. Irving*, 481 U.S. 704, 708 (1987) ("But the end of future allotment by itself could not prevent the further compounding of the existing problem caused by the passage of time. Ownership continued to fragment as succeeding generations came to hold the property, since, in the order of things, each property owner was apt to have more than one heir").

40 *See* Thomas W. Mitchell, *From Reconstruction to Deconstruction: Undermining Black Landownership, Political Independence, and Community Through Partition Sales of Tenancies in Common*, 95 Nw. U.L. Rev. 505 (2001).

41 Leeds, *supra* note 20, at 492. Extensive analysis of the ILCA can be found in Katheleen R. Guzman, *Give or Take an Acre: Property Norms and the Indian Land Consolidation Act*, 85 Iowa L. Rev. 595 (2000).

42 For more on the limited compensation paid to tribes as well as the general disfavor of returning land, see Nell Jessup Newton, *Compensation, Reparations, & Restitution: Indian Property Claims in the United States*, 28 Ga. L. Rev. 453, 468–480 (1994).

43 Despite supposedly welcoming all Indian grievances, in practice the Indian Claims Commission limited Indians to financial compensation even when the claim and just resolutions revolved around land wrongly taken from tribes. For more on the limitations of the Indian Claims Commission in practice, see Sandra C. Danforth, *Note: Repaying Historical Debts: The Indian Claims Commission*, 49 N.D.L. Rev. 359 (1973). More recently, when the Oneida Indian Nation sought to reacquire, on the open market, land within its reservation, it was told that too much time had passed since the land had been under Oneida control. *City of Sherrill v. Oneida Indian Nation of New York*, 544 U.S. 197 (2005).

44 For an overview of the designation and nature of surplus lands under the Dawes Act, see Royster, *The Legacy of Allotment*, *supra* note 30, at 13–14.

45 In theory the Secretary of the Interior had to "negotiate the purchase" of such lands from tribes. *See* Bobroff, *supra* note 27, at 1564.

lands to non-Indians, regardless of their future needs.[46] In fact, the predictable effect of these demographic facts, when coupled with neighboring non-Indian demands for land, motivated the selection of which reservations would be allotted.[47] The president was more likely to choose to allot the land of tribes located near non-Indian population centers.[48] Fully 38 million acres, 27 percent of the tribal land base, was declared "surplus" and sold off to non-Indians.[49] What the sale of surplus land clarifies—in case the division of the land in severalty left any doubt—was that despite the supposed benefits of the policy to tribal members, allotment's true beneficiaries were non-Indians.[50] The primacy of non-Indian interests was further highlighted by the Supreme Court's 1903 decision in *Lone Wolf v. Hitchcock* that Indian opposition could not stop allotment from taking place.[51]

Besides imposing significant losses of land on allotted tribes, the policy failed to generate the economic and social gains that proponents said it would. Eastern whites who self-identified under the banner "Friends of the Indian" had spent almost 20 years advocating for allotment based on their "messianic faith in the civilizing force of private property."[52] The Friends of the Indian included "some of the most progressive reformers of the day," who believed that allotment would both protect

---

46 *See* Miller, *supra* note 37, at 813 ("Most tribes did not have sufficient populations to allot their entire reservation to just tribal members. Hence, the United States sold the surplus lands to non-Indians."); Shoemaker, *supra* note 28, at 740 (surplus land distribution "left no reservation land on which future generations of Indian owners could spread out and develop as their numbers grew").

47 Allison M. Dussias, *Squaw Drudges, Farm Wives, and Dann Sisters' Last Stand: American Indian Women's Resistance to Domestication and the Denial of Their Property Rights*, 77 N.C.L. Rev. 637, 674 (1999). *See also* Terry L. Anderson, Sovereign Nations or Reservations? An Economic History of American Indians 94 (1995) (noting that whites had an incentive to try to open up reservations through allotment because at the time "western land values were rising").

48 Bobroff, *supra* note 27, at 1609–1610.

49 Gould, *supra* note 23, at 830.

50 *But see* Charles C. Painter, *The Indian and His Property*, *in* Americanizing the American Indians: Writings by the "Friends of the Indian" 1880–1900, at 114, 116 (Francis Paul Prucha, ed., 1973) (arguing that "the surplus of the reservation after allotment is a danger that threatens much, and a dead weight that hangs heavily about the newly made citizen's neck").

51 187 U.S. 553 (1903). Tulsa Law Review published a symposium issue commemorating the hundredth anniversary of *Lone Wolf* and Judith Royster's *Foreword* ably describes the background and effect of the case, "one of the most influential, and most contemptible, decisions in all of Indian law." Judith Royster, *Foreword: Look Back in Anger*, 38 Tulsa L. Rev. 1, 3 (2002).

52 Bobroff, *supra* note 27, at 1565. For a brief account of how Indian-rights advocates came to support allotment as the solution to the Indian problem, see Wilcomb E. Washburn, The Assault on Indian Tribalism: The General Allotment Law (Dawes Act) of 1887 (1975), 5–8. *See generally* Americanizing the American Indians, *supra* note 50 (collecting the writings of Friends of the Indian).

Indians from losing more land to settlers and would save Indians from their own "cultural backwardness."[53] Indians with large reserves were able to continue their prior lifestyle and did not have to resort to the intensive cultivation of land that was the non-Indian norm.[54] The problem—"Indians had too much land!"—had an obvious solution: break up the reservations.[55] Large, treaty-guaranteed, Indian land holdings supposedly "thwarted the highest and best economic uses of these lands," something that was antithetical to the beliefs of a country with a singular notion of how land should be used and owned.[56]

Proponents of allotment wrongly believed that Indian property law was essentially a blank slate upon which American property law and forms of ownership could be placed.[57] Lack of recognition of Indian respect for private property and their various forms of legal protection of individual ownership led reformers to argue that what was needed was to end the communal way of life on reservations.[58] "Giving" Indians the gift of the fee simple form of ownership, it was said, would open their eyes to the benefits of hard work, capitalism, and ultimately, through hardship, Christianity.[59] The myth of Indian common ownership, according to Kenneth Bobroff, is used to explain the unquestionable failure of allotment to generate the predicted economic growth. Allotment did not work, so the story goes, because Indians were unprepared for private ownership.[60] As Bobroff ably demonstrates, this is a myth whose roots can be found in the inability of non-Indians to recognize the forms of Indian ownership that pre-dated

53 Newton, *supra* note 42, at 465.

54 Not surprisingly, the change from "traditional tribal land uses in favor of intensive, land-degrading ranching and dry-land farming practices by non-Indian settlers and Indian allottees" mandated by allotment had a detrimental effect on the Indian land base. Raymond Cross, *Tribes as Rich Nations*, 79 Or. L. Rev. 893, 909 (2000). *See also* Angela R. Riley, *Good (Native) Governance*, 107 Colum. L. Rev. 1049, 1088 (2007) (noting that Indian "lifeways" are "undermined" by the imposition of foreign government structures and property systems, citing the Dawes Act as an example).

55 Raymond Cross, *Sovereign Bargains, Indian Takings, and the Preservation of Indian Country in the Twenty-first Century*, 40 Ariz. L. Rev. 425, 459 (1998).

56 *Id.* at 459.

57 Bobroff, *supra* note 27, at 1565.

58 As Terry Anderson notes, in fact "[p]rior to the arrival of Europeans, Indians understood the importance of individual rights to property and enforced those rights through formal and informal institutions" Terry L. Anderson, *supra* note 47, at 8. Descriptions of the various forms of Indian ownership emphasize the connection between cultural values and the forms of tribally recognized ownership. *See* Anderson at 32–41; Bobroff, *supra* note 27, at 1600 ("an analogy for almost every significant element of Anglo-American property law is present somewhere in the preceding survey of Indian property systems").

59 *See* Miller, *supra* note 37, at 814 (clarifying that it would be an "exaggeration" to say that the goal of allotment was to turn Indians into capitalists per se because the goal was more specific, to turn them more into "civilized," "christianized," "small scale farmers based on the model of white Americans").

60 Bobroff, *supra* note 27, at 1561.

allotment.[61] The problem with allotment, Bobroff argues, was not the introduction of private property per se, but the inflexibility and cultural indifference of the system of American property law that was imposed.[62]

The inflexibility was intentional and harsh. Allotment attempted to rid the country of the differences between Indians and non-Indians—culturally and in their forms of land use and ownership—that stood in the way of solving the "Indian problem" through assimilation.[63] The fact that successors to land could be, and by design would often be, non-Indians made a singular—fee simple—form of ownership all the more important.[64] Absorbing Indians and their land into America required that group land rights be replaced by individual rights and that the individual rights of Indians mirror those of non-Indians. It also required a certain callousness regarding the adverse effects of allotment experienced by many Indians. Allotment diminished, rather than increased, the productivity of reservation farming and did not "even help economic conditions" or "private economic interests in Indian country."[65]

---

61 *See* Bobroff, at 1571–1602 (surveying the property rights systems of a number of tribes).

62 Bobroff, at 1563. Professor Frank Pommersheim similarly calls attention to the cultural insensitivity of allotment: "The allotment policy is best understood, perhaps, when analogized to a land reform policy imposed from the top down without tribal input and consent; a policy grossly undercapitalized, provided as little as ten dollars and less per allottee for implements, seeds, and instruction; a policy insensitive to the hunting and food gathering traditions of non-agricultural tribes; and a policy devoid of any cultural understanding of the roles of the tiyospaye (e.g., the extended family of the Lakota) in which the allotments that were often assigned to individuals were located outside their home communities beyond their natural habitat. Seen from this perspective, it is not difficult to understand why the allotment policy failed." Frank Pommersheim, *The Reservation as Place: A South Dakota Essay*, 34 S.D. L. Rev. 246, 255–256 (1989).

63 In an important early book looking at allotment, D.S. Otis observed: "The supreme aim of the friends of the Indian was to substitute white civilization for his tribal culture, and they shrewdly sensed that the difference in the concepts of property was fundamental to the contrast between the two ways of life. That the white man's way was good and the Indian's way was bad, all agreed." D.S. Otis, The Dawes Act and the Allotment of Indian Lands 8–9 (Francis Paul Prucha ed., photo. reprint 1973) (1898). (In addition to editing, Prucha wrote an introduction for the 1973 reprinting of the 1898 text.)

64 Understanding whites, rather than Indians, as the intended beneficiary of allotment makes the structural inflexibility more understandable: "To the extent that Congress was making the rules on behalf of white constituents, the benefits and costs to Indians of alternative institutions were often of little relevance. For example, the Dawes Act of 1887 (otherwise known as the General Allotment Act), which assigned parcels of land to individual Indians, may have been designed to give Indians the benefits of private ownership. But an explanation more consistent with modern theories of political economy is that it provided a mechanism for land hungry whites to obtain access to reservations and for bureaucrats to expand their domains." Terry L. Anderson, *supra* note 47, at 14–15.

65 Miller, *supra* note 37, at 816–817. *See also* Trosper, *supra* note 6, at 184 ("Historians have shown that the Five Civilized Tribes were managing quite well in Indian Territory prior

Written at the end of the allotment period, the Merriam Report's conclusions were damning of a policy that proponents argued would lead to economic success. As the authors noted regarding the issuance of fee patents, "Too much reliance has been placed on the theory that the way to teach a boy to swim is to throw him overboard and let him swim or drown."[66] With reservation land too often arid and with limited agricultural potential, "Too many [Indians] are poor and living below any reasonable standard of health and decency."[67] To better understand the complete failure of allotment, even without taking into account the loss of land, it is worth quoting at length the report's description of Indian poverty:

> The standard of living is often unbelievably low. Almost nothing is spent for shelter and firewood, and very little for clothing and food. Many homes were visited where there was almost no food on hand. The homes where a reserve of food had been accumulated were the exception. Many Indians are just above the famine level, and if anything goes wrong they must go without or fall back upon government rations.[68]

Allotment resulted not in the self-sufficiency and economic development through individually owned agriculture anticipated by Friends of the Indian but rather in continued poverty and dependence on government support, albeit on much diminished reservations.

History and de Soto

The challenge in understanding the efficacy of Hernando de Soto's assertions that formalization of title will allow the poor an escape from poverty is the limited historical record for testing the hypothesis.[69] *The Mystery of Capital* is less than 10 years old, and programs designed to implement de Soto's ideas regarding

---

to the application of the allotment policy to them"). For a contrary view, see Wilcomb E. Washburn, *Foreword* to Terry L. Anderson, *supra* note 47, at x (describing the views of Terry L. Anderson: "Anderson argues that Indians who received land in fee simple after the breakup of tribal lands were more productive than those individuals whose land was encumbered by the continuing 'trust' relationship with the federal government, and even more productive than the land retained under tribal control under a similar trust relationship").

66 Meriam Report, *supra* note 24, at 100.

67 *Id.* at 433–434.

68 *Id.* 449–451.

69 Hernando de Soto is the author of two influential books, *The Other Path: The Invisible Revolution in the Third World* (1989) and *The Mystery of Capital: Why Capitalism Triumphs in the West and Fails Everywhere Else* (2000). The discussion of de Soto's ideas in this article is drawn out of *The Mystery of Capital*. For a brief introduction to de Soto generally, as well as the acclaim that has greeted his ideas, see Rashmi Dyal-Chand, *Exporting the Ownership Society: A Case Study on the Economic Impact of Property*

land-titling found in the book are even younger. Research looking at the early consequences of such programs suggests that the results are mixed, with some programs showing signs of success and others stumbling.[70] But comprehensive studies will have to wait until such programs have had more time to run their course. Allotment of reservations offers a unique historical lens through which to consider some of the potential long-term outcomes of modern land-titling programs. Based on many of the same assumptions regarding private property and disadvantaged groups as are found in *The Mystery of Capital*, allotment's failure highlights many of the dangers disadvantaged communities face in the formalization of title.

Throughout the world the poor do hold title to land, even if that title is not officially recognized by the state. The analogy used by de Soto, that of dogs whose barking reflects property lines of the community even where such lines are not formally recognized, captures the prevalence of communally accepted ownership. Often where there is a gap between officially-recognized title and title recognized by the community, it is described in terms of a "formal" versus "informal" dichotomy. Such labeling threatens to wrongly discount the norms of the community holding the property and "informally" recognizing ownership. As *The Mystery of Capital* makes clear, such ownership is often accompanied by those implements—written documentation and even legalese in presentation and form of title—that are associated with formal ownership. What makes the land holdings of the poor different from the land holdings of the privileged is lack of official state recognition of their form of ownership.

The parallel to Indians preceding allotment is self-evident. Indian ownership existed but was not recognized by the United States. Allotment was seen as a way Indians could lift themselves out of poverty once their land holdings were converted into the dominant, fee simple, form. Similarly, according to de Soto, once the holdings of the poor are formalized, they will be able to escape poverty by their newfound ability to access the capital markets. This perspective makes it less a question of formalization as much as nationalization of title. The formal qualities of the title held by Indians or the poor are immaterial if the title does not originate out of the *singular* state. *Johnson v. M'Intosh* is a case in point: in a dispute between two claimants to the same land, the Court sided with the person whose title traced back to a non-Indian government over the person who purchased the land directly from an Indian tribe.[71] Nothing in the facts indicates

---

Rights, 39 Rutgers L.J. 59, 59–68 (2007); Ezra Rosser, *Immigrant Remittances*, 41 Conn. L. Rev. 1, 46–48 (2008).

70 A literature survey on land-titling results, with a research bibliography, is in Alain Durand-Lasserve and Geoffrey Payne, World Bank, *Evaluating Impacts of Urban Land Titling: Results and Implications: Preliminary Findings*, available at http://siteresources.worldbank.org/RPDLPROGRAM/Resources/459596–1161903702549/S7-Durand.pdf.

71 *Johnson v. M'Intosh*, 21 U.S. (8 Wheat.) 543, 604 (1823) (rejecting the argument "that a title acquired from the Indians would be valid against a title acquired from the crown, or without the confirmation of the crown"). The case is ostensibly between two parties

that the decision was based on the "formal" qualities of the winner's title versus the loser's; rather, the Court held that it was unable to recognize anything other than the "national" title. The decision did not reject Indian title or suggest that Indian title was worthless. "The person who purchases lands from the Indians, within their territory, incorporates himself with them, so far as respects the property purchased," Chief Justice Marshall noted, "holds their title under their protection, and subject to their laws."[72] The same can be said of one who purchases a *champa* (in El Salvador) or a *favela* (in Brazil): if the title is not formally recognized, the purchaser is protected by and subject to the laws and norms of the surrounding community, not necessarily of the state. Therefore, it makes sense to think of such ownership not as "informal" title but as "community" title.

Land-titling programs share with allotment the goal of incorporating those who hold land according to local norms, or to tribal law pre-allotment, into the property system of the dominant society. For de Soto, incorporation through formalization of title will let the poor unlock the "mystery of capital," by making it possible for them to use their *champa* not just as a place to live but as an asset that can be used to secure loans. This assertion raises the larger question suggested by the Indian experience with allotment: whether incorporation into the dominant society and the related potential increased access to capital are necessarily good for disadvantaged communities.[73] As allotment shows, much can be lost through formalization and incorporation of community title. In what follows, the *champas* of El Salvador are used as the representative community for whom land-titling is being considered.[74] By focusing on the most problematic areas highlighted by allotment—land loss and the need for caution regarding asserted economic gains—the downside of land-titling can be better understood.

The majority of the *champas* of San Salvador are located in the city's *quebradas*, the small valleys of steep terrain that cut their way through many parts of the city.[75] There are other areas with *champa* communities, whole villages made up of

---

whose land claimed overlapped, but despite the Court's acceptance of such a conflict, their land claims never actually overlapped. Eric Kades, *History and Interpretation of the Great Case of* Johnson v. M'Intosh, 19 LAW & HIST. REV. 67 (2001).

72 21 U.S. (8 Wheat.), at 593.

73 There are a number of other preliminary questions, such as whether the poor did not already have access to capital secured through their community title and whether formal title of small lots typical of *champas* will actually allow the poor access to formal capital markets given the banking sector's preference for larger loans. For the purposes of this article, such empirical questions will be put aside and the focus will be on what can be learned from allotment.

74 This article is the second time I have used El Salvador the case study in a paper looking at economic development; for a detailed explanation and for more about El Salvador, see Rosser, *Immigrant Remittances*, *supra* note 69, at 6 n. 10.

75 Spanish is the official language of El Salvador, but there are quite a few words—often starting with a "ch"—that are distinctly Salvadoran. For the definition of *champa*, see JIM CASALBÉ, PURO GUANACO: DICCIONARIO DE SALVADOREÑISMOS 93 (2002).

small plots and houses constructed with whatever was available, but the *champas* located in *quebradas* stand out because they often exist right next to the houses or commercial centers of the upper-class.[76] *Champas* are constructed on unused land owned by another, most often on land initially not deemed suitable by those with money to build "normal" houses. There is no single type of *champa* housing; the category includes everything from a shack made of *laminas* or cardboard to small concrete block structures. While such communities, albeit with different names, are found throughout Latin America, the same sort of housing can be found in the *colonias* of Texas.[77] What begins as a trespass eventually becomes an area permanently filled with *champas* and an area whose residents' occupancy rights are acknowledged by poor and wealthy alike.[78]

For current *champa* residents, land-titling would probably seem ideal, offering them the possibility of converting their community-recognized occupancy rights into formal ownership rights. But suppose formal title was given and the credit markets in response advanced loans to such residents for business or other needs. Some residents would be able to start or expand upon successful small business, but the investments of some would not work out as well. Additionally, instead of trying to earn money with loans backed by their newly formalized title, others would use loans in order to finance additional consumption.[79] Given the poverty

---

76 Such geographical proximity highlights the country's inequalities and the fact that in the United States such living-space proximity across classes is rare. *See, e.g.*, SHERYLL CASHIN, THE FAILURES OF INTEGRATION: HOW RACE AND CLASS ARE UNDERMINING THE AMERICAN DREAM 3–126 (2004).

77 Texas *colonias* are somewhat distinct from El Salvador's *champa* communities in that *colonias* are often constructed on purchased, rather than adversely possessed, land, but both share a disregard for building code requirements. For more on the *colonias* of Texas, compare Jane E. Larson, *Free Markets Deep in the Heart of Texas*, 84 GEO. L.J. 179 (1995) (arguing for flexible building codes to accommodate *colonias*) with Richard Delgado, *Rodrigo's Twelfth Chronicle: The Problem of the Shanty*, 85 GEO. L.J. 667 (1997) (arguing that such accommodation enshrines a permanent lower class status for immigrant residents).

78 Occupancy rights in *champas* reflect Salvadoran social norms as well as the principles underlying rights through adverse possession. For a defense of adverse possession rights even when done deliberately, as opposed to accidentally, see Lee Anne Fennell, *Efficient Trespass: The Case for 'Bad Faith' Adverse Possession*, 100 NW. L. REV. 1037 (2006). Occupancy rights of the poor in El Salvador can also arise in more individual ways not requiring that the surrounding neighbors also live in a *champa*. If there is someone, a squatter family for example, on rural land that you want to buy, as the buyer you are expected to provide in some way for that family. If they have built a structure in the ideal place for a house, the buyer can move them to another part of the land but should build them a house at least equivalent to their original house and allow them to live there in return for some caretaking duties.

79 In many respects, although on a smaller scale, such consumption-driven lending would approximate the refinancing many American homeowners chose to do in the run-up to the mortgage crisis.

in El Salvador, some *champa* owners would need to meet their most basic needs by extracting equity.[80]

What would happen when current residents whose failed projects or consumption made them default? Two distinct possibilities arise: (1) the properties would be resold to a new, but similarly situated individual, of the same community or socio-economic class as the rest of the *champa* zone; or (2) the property would eventually be transferred out of the community and into the hands of the wealthy.

For a number of reasons, the land could well stay in the community. When a current resident defaults, as is sure to happen in a certain percentage of the loans made, the bank will seek out a new purchaser of the *champa*. Those who can afford not to live in a *champa* are unlikely to purchase such a parcel for their own use. Nothing will have changed about the small parcel, the condition of the *champa* itself, and most importantly the neighbors. Even though *champa*-filled *quebradas* can be found across the street from "normal" upper class housing, the wealthy likely will not want to purchase housing where the poor are quite literally living in what otherwise would be their backyard.[81] It is hard to keep up with the Joneses if you are living next to a *champa*.

The poor and the wealthy are unlikely to make the best neighbors. Though minimal, a street offers a visible separation of the classes that arguably provides added security for those living on the non-*champa* side of the street. To the degree that *champas* do not conform with the security norms of the better-off blocks of the city (tall walls, often topped off with either barbed wire or glass, separating every house), a wealthier buyer might rightly feel concerned about break-ins. Although by no means a given, distrust and social distance might also ensure *champas* stay within the same class. Concern that wealthy newcomers might be singled out for maltreatment or indifference to violations of their rights could similarly limit the desirability of purchasing a *champa* to those with less money.

Parcel attributes also could limit the class of purchasers to those similar to the original *champa* residents. Take lot size, for example: living space is closely tied to social class and *champas* usually have tight quarters. The *champa* housing quality probably has a *de minimus* impact, since a wealthier purchaser would presumably tear down or significantly upgrade such housing. But for the purchaser of a single *champa*, the original footprint would limit the size of any future unit

---

80 *See* Rosser, *Immigrant Remittances*, *supra* note 67, at 16 (discussing the extent and causes of Salvadoran poverty).

81 NIMBYism (not-in-my-backyard) plays an important role in delineating and creating the contours of urban space throughout the United States; what is being highlighted here is the extreme proximity that a purchase *in* a *champa* area would mean for a better-off individual or family. For a description of NIMBYism, *see, e.g.,* Denis J. Brion, *An Essay on LULU, NIMBY, and the Problem of Distributive Justice*, 15 B.C. Envtl. Aff. L. Rev. 437, 438 (1988) (explaining that NIMBYism reflects common agreement that undesirable facilities of various types are needed but that "we, as individuals, want these facilities to be located somewhere other than close to our own homes").

constructed. An individual buyer desiring more space could try to acquire adjacent lots, but would likely run into holdout problems when it came to price.[82] Indeed, the price per square foot, without any holdout problems, might itself prevent the wealthy from seeking to buy up *champa* lots in order to build a "normal" house on several lots.[83] That San Salvador has actually put an effort into providing services such as electricity, water, and sewer systems to the *champas* is a sign of how secure residents can feel in their community title. But in some *champas*, wealthier prospective buyers might not find such services or might be concerned that such services, even if present, might not be as reliable in the *champas* as in other residential areas. Finally, as already noted, since *champas* were initially built in San Salvador's *quebradas*, parcels are likely to be located on steeper, harder-to-build-on terrain.

For all these reasons, post-formalization *champas* might likely stay within the hands of the community or new community members of the same socioeconomic class. The absence of wealthy purchasers and visibly upper-class housing is perhaps the strongest evidence of the power the above forces have in restraining wealthy demand for *champa* parcels. If the wealthy really wanted the land, they arguably would have already found a way to get it. On the other hand, systematic formalization of title might alter how the wealthy view acquisition of *champa* land. Before land-titling, even though the resident and would-be seller might be able to produce a formal-looking community title of some sort, a wealthy person interested in buying one or more *champas* would sharply discount the amount they would be willing to pay because of the possibility that their title would not be state-recognized. And if the intention behind the purchase was to construct an expensive house, such risk-based discounting would likely make *champas* not even enter the minds of potential wealthy buyers. Contrast that with the situation post-formalization. Such a buyer could count on state recognition of title, making discounting for risk that what was purchased would not be afforded protection by the state, or from the state, no longer necessary.[84]

---

82 Secretive purchases that disguise the identity and characteristics of the buyer could limit the dangers of holdout pricing.

83 The poor have less money to spend on housing as a good, but often end up paying more per square foot than the wealthy pay. The wealthy pay more in total because they are purchasing more space, but this means that a wealthy buyer might be able to get a better deal for land to construct a house through the full-size housing market than through land aggregation of multiple *champa* parcels. For a leading account of the role differential pricing across income groups plays in setting the contours of urban development, see Sam Bass Warner, Streetcar Suburbs: The Process of Growth in Boston, 1870–1900 (2nd ed., 1978) (focusing on the growth of Boston between 1870–1900).

84 El Salvador's experience with rural land reform (*reforma agraria*) attests to the potential for the wealthy, given the chance and the possibility of formal title, to buy up land once in the hands of the poor. El Salvador's civil war, which ended in a peace agreement between the conservative government and the leftist Frente Farabundo Martí

Formalization makes *champa* land more attractive to the wealthy buyer, but how could that hurt the *champa* community? Just as gentrification of historically black parts of a city can help individual black owners by increasing the value of their property, while simultaneously harming their community, so too with *champas*. Surrounded by the high walls of upper-class housing or commercial centers and their associated ubiquitous security guards, *champas* are a unique and perhaps irreplaceable community asset for San Salvador's lower classes. The community aspect of their title makes the *champas* serve a role—limiting future residents to approximately the same class—similar to an affordable housing trust. San Salvador's affordable housing principally can be found in (a) *champas*, often in wealthier parts of town; (b) distant poorer suburbs with long commutes, such as Apopa or Lourdes; or (c) in more dangerous areas closer to the city, such as Soyapango. Each option has its associated costs and benefits, but *champas* play an important role in ensuring both affordability and social mixing in San Salvador. That the titles are not formalized serves as an implicit limitation on the price of *champas*, ensuring their relative affordability.

A sufficient improvement in the welfare of current residents through land-titling could justify abandoning the twin goals of protecting the community's continued ownership of *champas* and ensuring their future affordability.[85] The ability of current residents to translate land-titling into welfare gains requires that a number of factors line up. Titling must be linked to new credit being extended and perhaps most importantly, residents need both good ideas regarding how to use such credit and space for new or expanded businesses to succeed in the surrounding economic environment. Giving *champa* residents access to business capital will not improve their welfare if their ideas fail because they are entering a market already flooded with barely surviving entrepreneurial ventures of the same sort. If not fitting with

---

para la Liberación Nacional (FMLN) guerrillas, lasted from 1980–1992. In connection with the civil unrest, large farms owned by members of the oligarchy were expropriated and distributed to the poor, either in the form of collectives or as individual holdings. Following the peace agreement, soldiers on both sides also received land. To prevent the land from once again becoming locked up in the hands of a few families, El Salvador also created a limit on the amount of land any one individual could own. Nevertheless, the originally expropriated land base has diminished. Collectives unable to make loan payments have been forced to sell land or have suffered foreclosures and individuals have sold off land. El Salvador's land reform experience, however, is at best an imperfect example of the dangers of land-titling, as the land was never held under any sort of "community title." The land went from being owned in fee by the extremely wealthy to being owned in fee by collectives and poor individuals to being owned in fee by new purchasers. In the case of *champas*, the expropriation was not official state policy in the same way as it is under a land reform program.

85 What would constitute a "sufficient" improvement requires answering normative questions that this article will not resolve; instead the point here is simply it could be the case that title formalization involves a trade-off between the welfare of current residents and long-term community ownership.

or timed well with macro forces, land-titling will not necessarily improve the lives of residents. Economies that deny the poor meaningful opportunities to participate, whether through generally high barriers to entry or pervasive structural favoritism of the rich, may prevent residents from benefiting from their new access to title-based credit. Similarly, a stagnant or slumping economy at the national level of any duration could lay waste to envisioned improvements by even the hardest-working residents with the best business models.

For Indians living on reservations, economic gain and freedom from dependency were supposed to follow the allotment of Indian land. Though allotment allowed Indians to obtain new credit, Indians did not become the yeoman farmers that Friends of the Indian had imagined. By the end of allotment, Indians were worse off, having lost land and not having made economic gains. Although the future economic well-being of *champa* residents following a land-titling program cannot be known with certainty, the shared paternalism and institutional fetishism evident in proponents of both allotment and land-titling suggest caution. Paternalistically, both rely on an acceptance that non-poor, or non-Indian, policy-makers should decide the form of landownership and whether a change in form will lead to growth. Both also take as a given that moving to a single, preferred, form of landownership—fee simple—will lead to growth and is appropriate for the target population.

Pointing out the shared paternalism, reification of formal property, and requirement of institutional convergence in allotment and land-titling does not of itself provide an answer about whether land-titling should take place. But doing so does suggest a number of worthwhile starting realizations and assumptions. First, title formalization will not—despite the forcefulness of de Soto's argument in *The Mystery of Capital*—necessarily elevate disadvantaged communities out of poverty. Second, converting land from community to formal title carries with it the probability that the community will lose some of the land as it is sold—directly, or indirectly through foreclosure—to outsiders.[86] Lastly, the community affected ought to be empowered and charged with deciding whether to alter the form of its land tenure. Arguably, the impetus as well ought to come from within those communities, rather than from without by outside experts such as the Friends of the Indian or de Soto. Allotment was imposed upon tribes to disastrous effect. Land-titling is similarly risky and the poor communities in El Salvador and elsewhere that might benefit or be harmed by land-titling should decide for themselves whether to proceed with title formalization.

---

86 Professor Joseph Singer has argued, in the context of allotment, that the "community" will necessarily suffer a loss with such a conversion, because treating ownership by the collective entity of the tribe as if it were equivalent to ownership in joint tenancy by the individual tribal members wrongly effectuates a taking from the collective. *See* Joseph William Singer, *Lone Wolf, or How to Take Property by Calling It a "Mere Change in the Form of Investment*," 38 Tulsa L. Rev. 37, 44 (2002).

The failure of the allotment policy to obtain its desired end—economic and cultural "advancement" of Indians through the forced conversion of Indian land into individually owned fee land—highlights the downside to land-titling on behalf of the poor currently being advocated by de Soto. The analogy between the allotment experience of Indians and modern land-titling of poor areas is imperfect in terms of community types, degree of independent governing authority, and the role culture plays in land use decisions. Nevertheless, as Felix Cohen noted, the Indian experience has "contemporary significance" and can serve as a societal "miner's canary," marking "the shifts from fresh air to poison gas."[87] When considering proposals to impose a change, supposedly for their benefit, in how land is held by a disadvantaged group, the Indian allotment experience is worth drawing upon.

At the risk of being guilty of the same sort of paternalism shown by proponents of land-titling and allotment, let me note in conclusion that I believe intergenerational equity among the lower classes supports the preservation of *champas* even if current residents *might* benefit from title formalization. The persuasive burden should lie with those seeking to integrate disadvantaged communities through the imposition of a single form of individual ownership. This is as true for those who would like to see land-titling imposed as it is for those who would like to see de Soto's ideas applied to Indian reservations today.[88] Just as current reservation populations would be better off if allotment had not occurred and Indians still had their community's original land, the long-term viability of *champas* perhaps depends upon their retaining their distinct community, but not official, title. Unlike the case for Indians, there is no obvious reason San Salvador's lower-class communities should necessarily retain separate governance systems and cultural spaces. But the city's poor of tomorrow are going to need housing and at the very least a cautious approach to formalization of title is needed if islands of affordability are to be preserved.

---

87 Felix Cohen, *The Erosion of Indian Rights, 1950–1953: A Case Study in Bureaucracy*, 62 YALE L.J. 348, 390 (1953) (focusing on what the treatment of Indians reveals about "the rise and fall in our democratic faith").

88 Applying *some* of de Soto's ideas to *some* reservations *might* be appropriate for *some* tribes, but I believe that considering allotment, caution is appropriate. However, the editors of *Self-Determination: The Other Path for Native Americans* advocate a less cautious reservation application of de Soto: "[T]his book has been inspired by the work of Hernando de Soto ... This book tries to illuminate 'the other path' that Native Americans could take—the path of self-determination, individual ownership, investment in human and physical capital, and competitive achievement in the market economy." SELF-DETERMINATION: THE OTHER PATH FOR NATIVE AMERICANS (Terry L. Anderson, Bruce L. Benson and Thomas E. Flanagan, eds, 2006).

Chapter 6

Leaving the Body of Property Law? Meltdowns, Land Rushes, and Failed Economic Development

Rashmi Dyal-Chand[1]

Indefatigably, in *The Mystery of Capital* and other written works, speeches, and consultations with political leaders around the globe,[2] Hernando de Soto has championed the American "property systems"[3] as the paradigm for economic development among the poor in developing countries. Formalize property rights, he tells the Third World, and you will lift the "bell jar" that "makes capitalism a private club."[4] Given property's starring role in the current financial crisis in this country,[5] it would be reasonable now to expect de Soto to step back and think hard about his use of the United States as exemplar. Was this crisis the result of a "perfect storm," a confluence of factors that could only occur rarely? Was it attributable to failures in the banking infrastructure or in the secondary market for mortgage-backed securities, as de Soto himself suggests? Or could it be that the seeds of destruction, as well as progress, inhere in the property systems that de Soto has promoted so devotedly?

In this chapter, I outline one approach to answering these questions. By comparing two prominent examples of property's role in failed economic development, I extract a basic pattern in which property rights engender an industry-wide failure to manage long-term risks. With this effort, I begin an inquiry that I would urge de Soto and those interested in his prescription to continue. This

1 I am grateful to Nestor Davidson and Benjamin Ericson for thoughtful comments on an earlier draft, and to Robin Paul Malloy and Daniel Mandelker for foundational conversations. Alfreda Russell in the Northeastern University Law Library provided excellent research support, and Michael Birch and Kevin Mulligan provided valuable research assistance.

2 Hernando de Soto, The Mystery of Capital: Why Capitalism Triumphs in the West and Fails Everywhere Else (2000) [hereinafter Mystery of Capital]. For examples of de Soto's statements about the U.S. property system, see his institute's website, http://ild.org.pe/en/home.

3 Mystery of Capital, *supra* note 2, at 8.

4 Mystery of Capital, *supra* note 2, at 67 (citing Fernand Braudel, 2 *Civilization and Capitalism: The Wheels of Commerce* 248 (Sian Reynolds trans., 1982).

5 *See* Nestor Davidson and Rashmi Dyal-Chand, *Property in Crisis*, 78 Fordham L. Rev. (forthcoming 2010).

chapter proceeds as follows. I first consider de Soto's analysis of the causes of the current crisis. I argue that de Soto fails to recognize a very basic connection between property in the development process and the risk of meltdowns.[6] I then describe two examples of property-based economic development that have failed. The first is the proliferation of forms of property ownership in the lead-up to the current crisis in the United States. The second is the formalization of informal property holdings by the poor in certain urban areas in the developing world. Finally, I argue that a pattern emerges when these two examples are compared, a pattern that might provide some basic information to de Soto about the role of property and risk in economic development.

De Soto on the Meltdown

It is evident that de Soto has had opportunities to analyze the subprime crisis in the United States. In an October 2008 speech to the International Bar Association meeting in Buenos Aires, de Soto shared the following comments about its roots:

> Once you leave the records system, you are out of the system, and that's exactly what happened in the sub-prime crisis. A whole bunch of people … left the body of property law … and they went to an area of law called securitization. … [I]t's that we don't know how many banks are owning pieces of claims and property in the US market. … [Y]ou don't know who owns what. That's the crisis, not lack of money. … Once you have taken property and the clarity that property is supposed to bring to human connections, you have brought havoc to the market, and that's what happened in sub-prime.[7]

Though somewhat cursory, de Soto's comments in Buenos Aires do provide important information about his analytical framework. De Soto explicitly compared the meltdown to failed attempts at economic development in the Third World.[8] As a corollary matter, he appears to have viewed the expansion of the housing and credit markets (if not also the market in mortgage-backed securities)[9] prior to the

6 Unless otherwise specified, I use the term "meltdown" throughout this chapter to refer to the financial crisis in the United States that originated in the subprime mortgage market, as well as to similar national or global financial crises.

7 Hernando de Soto, President, Institute for Liberty and Democracy, Opening Ceremony Speech at the International Bar Association Annual Conference (Oct. 12, 2008), available at www.ibanet.org/conferences/BA2008.

8 *Id.*

9 De Soto's Buenos Aires comments blaming the "law of securitization" contrast with his enchantment in *The Mystery of Capital*, in which he claims that the securitization of mortgages and their sale in secondary markets injects life into assets, thereby generating capital. *See* Mystery of Capital, *supra* note 2, at 6.

meltdown as key moments of economic development in the United States. This was a useful contribution.

By the most basic definition of economic development, these markets were a powerful, if only temporary, engine of economic development. They raised per capita wealth across a relatively broad swath of the population.[10] The subprime market in particular generated "capital," as de Soto uses that term to mean surplus wealth, for the poor. In the last decade, as a consequence of the drop in underwriting standards, many poor people accessed credit through the subprime market. As a result, many poor people, who had previously been marginalized by the real-estate market, became homeowners. Contemporaneously with these developments, de Soto advocated the adoption of American-style property law as a means of leading the poor out of poverty, heralding developments in the United States as evidence of the synergies created by unified property systems.

But then something went terribly wrong. Suddenly, the very systems that de Soto had praised for "fixing the economic potential of assets,"[11] creating accountability,[12] and "protecting transactions"[13] were the source of wildly inaccurate pricing, widespread fraud, and vulnerability in transactions. Perhaps most alarmingly, the interconnected nature of these systems led in rapid-fire succession to a global financial crisis. Equally as importantly from a development perspective, the meaningful gains in per capita income among those who had participated in these markets turned into losses resulting from equity stripping, foreclosures, and intractable debt. At best, per capita development appeared to be largely a short-term phenomenon.

De Soto has thus far attributed this sudden inversion in market conditions, and more broadly in this development moment, to a failure to maintain the integrity of the property system. The system failed because the subprime market failed to follow the system. Instead of conforming to the "uniform" property records that had been in use, the subprime industry strayed to a new "law of securitization" that did not accurately and transparently communicate ownership and thus risk. De Soto's analysis is not off point by any means. It seems quite possible that future crises of this sort could be at least partially circumvented by closer compliance with recording laws,[14] elimination of "no-doc" and "low-doc" underwriting

10 Though it has been critiqued by many, and replaced in some contexts by other more comprehensive measures, growth in per capita income is probably the most basic and widely used measure of economic development. *See* James M. Cypher and James L. Dietz, The Process of Economic Development, 29 (2nd ed., 2004).

11 Mystery of Capital, *supra* note 2, at 49.

12 *Id.* at 54.

13 *Id.* at 61.

14 This was one of the lessons to be learned from a recent ruling by a federal district court judge in Ohio, who dismissed 14 foreclosure cases filed by Deutsche Bank on the ground that the bank failed to prove it owned the notes and mortgages—in part because it failed to record assignments in its favor. In re Foreclosure Cases, No. 07–2282, 2007 U.S. Dist. LEXIS 84011, at *3 (N.D. Ohio Oct. 31, 2007).

procedures,[15] and a more rational incentive structure for mortgage origination.[16] No doubt, greater transparency could alleviate some of the key information asymmetries that fueled the meltdown.

Yet, de Soto's analysis of the meltdown is not entirely satisfactory. Even less satisfactory is his dogmatic call for a return to property records as a means of alleviating future such crises, particularly when juxtaposed against more tempered analyses of the meltdown and appropriate responses.[17] Perhaps de Soto is right. But there are reasons to believe he may be wrong, or that his analysis is at least limited with regard to the weight he affords any causal relationship between the subprime meltdown and lack of adherence to the property system. First, the magnitude, longevity, and regulatory elusiveness of the meltdown suggest that it was too complex to be explained away as a consequence of divergence from the property system. Second, many subprime loans were documented using more traditional underwriting processes.[18] Many more followed the letter of disclosure laws such as the Real Estate Settlement Procedures Act.[19] Third, there is a strong theoretical argument that the crisis in fact resulted from deeply embedded values and systems in property law, rather than from a failure to comply with property law's true spirit.[20]

Is it possible, then, that a deeper connection lurks between property law, economic development, and meltdowns than de Soto recognizes? Could it be that, contrary to de Soto's supposition, the failures of the meltdown inhere *in* "the body of property law?"

Property in the Service of Economic Development

This section explores that question by considering two examples of failed economic development in which property played a central role. The first is the subprime meltdown in this country. Though it has been the subject of much

---

15 For descriptions of such instruments, see Gary Gorton, *The Panic of 2007*, 12–19 (Nat'l Bureau of Econ. Research, Working Paper No. 14358, 2008), available at http://www.kc.frb.org/publicat/sympos/2008/gorton.08.04.08.pdf; Allan N. Krinsman, *Subprime Mortgage Meltdown: How did it Happen and How will it End?*, 13 J. Structured Fin., Summer 2007, at 13, 15–17; L. Randall Wray, *Lessons from the Subprime Meltdown*, 30–31 (The Levy Econ. Inst. of Bard College, Working Paper No. 522, 2007), available at http://ssrn.com/abstract=1070833.

16 *See* Wray, *supra* note 15, at 8–9, 25.

17 On this point, it is quite revealing to compare de Soto's comments on the meltdown to those recently made by Joseph Stiglitz in a joint interview of both economists. Video available at http://www.abc.net.au/tv/fora/stories/2008/11/28/2431405.htm.

18 For statistical data concerning the number of subprime loans written using non-traditional underwriting process, see Gorton, *supra* note 15, at 7–12; Wray, *supra* note 15, at 31.

19 12 U.S.C. §§2601–2617 (1996).

20 *See* Davidson and Dyal-Chand, *supra* note 5.

analysis and description, few have understood our current crisis as a period of economic development. The second example is one recurring set of events following formalization as prescribed by de Soto. Thanks in part to the World Bank's promotion of de Soto-style formalization,[21] a number of developing countries have experimented with his formalization theory over the last decade. By now, also, a number of sound empirical studies have reviewed the diverse and interesting results of such efforts. It would be unfair to characterize de Soto's prescription as guaranteed to increase development or, on the other hand, as guaranteed to lead to disaster. It is, however, reasonable to search out patterns that can lead to failure, and this section seeks to do just that by focusing on one discrete pattern in some urban areas.

The Subprime Meltdown in the United States

In contrast with the ubiquitous front-page descriptions of the current crisis, the descriptive effort in this section is to identify the factors in the last decade that led first to intense economic development and then to development failure. In the lead-up to the crisis, development occurred in the form of an increase in per capita wealth (which I define broadly here to include both the ownership of illiquid assets such as homes and the acquisition of debt) among poor people, previously marginalized homebuyers, and other market participants. With the explosion in the subprime mortgage market, however, the gains in per capita wealth turned to losses, and it became apparent that the particular ownership structures that had been created were untenable as long-term and stable forces of development. Up to a chronological point, this description conforms to de Soto's idealized view of the property system, but then, in describing the ensuing meltdown, it diverges.

This development-focused tale begins with a sudden upsurge in the residential real estate and related credit markets to include low-income homeowners. Over the course of at least two decades, governmental policy promoted homeownership, including in the form of the Clinton, Bush, and Obama administrations' "ownership society" and similar campaigns, and the attendant regulatory subsidization of homeownership. Meanwhile, industry participants innovated new paths to profiting from market participation by new homeowners. These innovations included the relaxation of mortgage underwriting standards in lockstep with the development of exotic loan instruments, the entry of less regulated lenders specializing in subprime lending, the generation by lenders of instantaneous profit mechanisms from penalty and other types of fees, and the expansion of the secondary market.[22] Undeniably,

---

21 *See, e.g.*, Klaus Deininger, Land Policies for Growth and Poverty Reduction: A World Bank Policy Research Report (2003), 70, 75, 80, 96, 103, 118, 266 (citing de Soto's work as support for proposed policy reforms focusing on formalization).

22 For detailed accounts of these governmental and industry steps, see Davidson and Dyal-Chand, *supra* note 5; Jo Becker et al., *White House Philosophy Stoked Mortgage Bonfire*, N.Y. Times, Dec. 20, 2008, at A1.

many people who had previously been excluded from these markets were now given access.[23] At several levels, the expansion of these markets caused a sudden and widespread creation of new property rights, or at least new accessibility: poor and otherwise marginalized people became homeowners and obtained credit, new lenders joined the market for mortgage credit, and new investors in mortgage-backed securities joined the secondary market. At these various levels, per capita wealth rose. For low-income homeowners, the increase took the form of ownership of an illiquid asset.

In the context of this explosion in new property, a shockingly large number of new homeowners, and many other participants in the subprime market who had owned homes for some time, entered into subprime credit arrangements, ultimately with disastrous results. Many of these loans were obtained for the purpose of buying new homes. But a remarkable percentage of sub-prime loans were also "cash-out," in which borrowers used home equity as collateral for cash with few, if any, strings attached to its use.[24] For some, the long-term investment potential of the home as an illiquid asset—the fundamental notion of equity building—was either questionable or not apparent. For many, the appeal of immediate liquidity via "cash-out" home equity loans was overwhelming.[25] Given the specialization among lenders, many subprime borrowers had no choice but to accept detrimental loan terms, which lenders claimed were justified by the riskier borrower and collateral profiles. For cash-out borrowers, the result was a conversion of new property in the form of a home to new property in the form of credit, and more immediately, cash. Furthermore, in contrast to de Soto's predictions for Third World homeowners, the cash was often used for short-term consumption.[26] In our development story, these homeowners converted their wealth into a liquid form.

Sub-prime borrowers were not the only ones interested in immediate liquidity. Many of the credit arrangements in the subprime market were set up to fail, rationalized by market participants and regulators alike as workable only because borrowers could refinance at the moment when teaser rates skyrocketed, balloon payments came due on payment option adjustable rate mortgages, or equity began

---

23 *See* ELIZABETH RENUART, STOP PREDATORY LENDING (National Consumer Law Center, 2002), 17; National Low Income Housing Coalition, Low Income Housing Profile 1, 21 (2001), available at http://www.nlihc.org/doc/profile.pdf (tabulation of 1999 American Housing Survey found 44% homeownership by the "very poor", defined as under 30% of area median income).

24 *See* Wray, *supra* note 15, at 43; Gorton, *supra* note 15, at 18; U.S. CENSUS BUREAU, RESIDENTIAL FINANCE SURVEY 2001, available at http://www.census.gov/prod/2005pubs/censr-27.pdf (finding that of the 6.2 million properties used as collateral for home equity loans, 848,000 were owned by poor people).

25 See Rashmi Dyal-Chand, *Exporting the Ownership Society: A Case Study on the Economic Impact of Property Rights*, 39 RUTGERS L.J. 59, 91–92 (2007); Kathleen C. Engel and Patricia A. McCoy, *A Tale of Three Markets: The Law and Economics of Predatory Lending*, 80 TEX. L. REV. 1255, 1280–1286 (2002).

26 Dyal-Chand, *supra* note 25.

to be stripped (to name just a few examples).[27] Given this reality, short-term profit was the only rational goal. One source of immediate profit for lenders was the numerous and disproportionately large servicing, penalty, and other fees.[28] An even more potent source of immediate profit was sale of the loans on the secondary market, which occurred in large numbers.[29]

Perhaps the most stunning example of innovation in pursuit of short-term gain was that of the intermediaries, such as rating agencies and insurers, in the secondary market. By means of credit enhancements, insurance on the securities, and other techniques, these agencies were responsible for reducing the risk for secondary market investors interested in securities backed by subprime loans.[30] Of course, the novelty of most subprime instruments ensured that no one really knew just how risky they were. Nonetheless, as is now widely known, the fee structures for these services, including the much higher up-front fees for rating mortgage-backed securities than for rating corporate bonds, incentivized more creative (though by no means more reliable) ratings.[31] Thus from a development perspective, at all levels of market participation, the pursuit of per capita wealth increases took a quite particular form. Market participants were highly motivated to achieve immediate and liquid gains across the board.

Undergirding these developments in wealth improvement were two phenomena. The first was the steady and seemingly unending rise in housing prices. The second was the regulatory support for the markets for credit, mortgage-backed securities, and even real estate. From the indifference about qualifications and ethical responsibilities among brokers, to the non-intervention in market relationships involving intermediaries, to the consistent validation of the holder-in-due-course doctrine, regulation protected industry innovation.

As housing prices began to fall from late 2006 through 2007, it became clear just how untenable the subprime market had become as a durable foundation for economic development. The new market realities provided few or no opportunities for individual borrowers to refinance. Faced with interest rate resets and declines in home equity, many subprime borrowers defaulted, leading to record numbers of foreclosures.[32] The ripple effects from these individual losses resulted in bankruptcies among mortgage lenders, major losses and failures among

---

27 Gorton, *supra* note 15, at 3, 7, 12; Danielle DiMartino and John V. Duca, Fed. Reserve Bank of Dallas, *The Rise and Fall of Subprime Mortgages* (2007), 3–4, available at http://www.dallasfed.org/research/eclett/2007/el0711.html.

28 *See* Engel and McCoy, *supra* note 25, at 1266–1267.

29 *See generally* Gorton, *supra* note 15; Wray, *supra* note 14.

30 Wray, *supra* note 15, at 21–22; Engel and McCoy, *Turning a Blind Eye: Wall Street Finance of Predatory Lending*, 75 Fordham L. Rev. 2039 (2007), 2045–2048.

31 Wray, *supra* note 15, at 21–22.

32 DiMartino and Duca, *supra* note 27, at 5–6; Knowledge@Wharton, Subprime Timeline, available at http://www.knowledgeatwharton.com.cn/index.cfm?fa=viewArticle&articleID=1876.

intermediaries, and forced buy-backs and write-downs among secondary market investors. At all levels, market participants experienced a shockingly harsh reversal in economic development conditions. It was a moment of failed development.

Urban Land Rushes in the Wake of Formalization

Was the crisis a unique and unfortunate moment in American history, a "perfect storm," as many have claimed? Or was de Soto right that it was a consequence of sloppy, if not also disingenuous, adherence to pure property law? Perhaps de Soto could begin to answer these questions by comparing the American experience to reports about attempts at de Soto-style formalization in the developing world. Though field conditions vary widely, de Soto might be harder pressed to diagnose negative results as primarily stemming from failures in property documentation.

Results of formalization have been quite diverse thus far, which is an independent refutation of de Soto's claim that formalization is the guarantor of economic development.[33] This section focuses not on the unpredictability of formalization, however, but on a particular pattern seen in some of the targeted urban locales. The pattern described here is not a direct analog to the American situation. Most notably, it is not a chronicle of instabilities in the credit market because one relatively consistent result of formalization is a minimal or even nonexistent increase in mortgage lending.[34] Rather, it is a tale about land rushes. In this tale too, property served first as a basis for intense economic development and then, for the low-income market participants at least, as a basis for economic loss.

As in the American context, the tale begins with the sudden expansion of the residential real-estate market to new property owners whose rights to property had been formally recognized by the state. In the urban contexts where this pattern has developed, such titling has replaced high levels of informal or "customary" holdings in geographically desirable locations. For example, in one neighborhood of Dakar, Senegal, land-titling increased the number of formal owners by 25 percent in approximately a decade, a smaller number than was anticipated but still highly significant in its impact on the real-estate market.[35] Formalization occurred in even larger percentages in Sao Paulo, Phnom Penh, and some Indian cities.[36] As a consequence, in sizable and appealing pockets of some of these cities, new

33 See Gregory S. Alexander's chapter in this volume.

34 Geoffrey Payne et al., *Social and Economic Impacts of Land Titling Programmes in Urban and Peri-Urban Areas: International Experience and Case Studies of Senegal and South Africa* (March 2008), 26–33, available at http://www.gpa.org.uk/Publications/News/Report.pdf (reviewing the empirical literature on access to credit).

35 Payne et al., *supra* note 34, at 17.

36 Mike Davis, Planet of Slums (Sao Paulo, 2006), 81; Alain Durand-Lasserve, *Market-Driven Eviction Processes in Developing Country Cities: The Cases of Kigali in*

property rights were created on a large scale. In addition, it is not an overstatement in some Third World locations to depict formalization as creating a new class of owners, who had previously only held land informally. Given the increase in land value that regularly accompanies formalization,[37] per capita wealth rose for many newly titled owners. Here, as in the United States, such wealth initially took the form of ownership of an illiquid asset.

While there are certainly contexts, especially in rural areas, where land-titling appears to have resulted in greater stability, investment in real estate, and increases in income and human development, a different pattern has emerged in the urban locations described above. In these latter contexts, large numbers of newly titled landowners sold their homes in short order to middle- and upper-income members of their communities. In Sao Paulo, the soaring prices and consolidation of landownership in former slums have led one observer to describe "[b]oth land and houses" as "consumption goods."[38] Indeed, in some cities such as Dakar and Manila, many sales occurred simply in anticipation of formalization.[39]

Although the gains on sale were sometimes sizable, especially given the often positive effect of formalization on the market value of the properties, these gains were often only a small increment of the gains soon to be realized by the new buyers, who (unlike their sellers) were knowing participants in a speculative market. Recently in Phnom Penh, for example, the city offered informal residents US $2.50 per square meter (in anticipation of reselling the land to an interested developer) when a market appraisal found the land to be worth a minimum of nine times that amount.[40] Indeed, a generalizable piece of this story is the poor market participants' inattention to, lack of information about, or inability to capitalize on the anticipated long-term value of their real estate. Against the more abstract potential of longer-term gain, the immediate cash from sale of their homes was all too attractive an option to ignore. Thus, in these areas, the result was a conversion of new property in the form of formal landownership to new property in the form of cash. In other words, in this development story too, the newly titled owners systematically converted their wealth into a liquid form.

As was the case in the secondary market for American mortgage-backed securities, the newly titled lower-income landowners were not the only parties interested in immediate liquidity. Because their buyers were actively speculating, these buyers often sold in short order to other speculators, including developers, large landowners and even local governments. In a number of markets, including

---

Rwanda and Phnom Penh in Cambodia, 3 Global Urban Dev. 1 (2007) (Phnom Penh); Payne et al., *supra* note 34, at 41 (India).

37 See, e.g., Jean O. Lanjouw and Philip Levy, *A Difficult Question in Deed: A Cost-Benefit Framework for Titling Programs*, 45 Wm. & Mary L. Rev. 889, 943–949 (2004).

38 Davis, *supra* note 36, at 81 (quoting Suzana Taschner).

39 Payne et al., *supra* note 34, at 47 (Dakar); John Gravois, *The de Soto Delusion,* Slate, Jan. 29, 2005, available at http://www.slate.com/id/2112792/ (Manila).

40 Durand-Lasserve, *supra* note 36, at 10.

those described above, the often-brisk pattern of turnovers resulted in land rushes and wild speculation. Land prices either skyrocketed, destabilized, or both. In some markets, it was impracticable to predict land uses, and thus land values. Accordingly, the interest in short-term profit appears to have been paramount. From a development perspective, market participants at all levels were highly motivated to achieve wealth increases in the particular form of immediate and liquid gains.

Finally and not surprisingly, the wildest speculation occurred in the least regulated circumstances. Thus, in Phnom Penh, limited governmental resources (and perhaps also indifference) repeatedly prevented the city from implementing a widely supported plan to upgrade impoverished urban dwellings in the course of urban development.[41] In the absence of governmental involvement, spiraling real-estate prices continue to push the poor out of the urban area. In locations such as Dakar, Senegal, and Madhya Pradesh, India, where governments did attempt to regulate against land speculation, the weak nature of such regulations resulted in work-arounds and market distortions with minimal overall effect in reducing speculation.[42]

At some point, prices will stabilize, land will be developed, and communities will cope in these cities. But it is already clear that the original low-income owners realized only short-term gain from formalization, and moreover that their gain was often trifling compared to the profits achieved by other market participants. In these cities, property formalization did not serve as an aid to economic development so much as a destabilizing force. While some market participants thus far have experienced development success, and indeed cities such as Phnom Penh may even have an overall increase in wealth, the informal property-holders originally targeted for aid have experienced economic development as a failure.

Property Patterns in Economic Development

Even in his public commentary about the current financial crisis, de Soto has insisted on the inevitability that formalization will result in increased gross national product, surplus wealth, and inclusion in the "bell jar" of modern-day capitalism. But in the aftermath of property creation in the two quite different attempts at economic development just described, a much more disquieting pattern emerges. In both instances, the intended beneficiaries of development have experienced results ranging from minimal wealth improvement at best to substantial harm at worst. In one instance, the pattern preceded a global financial crisis. Given the exceptional consequences of these development examples, it is prudent to examine the pattern, and its replicability, in greater detail. In this section, I extract the commonalities from these two development examples and briefly raise some

41 Durand-Lasserve, *supra* note 36, at 9–10.

42 Payne et al., *supra* note 34, at 41.

basic questions about property and risk in economic development. In doing so, I seek to focus attention on the possibility that these commonalities are indeed a standard feature of property in service of economic development—very much within the body of property law.

Commonalities in a Pattern of Failed Development

Despite the diversity of results flowing from property-based economic development, at least five commonalities materialize from the two development examples just described. These commonalities form a basic pattern of failed development, which, in its most abstracted version, is a common tale of property and risk.

New and Ripe Property Rights One of the most obvious commonalities in both development examples was the creation of new property rights across a broad swath of the population. In the United States, many poor and previously marginalized homebuyers purchased homes and obtained mortgage loans. It might be more accurate to describe the marked increase in homeownership for this population as producing new property accessibility, rather than new property rights; the new forms of exotic loan instruments, on the other hand, produced rights that were truly novel. In the land-titling context, vast numbers of informal property-holders acquired formal title to their lands. Moreover, in both contexts these new owners acquired property rights at a moment when one or more markets, for real estate, credit, mortgage-backed securities, and related services, were poised and eager to transact in the newly created property. In other words, the new property rights were ripe for market transactions.

Information Gaps and Asymmetries Concerning Property Values A second commonality was a fundamental lack of information among the new property owners about the longer-term value of their new homes. Even a quick comparison of the American context and the many different land-titling experiments reveals important motivational distinctions among property owners who sold their homes shortly after acquiring title. One basic similarity, however, is that the new owners had no obvious knowledge about the value of illiquid assets and their potential to appreciate over decades on the one hand, nor of the longer-term development trajectories of their neighborhoods, public and private development goals and negotiations, and planning efforts on the other hand. Another basic similarity is the ubiquitous necessity for cash.

In addition to liquidity, the asymmetrical relationship between the low-income sellers (and in the United States, borrowers) and buyers produced another common result: considerably worse terms for the low-income market participants. Thus, in the United States, subprime borrowers participated in onerous credit arrangements that ultimately were impossible to meet. In many of the land-titling contexts, the low-income sellers realized a tiny increment of the overall gains as land prices skyrocketed in the wake of formalization.

Drive for Immediate Profit Perhaps the most significant revelation from comparison of these two development examples was the imperative, experienced across the board by market participants, for short-term gains. In the American context, this focus on instant gratification produced massive and stunning innovations in real-estate sales practices, servicing arrangements, and securitization techniques. Often in the land-titling scenarios, those who bought out the low-income property owners had very little information about development trajectories. Thus, they sold quickly to avoid gluts in local real-estate markets.

Indeed, it appears that a critical part of this pattern of failed development is a lack of information in the industry taken as a whole about the long-term risks associated with the newly created property. In the United States, for example, it was virtually impossible for securitizers and secondary market investors to value the risks of particular exotic loan terms. It was an abstract question indeed to contemplate the extent of a cushion necessary to cover defaults in payment options or exploding adjustable rate mortgages when such loans had only arrived on the scene within the previous five years. Although radically different at the level of details, a similarly confounding puzzle about risk and reward surfaced in city after city experimenting with formalization. In Dakar, for example, a new wave of informal settlement followed on the heels of formalization as a strategy for bypassing governmental regulation of land speculation.[43]

Bubbles and Bursts in Property Values A fourth commonality in these instances of property and development is the fluctuation in land values. This factor is puzzling in its own right, as it is not at all clear whether and to what extent property values have instigated, or responded to, failures in development. Notably, some American analysts have attributed the meltdown in the subprime market primarily to the decline in home values.[44] It is interesting to wonder whether a similar drop in prices in parts of the developing world that are currently experiencing crisis would result in similar meltdowns. For my purposes, it is useful simply to note that the spiraling rise of home prices appears to be an integral part of both stories.

Lack of Market Regulation A final fundamental commonality is the regulatory choice in both development examples to protect and promote industry innovation. In both sets of circumstances, there was an abiding faith in the potential of property ownership to produce wealth. Presumably at least partly because of the overarching faith in liberal democratic institutions, there also appeared to be a deep insecurity that regulation could ensure that the benefits of development would accrue to the intended beneficiaries. In this context, non-intervention appeared to be the safest alternative.

---

43 Payne et al., *supra* note 34, at 41.

44 *See, e.g.,* Christopher L. Foote, et al., *Subprime Facts: What (We Think) We Know about the Subprime Crisis and What We Don't* (Fed. Res. Bank of Boston Pub. Pol'y Discussion Paper No. 08–2, 2008), 3, available at http://ssrn.com/abstract=1153411.

Property and Risk: Some New Questions

While the details of the two failed examples of property-based economic development described earlier are clearly crucial, quite possibly separating the "mere" land rushes leading to further marginalization from the global financial meltdown, at bottom they are stories about property and risk. Specifically, the peculiar sequencing of the commonalities just described appears to have produced an industry-wide milieu in which market participants paid little or no attention to and/or underestimated both the risk of loss by individual market participants and the risk of catastrophic system-wide loss.[45] Thus, for example, in the American context, the industry appears not to have contemplated the extraordinary level of individual losses by homeowners, mortgage companies, and investors—nor the reverberating externalities flowing from such losses. In the land-titling contexts, participants in the experiment seem surprised by the lackluster, if not downright harmful, consequences to the intended beneficiaries of formalization, some of whom are living in worse and more unstable conditions. In hindsight, in the United States, it is shocking that the industry failed so completely to see what seems so clear now.

Analyses of property and risk are not new, though they take on renewed meaning in the current environment. In addition to studying this important literature, de Soto and those interested in his prescription ought to consider a few basic questions about the risks of property-based development. First, how basic is the pattern of failed development? Which of the commonalities described here recur with the most frequency in markets for new property? Which seem most associated with improper assessment of risk? In considering this question, it will be quite instructive to compare American regulatory responses to market creation and market repair to the more development-focused regulation in land-titling contexts. These different regulatory moves may shed light on the ways in which risk is assessed, avoided, and shared when dealing with new property.

Second, what more is needed to turn a failed development experiment into a full-blown crisis? Is it simply a decline in real-estate values? Is it the creation of an interconnected market for credit- or mortgage-backed securities? In answering this question, it will be important to consider the risk factors presented by the particular networks dealing with property in any given context.[46] It may also be true that risks that are not considered because they are unknown are more likely to lead to catastrophe.[47]

Finally, if in certain circumstances new property rights can lead relatively easily to development failures rather than development successes, do such circumstances

45 For an analysis of systemic risk, see Steven L. Schwarcz, *Systemic Risk*, 97 Geo. L.J. 193, 210–234 (2008).

46 *See, e.g.*, Robin Paul Malloy, Law in a Market Context: An Introduction to Market Concepts in Legal Reasoning (2004).

47 I am grateful to Robin Paul Malloy for sharing this insight with me.

require different regulatory responses? In the United States, this is a question that has only recently received meaningful attention as the current crisis has globalized and governments have begun to recognize the need for new "rules of the road."[48] In the land-titling context, some developing countries have experimented more liberally with prospective regulation of new property rights, though often with limited success.

These are only three among many questions that ought to concern de Soto as he contemplates the relevance of the current financial crisis to his ongoing efforts to aid economic development in the Third World. Whatever approach one takes to analyzing the relevance of the current meltdown to future development efforts, whether comparison of patterns or reconsideration of the laws of securitization, these questions are critical in an era in which risk is increasingly difficult to isolate.

48 *Obama Calls for New Regulations*, Boston Globe, Feb. 26, 2009.

Chapter 7
The Bell Jar and the Bullhorn: Hernando de Soto and Communication Through Title

Nestor M. Davidson[1]

As the chapters in this book attest, Peruvian economist Hernando de Soto's argument in *The Mystery of Capital* and other works that securing formal title stands as the lynchpin to unleashing the entrepreneurial spirit of those living in the developing world's informal sector continues to draw intense interest and controversy.[2] De Soto famously argues that the titling process, taken for granted in the unified legal systems of the developed world, would bring a vast marginalized population within what de Soto metaphorically describes as the formal legal order's otherwise hermetic bell jar.[3] Securing recognition for informal property arrangements would enable those holding extra-legal entitlements to land and other assets to enter capital markets, collateralizing those sources of economic value just as Western entrepreneurs do.

From a property theory perspective, de Soto's formal title does not serve most uses conventionally associated with property rights, such as providing security of expectation, directly rewarding investment in creating value, demarcating boundaries, and the like. After all, on his description, de Soto's informal property-holders seem more or less able to achieve those ends, at least within their own communities. As de Soto puts it, "[f]ormal property's contribution to mankind is not the protection of ownership; squatters, housing organizations, mafias, and even primitive tribes manage to protect their assets quite efficiently."[4]

---

1 I want to thank Michael Diamond and Rashmi Dyal-Chand for helpful suggestions on earlier drafts of this chapter.

2 *See generally* HERNANDO DE SOTO, THE MYSTERY OF CAPITAL: WHY CAPITALISM TRIUMPHS IN THE WEST AND FAILS EVERYWHERE ELSE (2000) [hereinafter MYSTERY OF CAPITAL]. This chapter also draws on HERNANDO DE SOTO, THE OTHER PATH: THE ECONOMIC ANSWER TO TERRORISM (2002) [hereinafter OTHER PATH].

3 *See* MYSTERY OF CAPITAL, *supra* note 2, at 1, 66–67 (quoting FERNAND BRAUDEL, 2 CIVILIZATION AND CAPITALISM: THE WHEELS OF COMMERCE, 248 (Sian Reynolds, trans., 1982)).

4 MYSTERY OF CAPITAL, *supra* note 2, at 59; *see also id.* at 156. For a decidedly less optimistic vision of the precariousness of life in the informal sector, see MIKE DAVIS, PLANET OF SLUMS, 122–150 (2006).

Instead, to de Soto, formal title serves primarily to facilitate communication with strangers at a distance. Without title, informal property-holders can signal the nature and extent of their entitlements, but can only do so to a relatively small audience able to understand the context in which such entitlements have taken hold.[5] The documentation and standardization provided by formal title solves this problem, de Soto argues, translating facts on the ground into a symbolic language that can be understood in national and global markets. To de Soto, then, property's "real breakthrough is that it radically improve[s] the flow of communications about assets and their potential."[6] In short, what the informal sector lacks is not so much clear or secure property rights, but rather the means to make those rights understood to a mass audience—a bullhorn to amplify their otherwise localized voice.

This vision of title as a tool to amplify communication is quite seductive. De Soto makes a compelling argument that people all over the world possess valuable, albeit small-scale, property, but the value to these "owners"—as de Soto describes informal possessors—is essentially rendered meaningless by their inability to make the fact of that possession outside of a narrow community. Solve this translation problem and you have solved the mystery of capital.

Whether making this means of communication meaningful will necessarily be the powerful remedy to the problems of the developing world that de Soto argues is a question I must leave to experts on development.[7] What I propose to do in this chapter, however, is suggest that de Soto's vision has intriguing relevance to a line of theory that focuses on the expressive nature of property. That theory, in turn, can help explore some tensions that de Soto's metaphorical construction of title as networked communication raises for conceptions of the work of property.

To begin, de Soto's communication through title requires a kind of compression of information that risks not only obscuring the rich texture of the property rights at issue but also changing the underlying entitlements themselves. De Soto seems to assume that the information to be communicated about informal entitlements is relatively simple. An informal holder has a more or less secure entitlement to a certain plot in a given place. In reality, that entitlement—and the message that formal title relates about the entitlement—must take into account a network of rights and limitations. Formal and informal property-holding alike must account for culture, context, the entitlements of others, regulatory constraints, and any number of other contingencies.

---

5 De Soto, Mystery of Capital, *supra* note 2, at 181 ("The problem with extralegal social contracts is that their property representations are not sufficiently codified and fungible to have a broad range of application outside their own geographical parameters").

6 *Id.* at 59.

7 *See, e.g.*, Davis, *supra* note 4, at 79–82, 179–185; Rashmi Dyal-Chand, *Exporting the Ownership Society: A Case Study on the Economic Impact of Property Rights*, 39 Rutgers L.J. 59, 62 (2007) (arguing that "there is no clear connection between property formalization and greater social welfare" for low-income individuals in the United States); Boris Kozolchyk, *Secured Lending and its Poverty Reduction Effect*, 42 Tex. Int'l L.J. 727, 737–738 (2007) (collecting studies that show almost no effect of titling on private lending).

Translating facts on the ground into a form that can be communicated to a distant audience accordingly requires paring away everything except the most economically salient information. For the reductive language of title to serve de Soto's purpose, a substantial amount of information must be lost, which in turn may pare away much of what gives that information meaning. In reducing property to a communicable core, compression thus changes not only the relevance of information but the underlying substance as well.

The process of communication through title, moreover, is not autonomous in the way that in-person communication is. Using title to reach distant audiences in any kind of a meaningful way requires a set of institutions to undergird the communication. De Soto has been criticized, perhaps unfairly, for ignoring the larger institutional culture in which formal title might take hold.[8] Without resolving this debate, conceptualizing formalization as a means of communication at a distance provides a fruitful way to think about what it takes to make that communication effective. It is not enough to send out what we might think of as raw data. Without the technology—in a metaphorical and often literal sense—to transmit, receive, and most importantly give effect to that data, de Soto's process of unlocking dead capital cannot work. De Soto's view of formal property's communicative power obscures this technology, leaving to the state little more than a triggering role. At least in the United States, however, it is the state that provides the infrastructure through which communication about property at a distance occurs, and the state remains inextricably intertwined not only with the recognition and enforcement of property rights, but with their texture and meaning as well.

Focusing on the titling process as a means of enabling distant communication thus provides a lens through which to explore what is required to make that dialogue possible, what limitations are embedded in this kind of reductive message, and what de Soto's vision suggests for larger questions of property's expressive meaning.

Informal Property as Failure to Communicate

The basic idea that formal property enables exchange at a distance and among strangers has long been recognized. As de Soto elaborates on the idea, this is done primarily through a set of fungible texts that embody formal recognition. These property texts have great power for de Soto, forming a deep, hidden architecture that allows assets to generate capital. As he writes, "every parcel of land, every building, every piece of equipment, or store of inventories is represented in a property document that is the visible sign of a vast hidden process that connects all these assets to the rest of the economy."[9]

---

8 *See, e.g.*, Christopher Woodruff, *Review of de Soto's* The Mystery of Capital, 39 J. Econ. Lit. 1215, 1219 (2001).

9 Mystery of Capital, *supra* note 2, at 6.

For de Soto, the problem for those outside the formal legal system is a failure to communicate; they lack the capacity to engage in the communicative process that links physical assets to capital markets in the formal sector. De Soto's mystery of capital can thus be understood at its core as a theory of the representational power of title, and situates that theory in the ongoing legal academic discourse of property, language, and information.

De Soto focuses on the information necessary to facilitate exchange, arguing that without formal property, "any trade of an asset, say a piece of real estate, requires an enormous effort just to determine the basics of the transaction: Does the seller own the real estate and have the right to transfer it? Can he pledge it? Will the new owner be accepted as such by those who enforce property rights? What are the effective means to exclude other claimants?"[10] Standing from what he calls an "extralegal" viewpoint, de Soto describes six effects that formal property systems produce that are lacking in the informal world. As we shall see, each effect is fundamentally about providing the means through which assets can communicate.

To begin, de Soto argues that formal property "fix[es] the economic potential of assets … transpos[ing] the physical object into a man-made representative universe."[11] Thus the ability to produce value from assets "is born by representing in writing—in a title, a security, a contract, and in other such records—the most economically and socially useful qualities *about* the asset as opposed to the visually more striking aspects *of* the asset."[12] Title does not merely describe a physical resource, although one practical advantage of formal title is that it enables others literally to locate specific owners, but abstracts out everything save the market-salient information.

De Soto's second effect of property is that titling enables the integration of dispersed information into a single system. In the developed world, legal institutions pulled together scattered representations and "deposited all the information and rules governing the accumulated wealth of their citizens into one knowledge base."[13] De Soto here combines information and legality, as by integrating he means not only accessing, but more importantly granting formal acknowledgment. This integration nonetheless allows people in the developed world to reach and evaluate the potential of any asset without actually seeing the asset itself.

Closely related to the identification value of fixing assets, property's next effect is that it provides the information necessary to make individuals accountable in "the impersonal context of law."[14] Owners entering formal legal systems make a bargain: in exchange for being freed from relying on "neighborhood relationships" and "local arrangements" for protection, owners lose "their anonymity."[15] Enforceable

10 Mystery of Capital, *supra* note 2, at 47.
11 *Id.* at 49.
12 *Id.* at 49–50.
13 *Id.* at 52.
14 *Id.* at 54.
15 *Id.* at 54–55.

property systems turn on this lack of anonymity; people "can be identified" and the consequences of violating property rules and bargains accordingly meted out. Only with property to lose—and the data necessary to use that property as a penalty—is exchange meaningful.

Perhaps most important to de Soto is formal property's ability to render assets fungible. Formalization allows disparate assets to be compared, to be divided, to be combined, to be traded, and to be measured easily. Sounding a bit like a folksy version of Tom Merrill and Henry Smith's information-cost theory of standardization,[16] de Soto argues that formalization creates a uniform metric to make it easy to measure the attributes of an asset, providing the underlying basis for such measurement in the first place.[17]

All of this fixing, rendering fungible, and aggregating, de Soto continues, links participants in the property system in a single network. This network allows assets to travel between distant markets and in turn provides a way of tracking those assets back to where they fit in the network.[18] In this network—de Soto's final property effect—transactions are "continually tracked and protected," providing transparency and permanence for the value of a resource beyond the physical asset itself.[19]

All of the effects that de Soto associates with property relate in various ways to making information flow meaningfully to strangers at a distance. The magic that de Soto ascribes to formal title is in no small part a question of solving the limits of informal communication about the facts of possession. Pulling all of those bits of paper together, to de Soto, "tremendously reduces the costs of knowing the economic qualities of assets," and thus "facilitates the capacity to agree on how to use assets to further production and increase the division of labor."[20] Although de Soto focuses on the "sealed bell jar" of formal legality, he can be understood to be calling for a bullhorn to blast information—translate the fact of ownership—into that bell jar.

This translation is no small feat. Carol Rose has noted that "[o]ne person's property can only exist, by and large, because other people accept it. In turn that social relationship of claim and recognition only exists because people are able to communicate their claims and because others understand and more or less agree to honor them."[21] To de Soto, formal title solves this communication challenge through acts of abstraction and recordation. The limits of context and cultural detail are rendered practically irrelevant by affixing physical facts relating to possession to a document. In this way, formal title allows those outside the bell jar to speak in a way that reverberates and can be heard inside the formal legal world.

---

16 *See* Thomas W. Merrill and Henry E. Smith, *Optimal Standardization in the Law of Property: The* Numerus Clausus *Principle*, 110 YALE L.J. 1 (2000).

17 MYSTERY OF CAPITAL, *supra* note 1, at 58.

18 *Id.* at 59–60.

19 *Id.* at 61.

20 *Id.* at 63.

21 Carol M. Rose, *Introduction: Property and Language, or the Ghost of the Fifth Panel*, 18 YALE J.L. & HUMAN 1, 3 (2006).

De Soto's vision of title as a bullhorn reflects a longstanding interest among property scholars in the communicative aspects of property. Carol Rose has wonderfully explored the ubiquitous language of property and how signaling through and about property stands at the root of a number of cornerstone doctrines.[22] An essential insight running throughout Rose's scholarship is that so much of what gives property its meaning resides in the stories property appropriates, the messages property sends, and the language through which people communicate about property.[23]

From a perspective closer to de Soto's, Henry Smith has examined the information costs associated with interacting through property and the way property law responds to such information costs.[24] Smith describes a basic communication problem driven by the differing nature of the audience for any particular communication. Information intensiveness, in Smith's phrase, is likely to be inversely correlated to the extensiveness of the audience. Given "finite resources," Smith argues, "one can communicate a lot to a few or a little to many."[25] Accordingly, property rights, which must be understood by a wide and heterogeneous audience, tend to be more standardized than contractual rights, which can be particularized to the relatively smaller audience of the contracting parties.

De Soto, like Rose, is deeply interested in the messages that property sends and the necessity of transcending the context in which that communication arises. De Soto sees the messages that property communicates in fairly reductionist terms, but understands that possession must be signaled and that signal received to make it meaningful. Like Smith, moreover, de Soto sees a basic tradeoff between the ability to communicate entitlements locally—which his informal owners can do—and the ability to reach a broad audience. De Soto perhaps sees more of a congruence between contract and property than Smith, but this may be because the kinds of social-contractual arrangements de Soto explores are framed in relatively simple property terms—primarily facts of physical location, possession, and alienability. Ultimately, though, both Smith and de Soto understand a deep connection between information and the nature of the relevant audience.

Evaluating de Soto's particular contribution to this discourse, however, brings to focus the problem of translation. In invoking the texts of property—literally, documents of title, articles of incorporation, and the like—to do the work of communication at a distance, what information is lost or suppressed and what institutions are required to make that communication meaningful?

---

22 *See, e.g.*, Carol M. Rose, Property and Persuasion: Essays on the History, Theory, and Rhetoric of Ownership, 9–45 (1994).

23 *See, e.g.*, Rose, *supra* note 21, at 5.

24 *See, e.g.*, Henry E. Smith, *The Language of Property: Form, Context, and Audience*, 55 Stan. L. Rev. 1105 (2003).

25 *Id.* at 1108.

Two Problems of Translation

Unlike the work of communication that property does for people in close proximity—physically capturing wild animals, for example, as an immediate signal of ownership to other hunters[26]—communicating through title with distant strangers raises several related problems of translation. Such communication, for example, inherently simplifies, compressing information into a narrow packet that may obscure much of what is important about ownership. This can reflect a normative choice about the nature of entitlements and accordingly change the underlying entitlements being communicated. Moreover, this form of communication requires a "technology" of amplification—a whole set of legal and cultural institutions that make that communication meaningful. Like information compression, amplifying the message of title requires choices about relevance and priority. In short, translation is not the neutral networking process that de Soto describes.

The Compression of Information (and Property)

On one level, de Soto's title documents seem the simplest form of amplified voice—texts that contain a few relatively narrow facts about possession and entitlement, clearly transcribed, and translatable throughout the world. The vision of property that undergirds de Soto's magic paper is clean, simple, and untroubled by property's inherent complexity.

At least in the United States, however, the property records that form the formal system impart only a fraction of the information necessary to interact around property. What is left out from the information available in any county clerk's office is much of what gives property its real texture. The nature of local regulation, for example, is often as critical to the economic potential of an asset as identifying the owner and the boundaries of that owner's plot. And property almost always implicates the rights of others, often in ways that are highly particularized.[27] That complexity exists in the developed countries that de Soto uses as his comparators—indeed, arguably more so than in the small-scale informal arrangements on which de Soto focuses.

De Soto argues that one of the great benefits of representing property through deeds and the like is precisely this process of simplification. As he notes, the title document to a house "focuses your attention on the economic potential of the house by filtering out all the confusing lights and shadows of its physical aspects and its local surroundings."[28] Communication through title, to de Soto, involves purifying signal to eliminate noise. But signal and noise in property, despite Henry Smith's arguments to the contrary, are not so easy to disaggregate.

---

26 *See* Carol M. Rose, *Possession as the Origin of Property*, 52 U. Chi. L. Rev. 73 (1985).

27 *See* Joseph William Singer, Entitlement: The Paradoxes of Property (2000) (discussing the interrelations at the heart of ownership).

28 Mystery of Capital, *supra* note 2, at 50.

Speaking about property at a distance is in many ways a fundamentally different exercise than sending and receiving signals about property in close proximity. De Soto's market participants stand at one end of Smith's spectrum of audiences capable of understanding nuanced, information-rich messages and audiences better situated to process relatively simple, formalistic messages. Messages for this wide and heterogeneous audience are more effective when simplified.

The fact that certain messages may more easily be transmitted valorizes those simplified messages, influencing the underlying content of the property rights at issue. Information that does not fit the reductionist image—that does not contain what de Soto argues are the most important economic and social facts—is harder to communicate and thus less likely to gain recognition and value.

In Smith's terms, there is an inherent intensiveness to much information about property even in the most developed legal systems, requiring experts and well-developed institutions to decipher. Smith has argued that clearer, harder entitlements are easier to communicate and property law accordingly has a normative tendency to prefer such entitlements.[29] But that normative preference is far from a given and the fact that simpler, clearer entitlements may be better understood is simply one value to be balanced against many others that property recognizes.

This raises the basic question whether titling can perform the communicative work de Soto invokes where the underlying legal relationships do not reflect a paradigmatic isolated owner. In some sense, de Soto's information packets make sense only if they reflect certain widely shared norms about ownership,[30] although such norms remain contested in the United States and other Western legal systems. De Soto purports to solves this problem by asserting that basic property norms are more or less universal.[31] Although he does not spell these norms out in detail, it seems from his project that he envisions fairly clear rights of exclusion and alienability, relatively free from regulatory constraints.

Scholars have argued that communal rights in the developing world stand as a constraint on the individualistic underpinnings of de Soto's informal owner.[32] Again, I will leave that debate aside. But even in the best established modern property systems, the sole, absolute, isolated owner is largely a fiction.

29 *See* Henry E. Smith, *Property and Property Rules*, 79 NYU L. Rev. 1719 (2004).

30 De Soto ascribes the development of formal property in the West to political decisions to "acknowledge that social contracts born outside the official law were a legitimate source of law" (Mystery of Capital, *supra* note 2, at 106) and to shape law to match these cultural norms. *See also* Mystery of Capital, *supra* note 2, at 157 ("Property is not the assets themselves but a consensus among people as to how those assets should be held, used, and exchanged.").

31 *Id.* at 180 (arguing that informal property norms in many countries tend to reflect Western property rules).

32 *See, e.g.*, Karol C. Boudreaux, *The Legal Empowerment of the Poor: Titling and Poverty Alleviation in Post-Apartheid South Africa*, 5 Hastings Race & Poverty L.J. 309, 318 (2008) (collecting studies); *see also* Joel M. Ngugi, *Re-Examining the Role of Private Property in Market Democracies: Problematic Ideological Issues Raised By Land*

Interconnected property that reflects community exigencies is much more common than exclusionary property. The process of what de Soto describes as "boil[ing] down"[33] through the veneration of titling can obscure this reality, creating a normative preference for simplicity for the sake of alienability (or, to be more precise, collateralization).

Moreover, abstraction through title may present a picture of the stability of property rights that can be deceptive. The subprime mortgage meltdown that generated the global economic crisis that began in 2008 demonstrates that the value of an asset, however perfectly fungible, depends as much on economic facts beyond the asset itself and risks associated with the asset as it does on anything having to do with the owner or the internal characteristics of the asset. Debt can become "toxic" and credit markets can freeze less because of any clear change in the facts on the ground, and more because of assumptions that lenders and investors make about the nature of the market in which collateral is operating. Possession and the physical facts relating to that possession may be far down on the list of relevant messages driving credit markets. What is much more important is the ability of lenders to collect, the economic position of local housing markets, and unknown variables about risk aggregation in the wider market. Symbolic representation that squeezes out everything except the purportedly most economically salient information may ultimately not accurately convey even that.

Of course, very little of this has anything to do with what is actually communicated in title. Most of the questions de Soto asks—about rights of conveyance and exclusion, priority of title, and the like—are largely exogenous to any individual property-holder. These questions require a functioning legal system and consensus about the substance of property rights, all of which is independent from the particular details of any individual owner contained in title documents. This points to the second problem of translation: that communicating at a distance metaphorically requires means of amplification that are not self-generating.

Obscuring the Technologies of Amplification

De Soto's description of property is striking in its technological resonance. "Property," de Soto writes, "is not mere paper, but a mediating device that captures and stores most of the stuff required to make a market economy run."[34] This data-storage system serves to create a network of assets as markets seamlessly incorporate

---

Registration, 25 MICH. J. INT'L L. 467, 486–489 (2004) (discussing the violence done to customary rights through the process of land registration in Kenya).

33 MYSTERY OF CAPITAL, *supra* note 2, at 218–219 ("The revolutionary contribution of an integrated property system is that is solves a basic problem of cognition. Our five senses are not sufficient for us to process the complex reality of an expanded market, much less a globalized one. We need to have the economic facts about ourselves and our resources boiled down to essentials that our minds can easily grasp").

34 *Id.* at 63.

that data. But in de Soto's description, that network seems almost self-generating, beyond some initial documentation by the state to create the data packets that make up the network.[35] This conception of the autonomous network—the state-as-neutral ratifier view of property—obscures the necessity of an active backbone.

Translating the texts of property to a distant audience, to play out the metaphor, in reality takes a well-functioning set of institutions to undergird the actual meaning ascribed to formal title. De Soto's process of translation—of making physical resources meaningfully fungible through title—requires everything from a functioning recordation system to neutral dispute-resolution mechanisms to a set of regulatory structures that can effectively balance debtor and creditor rights, among other regulatory challenges inherent in his project of releasing dead capital.[36] A document that says that any given individual "owns" a particular asset is not enough for a market to develop; that market will only function if the message that title communicates is backed up by a legal system that supplies much of the relevant meaning.[37]

De Soto has been criticized for ignoring this larger institutional context, although he has put increasing attention on legal reform as an aspect of his overall project.[38] The point here is simply that the communicative network that de Soto describes requires some form of "programming" to give it effect. De Soto sees the state standing outside this process—indeed, he sees the state as a barrier to communication through title—but it is less the texts of property and more the channels that the state creates to give those texts power among strangers that allows amplification.

De Soto seems to assume that the state is largely an outsider to the expressive content of property, reflecting his larger perception of the government. At least in the United States, however, the state plays an active role in not only mediating, but shaping property's expressive meaning.[39] Although the expressive content of property is largely driven by facts on the ground, not just about possession, but about all of

---

35 *Cf.* Dyal-Chand, *supra* note 7, at 62 (noting that to de Soto, "after some initial governmental intervention in the form of registration of property rights, the market will function properly by allowing the poor to accumulate wealth").

36 *See* Kozolchyk, *supra* note 7.

37 There is some evidence, although the evidence is mixed, that titling does not have the collateral-unlocking effect that de Soto asserts. For discussions of relevant empirical research, see, for example, Michael Trebilcock and Paul-Erik Veel, *Property Rights and Development: The Contingent Case for Formalization*, 30 U. Pa. J. Int'l L. 397, 421–422 (2008); Kozolchyk, *supra* note 7.

38 De Soto, for example, co-chairs the Commission on the Legal Empowerment of the Poor, a project associated with the United Nations Development Programme that broadens de Soto's focus on property rights to include access to justice and the rule of law, labor rights, and business rights. *See* The Commission on Legal Empowerment of the Poor, Report of the Commission, Vol. 1, Making the Law Work for Everyone (2008).

39 *Cf.* Nestor M. Davidson, *Property and Relative Status*, 107 Mich. L. Rev. 757 (2009) (discussing governmental symbolic entrepreneurship relating to property).

property's various meanings, there is an inescapable top-down aspect to that meaning. What legislatures, courts, and other legal institutions say about the terms and limits of property—which has always been, and likely always will be, contentious—plays an important role in articulating the cultural meaning of property.

Once the pattern language exists, moreover, the forms of property can serve as a focusing or channeling device for regulatory purposes.[40] De Soto views the value of property as largely about access to credit markets, unmediated by interference with the lender-borrower relationship. The regulation of that relationship, however, takes place in the context of a specific conceptual category that is overlaid with the accretion of significant regulation, much of it focused on protecting vulnerable consumers. Indeed, courts in the United States sometimes block attempts to sidestep this category to avoid relevant regulatory constraints.[41] This kind of regulatory approach runs throughout property, as the state invokes formal categories to shape the conditions of ownership. It is unlikely that the state would formalize property and then simply walk away. To de Soto, this might be normatively troubling (not surprisingly, given his experience in Peru and other developing countries with inefficiency and outright corruption),[42] but it is an inevitable aspect of the role of the state in mediating property rights.

Mixed Messages in the Representation of Property

De Soto argues that integrated formal property is a representation system that can "help us manipulate and order the complexities of the world in a manner that we can all understand."[43] The messages that de Soto is most interested in have to do with the generation of capital—with using the value of an asset to leverage production. But property, in all of its forms, communicates many more messages than simply collateral value. These varied messages in turn help shape how people interact with and through property.

To de Soto, the key facts about property that bear communication are essentially related to the economic potential an asset might hold. This is certainly important, but possession and amenability to dispossession for failure to repay debt hardly exhausts the range of meanings that property imparts. Some of the expressive aspects of property, both in terms of tangible and intangible resources as well as property rights

---

40 *See* Nestor M. Davidson, *Standardization and Pluralism in Property Law*, 61 Vand. L. Rev. 1597, 1644–1650 (2008).

41 *Id.* at 1648 (discussing the recharacterization of installment land sales as a means of preserving the borrower protections found in the category of mortgage regulation).

42 *See* Other Path, *supra* note 2, at 132–151 (detailing the barriers to formalization in the developing world across a variety of economic sectors); *see also id.* at 189–199 (discussing the "redistributive tradition" in Peru).

43 Mystery of Capital, *supra* note 2, at 220.

themselves, are generally positive. Property, for example, can signal respectability, stability, inclusion. On the other hand, property can also signal exclusion, even the threat of violence.[44] Most messages related to possession are decidedly mixed, for example the way property often signals relative status and position.[45]

Moreover, what property communicates—possession, the reflected value of investment or labor, status, political empowerment, kinship, to name a few cultural meanings in the United States—is intricately intertwined with how people interact with the stuff of property. In an informal community, possession may signal belonging, which may lead people to be wary of risking dispossession through collateralizing their assets. Likewise, if people tend to want more property or certain kinds of property because of the status that property confers in a given culture, a kind of spiral of status-seeking can ensue.

Reducing property to its narrowest representation, finally, can become a tool for *misrepresentation*. In the United States, incomplete and at times inaccurate property records can give rise to manipulation and can create a power imbalance between those conversant in the legal system beyond its naked paper and those dependent on more easily communicated messages.

None of this is to argue that some messages are not more important or more relevant in a given context than others. Rather, it is simply to acknowledge that the communication of information into what is most economically relevant not only compresses information into a narrow channel, but can also obscure other, equally important messages.

Hernando de Soto has been deeply influential in no small measure because his vision of the work of property rights is so viscerally compelling. Outside of the hermetic bell jar of formal legal order, billions of people have established informal property rights, but lack the means to communicate those rights to those inside the bell jar. Solve the translation problem—use a metaphorical bullhorn to create the means of universal communication—and you will have unlocked a powerful tool to tackle intractable problems plaguing the developing world.

As compelling as this vision might be, it suffers from its own problem of translation. De Soto preemptively warns of suspicion of his vision of property as a symbolic language, writing that "property paper has been seen by many intellectuals as an instrument of deceit and oppression."[46] But it is not just the ability of elites to manipulate the texts of property that raises concerns. It is also the tendency of communication through title to compress and the necessity for an irreducibly complex technology of communication that must be understood. Property is an important means of expression and this representational system must be approached without a reductionism that risks muting much of what gives property its power.

---

44 *See* Rose, *supra* note 22, at 14 (discussing violence and the threat of violence against minority families in white neighborhoods in the first half of the twentieth century as "a message of ownership").

45 *See generally* Davidson, *supra* note 39.

46 Mystery of Capital, *supra* note 2, at 223.

Chapter 8
Red Tape and Gridlock

Larissa Katz[1]

This chapter concerns the role that property theory has to play in making sense of the challenges that face developing states as they try to bring people and assets into the formal sphere. Peruvian economist Hernando de Soto famously argued that because of red tape in the formal sector, people in poor countries are forced to rely on informal ownership, despite its being a degraded form of ownership that inhibits securitization of assets.[2] Owners in many poor countries are required to obtain the approval of dozens of regulators, community associations and even neighboring owners in order to operate formally.[3] De Soto's analysis of the flight

---

1 This chapter is a slightly modified version of an article that first appeared as Red Tape and Gridlock, CAN. J. OF L. AND JURIS. (forthcoming 2010). The ideas in this chapter were developed during a visit at the John Fleming Research Centre, Australia National University in December 2008. I am grateful to the John Fleming Research Centre and to the Law Foundation of Ontario for funding. An earlier version of this chapter was prepared for a special panel on Hernando de Soto and Mature Market Economies at AALS, January 2009. I benefitted from discussions with audiences at the AALS, Queen's/McGill Junior Scholars Forum and a McGill Legal theory workshop. I am especially grateful to Lee Fennell, Evan Fox-Decent, Amnon Lehavi, Oskar Liivak, Eduardo Peñalver, James Penner, Chris Serkin and Malcolm Thorburn for their careful and insightful comments.

2 De Soto initially studied informal property rights in Peru but has since successfully pressed his prescription for more formal private property with governments around the world. *See* HERNANDO DE SOTO, THE OTHER PATH: THE ECONOMIC ANSWER TO TERRORISM (1989) [hereinafter OTHER PATH]; HERNANDO DE SOTO, THE MYSTERY OF CAPITAL: WHY CAPITALISM TRIUMPHS IN THE WEST AND FAILS EVERYWHERE ELSE (2000) [hereinafter MYSTERY OF CAPITAL]. In fact the *wealth-maximizing* benefits that de Soto anticipates from formalizing property rights have not always materialized. *See* JEAN-PHILIPPE PLATTEAU, INSTITUTIONS, SOCIAL NORMS, AND ECONOMIC DEVELOPMENT (2000); NIALL FERGUSON, THE ASCENT OF MONEY, 274–278 (2008) (questioning the link between formal title and increased access to credit). Further, there is evidence that, after the initial wave of formalization and privatization, there is often a return to informality. *See, e.g.*, Daniel Fitzpatrick, *Evolution and Chaos in Property Rights Systems: The Third World Tragedy of Contested Access*, 115 YALE L.J. 996 (2006); Benito Arruñada and Nuno Garoupa, *The Choice of Titling System in Land*, 48 J.L. & ECON. 709, 710–712 (2005). What was not anticipated by de Soto is the evidence that formalizing title does enhance owners' security. *See* Erica Field, *Entitled to Work: Urban Property Rights and Labor Supply in Peru*, 122 Q.J. OF ECON. 1561 (2007) (showing how formal title frees women and children from monitoring the household's assets and so to join the workforce).

3 *See infra* notes 25–28 and accompanying text.

to the informal sector does not engage the nature and structure of ownership at all, but rather straightforwardly concerns the transaction costs and hold-out problems that make it too costly for many people to own formally.

What does property theory have to add to de Soto's straightforward explanation of informal ownership in terms of transaction costs? The answer depends on our views about ownership. One suggestion is that it is deficiencies in the *form of ownership* that contribute both to informality in the developing world and to its counterpart in the developed world, the under-use of assets. This account emerges from Michael Heller's work on the anticommons, a distinct form of ownership (and, by analogy, other kinds of decision-making authority) in which there are multiple holders of the power to make decisions about who can use a resource and how.[4] Heller's work suggests that gridlock from anticommons problems characterizes many of the kinds of hurdles that de Soto describes.[5] People in developing economies tend to hold property informally where too many "owners" have uncoordinated veto-power over the use of assets in the formal sphere, leading to gridlock.[6] Seen as an anticommons problem, the phenomenon of informality suddenly becomes relevant as a dramatic illustration of a more basic problem that also affects formal property systems in the developed world.[7] In the developing world, gridlock in the formal sector shows up most dramatically in the growth of the informal sector. In the developed world, gridlock produces a less obvious but related effect: the under-use of assets.[8]

---

4 *See* Michael A. Heller, *The Tragedy of the Anticommons: Property in the Transition from Marx to Markets*, 111 HARV. L. REV. 621, 639 (1998) [hereinafter *Tragedy of the Anticommons*]; Michael A. Heller, *The Boundaries of Private Property*, 108 YALE L.J. 1163 (1999) [hereinafter *Boundaries*]; MICHAEL A. HELLER, THE GRIDLOCK ECONOMY: HOW TOO MUCH OWNERSHIP WRECKS MARKETS, STOPS INNOVATION, AND COSTS LIVES (2008) [hereinafter GRIDLOCK]. Heller attributes the term "anticommons" to Frank Michelman, and was obviously influenced by Michelman's economic analysis of the anticommons in *Ethics, Economics and the Law of Property*. *See* Frank I. Michelman, *Ethics, Economics, and the Law of Property*, *in* NOMOS XXIV: ETHICS, ECONOMICS, AND THE LAW 3 (J. Roland Pennock & John W. Chapman, eds, 1982).

5 I take up a discussion of two of these kinds of hurdles below.

6 Heller's initial work on the anticommons did more than simply provide a useful shorthand to describe the costs associated with assembling veto-rights. It added a distinct form of ownership to our "property lexicon," as he calls it. *See* GRIDLOCK, *supra* note 4, at 23–49. *See also* Stephen R. Munzer, *The Commons and the Anticommons in the Law and Theory of Property*, *in* THE BLACKWELL GUIDE TO THE PHILOSOPHY OF LAW AND LEGAL THEORY 148 (Martin P. Golding & William A. Edmundson, eds, 2005).

7 *See* James M. Buchanan and Yong J. Yoon, *Symmetric Tragedies: Commons and Anticommons*, 43 J.L. & ECON. 1, 11–12 (2000) (modern bureaucracies are every bit as tangled in the anticommons as transitional countries).

8 This is what Heller has called the tragedy of the anticommons. *See Tragedy of the Anticommons*, *supra* note 4. Frank Michelman first developed the idea that there are symmetrical tragedies in commons and anticommons in a 1985 address to the AALS Property Panel: "If users in a common must fail to regulate their use activities with due

I will argue that, whereas de Soto may very well be right about the role of transaction costs in pushing people into the informal sector (red tape makes it costly or even impossible to pursue certain valuable ends in the formal sphere), this phenomenon does not point to a deficiency in the form of ownership. Heller's idea of ownership plays an important role in his application of the anticommons to the regulatory hurdles that de Soto identifies as a trigger of informality. I will argue that Heller's re-telling of de Soto's insights about informality proceeds from an overly capacious theory of ownership. According to Heller, an "owner" is anyone with the power to veto certain valuable projects, the highest-value uses of resources alone or in combination with others.[9] On this view, an owner's position is treated as incomplete if she lacks the requisite inputs for valuable projects.[10] Further, a person counts as an owner, albeit one locked in an anticommons, if she has the power to block the projects others can pursue. But this view of ownership in an anticommons leaves us unable to see that owners are in a radically different position *vis-à-vis* owners with parallel and overlapping authority over an object than they are *vis-à-vis* the state or other non-owners. The result is a tendency to stretch the concept of the anticommons to explain situations where there are no deficiencies in the form of authority but only straightforward transaction costs and holdout problems.[11]

---

regard to the costs of *using* a resource, rights-holders in an anti-common must fail, and for the same reasons, to act on applications for use permission with due regard for the costs of *idling* the resources when permission is denied." Frank Michelman, Remarks at Property Panel, American Association of Law Schools, "Is the Tragedy of the Common Inevitable?" (Jan. 1985) (unpublished manuscript, on file with author). I am grateful to Lee Fennell for sharing this document with me.

9 Heller would identify an anticommons even in cases where some uses of the object of property are possible, but where its highest-value use is not. Thus, *under-use* (rather than non-use) occurs in a typical tragedy of the anticommons. *But see* note 35 and accompanying text on the relationship between an anticommons and under-use and a commons and over-use.

10 I will argue below that, in emphasizing the highest-value uses of resources as a guide to the proper definition of property rights, Heller's view of ownership looks very much like a bundle of rights approach constrained by a *numerus clausus* principle. Heller has criticized the mainstream bundle of rights approach insofar as it sweeps aside the *numerus clausus* principle and so invites judges to treat low-value use-rights as constitutionally protected property rights. *See Boundaries*, *supra* note 4, at 1202–1203. *See also* J.E. Penner, *The "Bundle of Rights" Picture of Property*, 43 UCLA L. Rev. 711, 777 (1996) (criticizing the idea that we have discrete property interests in the various specific uses we can make of a thing).

11 The misapplication of the concept is reflected in the increasingly wide-spread skepticism that an anticommons refers to a form of ownership at all. *See* Lee Fennell, *Commons, Anticommons, Semicommons*, *in* Research Handbook on the Economics of Property Law (Kenneth Ayotte & Henry E. Smith eds, forthcoming 2009) [hereinafter *Commons, Anticommons, Semicommons*]. ("The term 'anticommons' has since become a shorthand for a broad class of problems requiring the assembly of permissions or entitlements …") *Commons, Anticommons, Semicommons*, *supra*, at 10.

I have argued elsewhere[12] that ownership is not just a mutable bundle of Coasean use-rights.[13] Nor is it the freedom constituted by the exclusion of others from a thing.[14] Rather, it is the special authority to set the overall "agenda" for an object of property,[15] to give an object its purpose and character, which, in turn, has implications (in quite a structured way) on the sorts of ends that others, including non-owners, can pursue with that object.[16]

On a view of ownership as agenda-setting authority, a true anticommons exists where owners are in a symmetrical relationship in which each person has the *same* kind of authority over an object or some aspect of an object of property.[17] Each person's authority commands deference from others. In order for one person to set an agenda at all in this circumstance, each other owner must simultaneously ratify the proposed agenda for the object. By contrast, owners are in an asymmetrical relationship with both the state and non-owners with authority over complementary goods.[18]

---

12 Larissa Katz, *Exclusion and Exclusivity in Property Law*, 58 U. Toronto L.J. 275, 277–278 (2008) [hereinafter *Exclusion and Exclusivity*] ("[O]wnership, like sovereignty, is an exclusive position that does *not* depend for its exclusivity on the right to exclude others from the object of the right. What it means for ownership to be exclusive is just that owners are in a special position to set the agenda for a resource"). I distinguish between ownership and property, which includes subordinate interests relating to the use or value of an object, such as an easement or mortgage.

13 See Ronald Coase's chapter "The Problem of Social Cost" in R.H. Coase, The Firm, The Market And The Law (1998). For a classic statement of the bundle of rights view, *see* Thomas C. Grey, *The Disintegration of Property*, *in* Modern Understandings of Liberty and Property, 291 (Richard Epstein ed., 2000). Law and economics has largely followed the legal realist view of property as a bundle of rights. *See* Thomas Merrill & Henry Smith, *What Happened to Property in Law and Economics*, 111 Yale L.J. 357, 359–360 (2001) (describing the influence of the Coasean view that rights ought to follow bargaining costs).

14 A modern *locus classicus* of the boundary approach is J.E. Penner, The Idea of Property in Law (1997). *See Exclusion and Exclusivity, supra* note 12, at 279–285 (describing the features of a boundary approach).

15 By "object of property," I mean a resource which is subject to agenda-setting control within our property system. An "object" can be tangible or intangible.

16 The law in many circumstances imputes a default agenda to an owner, e.g., the home is assumed to be a place dedicated to private activities and so not open to the public. *See Exclusion and Exclusivity*, *supra* note 12, at 298.

17 For an example of a "true" anticommons in a non-ownership context, see my example of a parliamentary filibuster, see *infra* section on Ends and Means.

18 By complementary goods, I mean goods which are often most productively used in combination. A good example is pendant paintings, often religious paintings or portraits, which were initially meant to hang side by side. While best viewed together, many fine examples of pendant paintings are now separately owned by different institutions or collectors. *See* John Oliver Hand et al., Prayers and Portraits: Unfolding the Netherlandish Diptych, 9 (2006) (describing separation of pendant paintings as secularization obscured the religious significance of certain pairings).

Regulators simply narrow the scope of agendas that are open to the owner but are not, simply by virtue of their ability to block the ends that owners can achieve, themselves "owners" exercising parallel agenda-setting authority. And non-owners have no authority over the object at all—although owners of complementary goods have the power to set the agenda for their own objects (which may have implications for the ends that can be pursued using other complementary things).

From all this we can conclude the following. De Soto might very well be right that spreading authority among too many regulatory bodies in developing countries creates costly red tape, but this is a normative argument about the *distribution* of authority required to produce a certain desired result, not a conceptual argument that proceeds from the idea of ownership. Heller, too, is best understood as pursuing a similar normative argument about the best distribution of ownership and regulatory authority in order to facilitate valuable projects.[19] The problems that Heller identifies with regulators' power to veto projects are properly understood just as transaction costs and straightforward hold-out problems, as de Soto has already recognized, rather than deficiencies in the form of public or private authority. His proposals would not change the form of authority, but rather would simply re-allocate it consistently in the direction of fewer owners and fewer regulatory hurdles. Heller, too, might be right that there is good reason to streamline regulatory authority and also to concentrate property holdings in the hands of fewer rather than more people. But this kind of distributional claim needs to proceed as a normative argument and not a conceptual one that follows from the idea of ownership.

This chapter is in two parts. In the first part, I argue that the concept of the anticommons does not join de Soto's analysis of regulatory hurdles because the concept of the anticommons properly applies only in situations of independent but overlapping authority (e.g. multiple owners with the same authority over a resource or separate public authorities with the same mandate).[20] The concept of the anticommons does not apply in cases of parties whose spheres of authority do not overlap (e.g. owners of separate but complementary assets or regulators with separate but complementary mandates). It also does not fit cases where parties are vertically related (e.g. the *hierarchical* relationship between owners and regulators or, analogously, the hierarchical relationship between owners and subordinate property rights-holders such as a landlord and tenant).[21] Thus,

---

19 *See* GRIDLOCK, *supra* note 4, at 43 (describing the core of an anticommons problem as: "too many uncoordinated owners or regulators blocking *optimal use* of a single resource" (emphasis added)).

20 Heller acknowledges as much at one point in the *Tragedy of the Anticommons*, *supra* note 4, at 639 ("Because multiple parties may hold *the same right*, almost any use of the storefront requires the agreement of multiple parties" (emphasis added)).

21 Just as there is an analogy between ownership and sovereignty when it comes to the preservation of authority, so too is political and ownership authority vulnerable to sterilization in a similar way: the existence of multiple, overlapping authorities risks preventing the exercise of authority in both contexts. It makes sense, on my own understanding of ownership in relation to sovereignty, that a political anticommons is

regulatory or ownership authority defined by separate (even if complementary) mandates is not structurally deficient although it may lead to straightforward transaction costs and hold-out problems. Further, regulators with power to veto the agenda for a resource do not usurp ownership authority, but rather simply impose transaction costs on owners much as de Soto described.

In the second part of the paper, I consider whether Heller's contribution to de Soto's analysis of red tape is to offer a better normative framework for resolving the question, central to both approaches, of how to distribute decision-making authority. Both a gridlock and a red tape analysis depend on some way of determining the measure of *good* regulation (i.e., valuable regulatory check-points), as opposed to *bad* regulation (i.e., pointless regulatory hurdles). While the answer to this distributional question is a matter of substantive political theory and policy,[22] Heller does no more than de Soto in pointing to economic reasons[23] for preferring fewer owners of complementary assets and fewer regulatory steps:[24] the transaction costs and potential hold-out problems that diffuse ownership and regulatory authority present *when seen through the lens of a particular project.*

Red Tape and Gridlock

Michael Heller's work on the anticommons suggests that property theory has a role in explaining some of the forces that push people into the informal sphere and

---

analogous to an ownership anticommons. *See Exclusion and Exclusivity*, *supra* note 12, at 278.

22 This is a question about the role of government and the value of government intervention even in the absence of clear market failure.

23 *See, e.g.*, *Tragedy of the Anticommons*, *supra* note 4, at 644–645 n.115 ("'[I]nformals suffer … from the absence of a legal system that guarantees and promotes their economic efficiency—*in other words, of good law* ….' I would place bundling property rights coherently at the same level as de Soto's examples") (emphasis added). The internal quotation is to OTHER PATH, *supra* note 2, at 158.

24 This projects-driven approach to evaluating regulation would justify now widely recognized instances of under-regulation, such as the failure by the Bush administration to regulate the market in asset-backed securities. The absence of regulatory hurdles in the development of markets in asset-backed securities is a major cause of the current economic crisis. And yet the regulation we now see was required would have contributed to what Heller would call a regulatory anticommons *when seen through the lens of the investment bank's project* of rebundling mortgages for the purpose of selling them off as collateralized debt obligations. The additional value that investment banks were able to extract from security interests by packaging them as they did could not have been possible had investment banks been subject to anywhere near the kind of regulatory obstacles that banks themselves would have faced had they tried to achieve the same debt to capital ratio. *See* FERGUSON, *supra* note 2, at 230–282. *See also* note 104 and accompanying text (further explaining the anti-regulatory slant to Heller's work).

more generally, lead people to under-use assets in the formal sphere. The promise of Heller's work on the anticommons is the addition of an important conceptual dimension to de Soto's work on informality. De Soto attributes the persistence of informality in much of the developing world to red tape: too many hurdles in entering and remaining in the formal sphere impose steep costs that drive people into the informal sphere even in the absence of corruption.[25] These costs add up when owners are forced to garner the approval of multiple government agencies,[26] adjoining owners[27] or community associations[28] in order to enter and stay in the formal sphere. Simply put, many people in poor countries just cannot afford to operate formally because of red tape. As a result, in most of the world, people control resources without recourse to the state. In some cases, they rely on brute possession to use and enjoy their assets. In other cases, they turn to local collective action mechanisms to provide the assurances, determinacy, and systematic enforcement characteristic of any system of property.[29] Informal asset-control and formal property systems are not, however, tidy parallel universes. The persistence of informality tells us more about what is wrong with formal property systems than about what is right with the informal systems that emerge and persist in their place. Informality, de Soto argues, is nearly always a drag on the economy. Although informal systems tend to be quite adept at securing owners' assets, they are not nearly as good at protecting the rights of third parties (e.g. mortgagees and lien-holders) and so the transactions that turn assets into capital.[30] De Soto's work on informality is intended to illuminate the costs of operating formally in the developing world while also showing the value of inviting the state in as the supplier of property rights.

What does gridlock add to an explanation of informality in terms of red tape and the transaction costs or hold-out problems it produces? What Heller's gridlock story promises is that there is a role for property theory in extending de Soto's basic insights so as to explain a deeper and more pervasive problem in formal property systems everywhere. It suggests that what is missing from de Soto's account of informality in terms of red tape is an understanding of how property rights themselves might be deficient in the formal sphere. Gridlock explains the flight to informality as a response to a deficiency in the form of ownership authority that exists when regulators, non-owners and owners are

---

25 *See* Mystery of Capital, *supra* note 2, at 18–28; Other Path, *supra* note 2, at 132–151.

26 *See* Mystery of Capital, at 22–27 (Figures 2.2, 2.3, 2.4).

27 *Id.* at 22 (Figure 2.2 (Philippines)).

28 *See id.* at 22–24 (Figure 2.2 (obtaining formal title to land in Philippines); Figure 2.3 (obtaining formal rights to build in the desert in Egypt)).

29 *See generally* Larissa Katz, *Governing Through Owners* (unpublished manuscript, on file with author).

30 See the sources in note 2 (suggesting that formalization projects have not in fact delivered on their promise).

trapped in an anticommons, which, on Heller's account, they are when each has the power to veto the highest-value use of an object of property.

Distinguishing Gridlock from Red Tape

The real question that confronts me here is the extent to which gridlock is distinguishable from red tape in the context of the regulatory hurdles that drive people into the informal sector. Is gridlock just the result of too many transaction costs from red tape, or does it proceed from a problem with property rights—an anticommons? The answer to this question depends on what we see as defining an anticommons. Heller's original argument was that an anticommons is a *form* that property rights sometimes take[31] and, by analogy, the form of other types of decision-making authority: regulatory, political and even adjudicative (e.g. juries).[32] What distinguishes an anticommons from a mere hold-out situation[33] (which a monopoly creates, for instance) is that in an anticommons, potential hold-out problems are built right into the form of ownership. According to Heller, in an anticommons we have the opposite of the commons: each member of the anticommons wields a power to *veto use* rather than, as in a commons, a *privilege to use* the resource.[34] On this account, private property is a mean point between the commons on one end and the anticommons on the other, between too many use-

31 Heller's work on the anticommons thus aims to do more than simply provide a useful shorthand to describe the costs associated with assembling veto-rights. He aims to add another concept to our "property lexicon," as he calls it, by explaining how private property is bounded by commons on one side and anticommons on the other. *See Boundaries*, *supra* note 4, at 1166–1167 (setting out the boundaries between different forms of ownership and completing the spectrum by adding the "anticommons"); GRIDLOCK, *supra* note 4, at 37; Munzer, *supra* note 6, at 153–154 (discussing Heller's contributions to property theory).

32 For an example of a political anticommons, *see* Fitzpatrick, *supra* note 2, at 1002–1003 (describing the "property rights failures"—the failure of any one system of private property to emerge—where more than one level of government or more than one source of authority has the power to define property rights).

33 *See* Robert Ellickson, *Property in Land*, 102 YALE L.J. 1315, 1330 n.56 (1993) (describing hold-out problems in "bilateral monopolies"). Note that Heller treats these as anticommons problems too. *Tragedy of the Anticommons*, *supra* note 4, at 669 (an anticommons exists even when "a few actors have rights of exclusion in a resource that each wants to use"). *See also Boundaries*, *supra* note 4, at 1187 n.122 ("[a]s few as two regulatory bodies may create this type of problem when they resist coordination"); Michael A. Heller, *Three Faces of Private Property*, 79 OR. L. REV. 417, 424 (2000) [hereinafter *Three Faces*].

34 The anticommons looks a lot like a "negative community," in which everyone in a state of nature has a veto power that must be extinguished before anyone can proceed. The commons, to complete the analogy, is like Pufendorf's "positive community," in which the starting point is a use-privilege. *See* RICHARD SCHLATTER, PRIVATE PROPERTY: THE HISTORY OF AN IDEA, 128 (1951).

rights and too many rights to "exclude."[35] The hold-out problems that are built in to an anticommons often lead to the tragedy of under-use, on Heller's account. In the developing world, a tragic anticommons in the formal sector may also create opportunity costs for owners who are able to pursue their ends more freely in the informal sector.

In what follows, I will argue that Heller misstates the significance of veto-power over uses to the concept of the anticommons. It is indeed Heller's emphasis on the effects of an anticommons on the ends that owners can pursue that invites some scholars' skepticism about the commons/anticommons distinction.[36] Lee Fennell argues in her paper, *Common Interest Tragedies*, that owners in a commons are also able to block others from using a resource for inconsistent purposes. For example, where one co-owner of a garden runs around screaming, the other co-owners cannot use it for quiet conversation and so are effectively "excluded" from a particular use. For Fennell, the convergence of use and exclusion puts Heller's proposed conceptual distinction between the commons and the anticommons on shaky ground. Fennell's conclusion is that we are better off with a functional taxonomy of common interest tragedies rather than a conceptual account that classifies groupings of rights as either an anticommons or a commons. I disagree. Fennell is of course right that an owner can maneuver to block the ends of others in a commons just as much as in an anticommons. Indeed, outsiders may also have the *de facto* power to block an owner's ends through fair competition or the ordinary use of neighboring property. But this does not challenge the distinction between owners and non-owners any more than Fennell's example is a challenge to the distinction between commons and anticommons. We trigger the conceptual confusion that Fennell identifies only if we try to root the concept of the anticommons in the power to veto use. What we should take from the convergence of a commons and an anticommons in Fennell's example is that we should not define an anticommons just, or even primarily, in terms of the effect it has on the ends that owners are able to pursue.

Let me start by explaining this important distinction between ends and means in the concept of the anticommons. I will then offer an alternative account of an anticommons in terms of the effect an anticommons has on the ability of owners to exercise their agenda-setting authority at all. An anticommons thus remains an important property tool distinct from a commons, on my telling. It is just far narrower in scope than Heller concedes. Following this I will turn in the next section to consider how, if at all, this refined and much narrower concept of the anticommons joins de Soto's analysis of informality.

35 Lee Anne Fennell, *Common Interest Tragedies*, 98 Nw. U. L. Rev. 907, 936–940 (2004) [hereinafter *Common Interest Tragedies*].

36 *Id. See also Commons, Anticommons, Semicommons*, *supra* note 11, at 11–12 (arguing that an anticommons problem is an assembly problem "nothing more and nothing less").

Ends and Means

The distinction between means and ends enables us to distinguish between an anticommons and ordinary hold-out/transaction cost problems. I will start by offering a few examples to show that an owner may have private property (the exclusive authority to set the agenda for a resource) even in situations where her ends are blocked.[37] Where a person does not own the inputs she needs to achieve the ends she desires, she may be able to acquire them through contract or she may find that the transaction costs are too high or the hold-outs intractable, with the sometimes unfortunate result that her ends are blocked.[38] This, however, is not due to any special deficiency in the form of property rights to those inputs, but rather to straightforward transaction costs or hold-out problems.[39] The examples that follow are meant to distinguish between deficiencies in the form of authority (in ownership and other cases of anticommons) and situations that generate external costs and hold-out problems.

Example 1: Country X has a minority government. The opposition party filibusters by introducing endless amendments to a proposed bill. For an indefinite period, no Member of Parliament is able to pass any legislation. As a result of the filibuster, MPs are prevented from achieving their ends. More importantly, MPs are also blocked from exercising their *means* of achieving their ends, i.e., exercising the authority of the house to pass legislation. The filibuster prevents the essential business of Parliament from taking place. A parliament that is not filibuster-proof is subject to a political anticommons, where the overlapping authority of members of parliament to propose bills and amendments to bills results in no one's being able to pass legislation. This situation is quite obviously distinct from one in which the executive fails to implement a scheme set out in legislation that has been passed (thus foiling the ends of the legislature) or where, for other (external) reasons, the legislation in question fails to accomplish what it was designed to do. In these latter situations, the legislature has not been prevented from exercising its authority to pass legislation; it has merely been prevented from achieving its desired *ends*.

Example 2: X is an owner of a patent over technology enabling the use of human sperm to fertilize animal eggs.[40] X has exercised her authority to set the agenda

37 *Exclusion and Exclusivity*, *supra* note 12, at 311–315 (discussing the relationship between autonomy and property).

38 Not all hold-outs create inefficient or even socially undesirable results. *See Common Interest Tragedies*, *supra* note 35, at 941 (discussing the distinction between "efficient" outcomes, where the subjective preferences of the owner prompt the hold-out, rather than an attempt to capture a greater share of the surplus wealth created by assembling veto rights, and distributionally unsatisfactory results).

39 *See* Ellickson, *supra* note 33, at 1330 (referring to the "consensus position that transaction costs tend to increase with the number of individuals involved").

40 This example was inspired by "Modernising Reproduction," Baroness Ruth Deech's Dec. 11, 2008 lecture at the John Fleming Centre for the Advancement of Legal Research at the Australian National University (unpublished).

for the patent by establishing its purpose: X has made the patented technology available for a small fee for research into infertility. X hopes to achieve a deeper understanding of human infertility and to recoup her costs. But it so happens that all owners of human sperm (male donors whose sperm has been collected) refuse to consent on ethical grounds to the use of their sperm to fertilize animal eggs. A regulatory body responsible for overseeing IVF research later rules that it is illegal to use human sperm in this way. X has been unable to achieve her ends, but her authority to set the agenda for her patent is unaffected because, in making the technology available for research for a small fee, she has exercised fully whatever control over the technology that her ownership of the patent gave her. She has given the technology an agenda, which organizes the uses that can be made of it. X is not in an anticommons with the owners of sperm or the regulatory body, even though both of the latter can interfere with her achievement of her ends.

On my telling, what is important about an anticommons is its effect on an owner's *means* rather than her *ends*. There is a distinction between changes to the form of ownership that undermine the possibility of agenda-setting and obstacles to the ends an owner would like to pursue. Whereas owners of private property are not guaranteed the ability to achieve their ends (perhaps because of limits on the scope of their authority or the inaccessibility of other necessary inputs), owners in an anticommons are not even guaranteed the ability to exercise their very means, precisely because any exercise of agenda-setting authority by one requires simultaneous ratification by the others.

I have identified an important feature of an ownership anticommons and, by analogy, other types of anticommons which I think provide guidance on how to distinguish it from cases where outsiders are able to impose straightforward costs on owners or to withhold inputs needed to achieve a particular end. Owners in an anticommons do not merely have veto-power. Even in the context of an anticommons, the essence of ownership remains the authority to set the agenda for a resource. Talk of "veto-power" makes sense only as a short-hand for a more complicated underlying reality in an anticommons: where multiple owners have independent but overlapping authority, a person is able to set the agenda for the resource only where at the same time the others exercise their separate authority to set the agenda by ratifying the choice. This is an important qualification because (as I argue below in the case of the empty Moscow storefronts) it rules out those who have leverage to influence the owners' decisions without themselves having any authority to proceed with the business of setting the agenda for a resource.[41]

In light of the above, I will now turn to the task of distinguishing an anticommons from other forms of ownership, in particular from the commons,

41 This distinction is lost in the Moscow storefront case: Heller treats as "owners" agencies with the regulatory power to block a particular sale for public reasons, without, however, the right to sell, and the regulatory power to set prices, which influences a decision to sell by a person with the authority to do so. *Tragedy of the Anticommons*, *supra* note 4, at 638 (Figure 2).

with which it is easily confused. The confusion appears when we focus on the effects an anticommons can have on our ability to achieve our ends rather than our ability to exercise our means.[42]

The Commons

In a (limited access)[43] commons, co-owners share the authority to set the agenda for a resource: they are collectively in charge of deciding the purpose the resource has, and so the ends which it can serve.[44] It is this shared agenda-setting authority, rather than access to the resource, that is the essential ingredient of common ownership. A non-owner may have use-rights in a communal property regime but still not share ownership authority. What distinguishes a non-owner from a co-owner is that the latter *also* has a right to share in the setting of the agenda. A good example of this distinction between use rights and co-ownership is found in Elinor Ostrom's description of the ancient irrigation systems in Spain, in which owners of "dry" land (*seca*) are free to use water during times of plenty but only owners of irrigated land (*regadiu*) are members of "irrigation communities" which participate, through their chief, in the decision-making bodies that control the irrigation system.[45] Non-owners thus may have use rights in a commons but these use rights do not amount to co-ownership without a share in the authority to set and pursue joint objectives. On this account, the common law's tenancy in common and joint tenancy are a commons with respect to the use and enjoyment of the resource.[46] In each, co-owners have independent use rights but collective authority

---

42 *See Common Interest Tragedies*, *supra* note 35.

43 *See, e.g.*, Carol M. Rose, *The Several Futures of Property: Of Cyberspace and Folk Tales, Emission Trades and Ecosystems*, 83 MINN. L. REV. 129, 155 (1998) (distinguishing between open-access and limited access commons).

44 *See infra* note 47 (describing the business of ownership as the setting of agenda. Owners are in charge of determining the character of a resource, its purpose in the world). Shared agenda-setting authority usually emerges in situations where each owner owns an undivided share of the whole and so is entitled to participate either equally or in proportion to her share to the management of the resource. On this view, the co-ownership of farms that Heller describes does not create an anticommons but rather a commons.

45 *See e.g.*, ELINOR OSTROM, GOVERNING THE COMMONS: THE EVOLUTION OF INSTITUTIONS FOR COLLECTIVE ACTION, 71–76 (2007).

46 Joint-tenancies and tenancies-in-common are "mixed" property: commons with respect to use and enjoyment, but exhibiting anticommons problems with respect to disposition or transactions that affect title; co-owners are effectively prevented from disposing of or mortgaging their share without the consent of others. It was to respond to the costs of assembling concurrently owned shares in property that the English in 1925 introduced several changes into the law of real property that converted concurrent interests in land into interests in the proceeds from the sale of land. Whereas before January 1, 1926, there could be an unlimited number of tenants in common whose consent had to be obtained for a sale or mortgage, after that date, there could be a maximum of four joint tenants with legal title, holding in trust for sale for any number of beneficiaries. This limited the number of people at the bargaining

over the agenda.[47] The right that co-tenants have to possess the whole ensures that each has an independent use right that is not dependent on the permission of others. At the same time, rules prohibiting ouster and waste preserve collective agenda-setting authority. Ouster does so by preventing any one co-tenant from effectively preempting the agenda-setting process through use that is inconsistent with the uses of others.[48] The prohibition on waste does so by preventing a co-tenant from unilaterally making changes to the character of the resource—that is, to its current agenda—even in some circumstances where the changes would produce a surplus of value for all.[49]

No one in a commons has *independent* power to set the agenda. In practice, the agenda for a resource in a commons emerges in one of three ways: organically, through individual uses that over time give land or a resource a collective purpose;[50] through deliberate collaboration;[51] or, in the absence of constraining rules like the rules against ouster, through preemption. Preemption occurs where one co-owner is able to ensure that the facts on the ground are unfavorable to the purposes of the others. Thus, in Fennell's example of the screamer and the quiet conversationalist, the screamer's active use operates as a brute fact that limits the desirability or even the possibility of conversation. It is not that the conversationalist has a duty to defer to the screamer's agenda but rather that the screamer coercively preempts the

---

table. The equitable owners who could be safely ignored by third parties because the interest of equitable owners was now only an interest in the share of any proceeds of sale. This innovation was limited in the more recent wave of land reform legislation of 1996. In recognition of the use-value, rather than just the exchange-value, of property, equitable owners have once again been accorded a say in any decision to alienate the land in English law. *See* The Rt. Hon. Sir Robert Megarry and Sir William Wade, The Law of Real Property, 115–145 (Charles Harpum et al., eds, 7th ed. 2008). I am grateful to James Penner for pressing me to make this point explicit.

47 Agenda-setting authority, which I argue is the essence of ownership, is thus distinct from use-rights that, on a bundle-of-rights approach, are allocated case-by-case to reflect a balancing of interests and values.

48 *See* Anne Warner La Forest, Anger & Honsberger Law of Real Property, 14–12, 14–36 (3rd ed. 2006) (overview of the law of ouster).

49 The law of waste limits the changes that co-owners can make to the physical character of the land. *See* Bruce H. Ziff, Principles of Property Law, 165 (4th ed. 2006) (rules prohibiting voluntary waste "prevent the over-cultivation of timber estates, the destruction of buildings, the opening of new mines and other conduct that will diminish the property in the long run"); *id.* at 329 (applying principles of voluntary and equitable waste to co-owners); Jedediah Purdy, *The American Transformation of Waste Doctrine: A Pluralist Interpretation*, 91 Cornell L. Rev. 653 (2006).

50 *See supra* note 48 and accompanying text (describing the effect of rules prohibiting ouster on the ability of members in a commons to preempt the agenda-setting process).

51 *See, e.g.*, Robert C. Ellickson & Vicky L. Been, Land Use Controls: Cases and Materials, 582–606 (3rd ed. 2005) (discussing the residential community association). *See also* Ostrom, *supra* note 45 and accompanying text (discussing governing bodies for Spanish irrigation systems).

process of agenda-setting. Tragedy results where neither custom, collaboration nor preemption produces a coherent agenda, with the result that there is no overarching structure or plan that guides sustainable uses.

Anticommons

By contrast, in an anticommons, owners do not share agenda-setting authority for a resource, but rather everyone has autonomous but overlapping authority over the same resource. As Heller puts it, that there are "too many owners" with the "same right."[52] The result is a conceptually distinct form of ownership. Where there are overlapping spheres of independent authority, no one can proceed if the others do not simultaneously ratify her agenda.[53] How could it be otherwise? *The authority of an owner commands deference from others, even—or perhaps especially—those who have an identical claim to authority.*[54] This requirement of deference has the effect of giving each owner the ability to prevent every other owner from exercising her authority at all.[55] The requirement of deference to the potentially inconsistent agendas of each owner in an anticommons stifles the emergence of a collective agenda from facts on the ground, that is from actual use by co-owners.

An additional basis for the distinction between commons and anticommons is simply a question of strategic advantage. To use Fennell's example once more, it is the quiet conversationalist, not the screamer, who would have a strategic advantage in an anticommons because the paralysis that results in an anticommons

52 Of course it requires some further analysis to determine the kinds of property rights that confer agenda-setting authority. Although there is a concept of ownership in law, it is rarely explicitly invoked in statutes or cases. *See* J.W. Harris, Property and Justice, 68–72 (1996) (explaining much of property law addresses transactional or conveyancing problems and so we do not get many cases that focus squarely on the concept of ownership).

53 This is in keeping with Frank Michelman's original articulation of the idea of the anticommons. Michelman pointed out that the use of a resource in an anticommons requires "near-simultaneous unanimous consent." *See* Michelman, *supra* note 4, at 6.

54 Put this way, the paradoxical nature of an anticommons, and indeed its incoherence, emerges much more clearly. *See Tragedy of the Anticommons*, *supra* note 4, at 644–645 n.115 (referring to "bundling property rights *coherently*" (emphasis added) in contrast to the fragmentation of rights in an anticommons).

55 One difference between this articulation of the anticommons and Frank Michelman's description of a regulatory regime in *Ethics, Economics and Property Law* is that it assumes as a starting point that all members have agenda-setting authority, which in turn generates a right that others abstain from using without their consent. The rule that constitutes a regulatory regime, according to Michelman, is just the right that "each of the others shall leave the covered objects alone except insofar as authorization is obtained" Michelman, *supra* note 4, at 6. The purely negative articulation that Michelman offers does not make sense as a form of property: through property rights, the law ensures that someone has agenda-setting authority over objects. The trouble of course in an anticommons is that too many people do.

mimics the effects of the agenda she would have set for the garden.[56] But this is only a strategic and not a legal advantage: neither the conversationalist nor the screamer is able to exercise her authority to dedicate the land to her favored purpose although the conversationalist is in a better position to enjoy the *détente*. The danger of an anticommons is that resources may be left agenda-less. That is to say, the very business of ownership, which is to give a resource its purpose and so to organize the uses to which it can be put, may be stalled in an anticommons.

What the Anticommons Does Not Explain about Flight to the Informal Sector
The integrity of the anticommons concept is undermined if we apply it too liberally in cases where owners confront external obstacles in achieving their ends. We lose sight of the core features of an anticommons in applying it as another dimension in the analysis of factors that drive people into the informal sector. This is not to say that the anticommons has no role in explaining informality: a true anticommons in the formal sector might create opportunity costs for owners who could otherwise control their assets informally. The inability to set the agenda for a resource in the formal sector might well be a factor in the flight to the informal sector—assuming that the informal sector offers a form of ownership superior to what is on offer in the formal sector. This itself would be a troubling assumption. Evidence suggests that informal sectors, rather than offering neat alternatives to formal property systems, often produce seriously degraded forms of resource control.[57] Contestation over resources may force informal owners to rely on self-help to protect their holdings, but this is a costly and often ineffective substitute for third-party enforcement mechanisms.[58] What this suggests is that people cling to informal property systems not because they offer structurally superior property rights (as flight to the informal sector because of an anticommons in the formal sector suggests) but because of the aggregate costs of formality.

---

56 Much as the conservationist and not the developer, enjoys a strategic advantage in an anticommons. Abraham Bell & Gideon Parchomovsky, *Of Property and Antiproperty*, 102 Mich L. Rev. 1 (2003); Heller, *Tragedy of the Anticommons*, *supra* note 4, at 673 (strategic uses of anticommons). In fact, the conservationist's advantage is only possible where there is a true anticommons and so where others are not able to set an agenda without her permission. This is not the case where there is no anticommons but separately owned parcels that the conservationist wants to assemble into a larger tract. In such a case of complementary resources, a failure to cooperate can foil the conservationist's ends. This is another ground for distinguishing between a true anticommons that impedes the exercise of authority and the assembly problems that can foil an owner's desired ends. I am grateful to Lee Fennell for pressing me on this point.

57 Jedediah Purdy describes most "informal" property rights as possessory rights. *See* Jedediah Purdy, *A Freedom-Promoting Approach to Property: A Renewed Tradition for New Debates*, 72 U. Chi. L. Rev. 1237, 1287 (2005).

58 *See* Robert C. Ellickson, Order Without Law: How Neighbors Settle Disputes, 126–127 (1991) (describing different systems of social control, with third party control provided by a state, an informal organization or social norms).

My primary concern, however, is not the use of the concept of the anticommons to explain informality in cases where there are horizontally related, overlapping spheres of authority, i.e., in limited cases of true ownership anticommons. It is rather the reformulation of de Soto's analysis of regulatory hurdles in terms of an anticommons that is more troubling. The distinction between blocked ends and blocked means is the key to understanding why the concept of the anticommons does not offer a general rationale for the kinds of regulatory hurdles that de Soto would explain in terms of straightforward transaction costs/hold-out problems: regulatory anticommons, where the regulators have separate but complementary mandates that affect an owner's ability to achieve a particular result (BANANA[59] republics) and ownership anticommons, where the rights-holders are a mixed bag of private owners and public regulators (e.g., Heller's Moscow storefront case).

I will now turn to two situations in which I think it is wrong to apply the concept: horizontal relationships in which the parties have complementary but non-overlapping spheres of authority and vertical relationships, in which the parties are hierarchically related. These two situations bear on the discussion of the root causes of informality because these are precisely the kinds of situations that generate straightforward external costs that may drive owners towards informality. I will argue that it is more productive to analyze these cases simply in terms of the external costs they present (following de Soto) rather than in terms of an anticommons. The concept of the anticommons neither deepens our understanding of these situations, nor does it explain their relevance to our understanding of the costs of formal ownership in the developed world.

Hierarchy and Vertical Relationships One of the most evocative examples of an anticommons is Heller's case study of the empty Moscow storefronts in the 1990s.[60] According to Heller, Moscow storefronts were left unused while Russia made the transition to capitalism because too many regulatory and private entities had the power to veto any particular use (e.g. sale or lease) of these storefronts. The government entities in question had both formal and informal[61] leverage over the kinds of uses to which the storefronts were put. Heller quoted the following description of the role of government in the creation of the anticommons in storefronts: politicians "use their control rights to produce inefficient outcomes

59 This is an acronym for "Build Absolutely Nothing Anywhere Near Anyone." See GRIDLOCK, *supra* note 4, at 131.

60 Others have questioned on different grounds whether this should be the canonical example of the phenomenon, while others have endorsed it (for instance, *see* Munzer, *supra* note 6).

61 *Tragedy of the Anticommons*, *supra* note 4, at 635–636 n.77 (describing the informal but real influence of the bureau responsible for keeping track of physical and technical specifications of buildings and of the committee for the preservation of architectural and historical monuments).

that serve their goals," the Moscow storefronts are an example of "private assets that are politically controlled by regulators."[62]

What would de Soto say about this situation, and, correspondingly, the flight to the informal sector that Heller says resulted (evident in the thriving sidewalk kiosks in front of empty storefronts)? De Soto's analysis would undoubtedly have been in terms of straightforward transaction costs that accumulate and trigger a flight to informality. The experience of one kiosk owner, who said "it was simply not worth spending a year and a half fighting the bureaucracy to get space on a first floor," sounds very much like the red tape that de Soto documents in explaining informality elsewhere in the developing world.[63] Take for example de Soto's study of formal ownership in the Philippines. De Soto and his researchers document multiple hurdles to formal ownership. Owners were required to seek approval from over 50 regulatory agencies as well as neighboring owners and community associations before they could acquire and register formal title to land.[64] The assembly of permissions required to formalize property rights generated costs that pushed people into the informal sector. Whereas Heller would see the process for formalizing title in the Philippines (like the process for acquiring rights to use the Moscow storefronts) as a gridlock problem, de Soto would see red tape.

There is little doubt that politicians and regulators in the context of the Moscow storefronts imposed crippling costs on owners of storefronts. But what does the concept of an anticommons add to de Soto's analysis of such situations? It suggests is that the veto-power of the government entities in this case does not simply impose external costs; rather, it changes the *form* of ownership by contributing to an anticommons.[65] If Heller is right, what de Soto misses is the deeper commonality among cases such as this one, and cases in the developed world where the form that ownership of an asset takes may not trigger informality but leads, more subtly, to the under-use of assets.

There is, however, good reason not to reformulate de Soto's analysis of vertical relationships (between regulators and owners) in terms of an anticommons. To find an anticommons in this context, we would in effect be treating the veto-power of regulators as indistinguishable from the veto-power of owners.[66] On such an approach, increasing the number of regulators or owners moves us along the

62 *Id.* at 624–625 n.13 (quoting Andrei Shleifer, *Establishing Property Rights*, *in* PROCEEDINGS OF THE WORLD BANK ANNUAL CONFERENCE ON DEVELOPMENT ECONOMICS, 93, 98–100 (1994)).

63 *Tragedy of the Anticommons*, at 634 and n.68 (quoting Celestine Bohlen, *Moscow Journal: It's a Kiosk! It's a Mall! No, It's Slavyansky Ryad!*, N.Y. TIMES, Dec. 23, 1992, at A4).

64 MYSTERY OF CAPITAL, *supra* note 2, at 20.

65 Or in this case contribute to the formation of an anticommons. The multiple private owners of storefronts in Moscow form an ownership anticommons with or without the regulatory overlay.

66 Heller for instance quotes Richard Epstein: "[Twenty] or more agencies … are given the power to veto new construction on grounds such as environmental protection, antigrowth or sewage. In principle these permits do not allow the regulator to hold out as

spectrum from consolidated to diffuse veto-power, from private to anticommons property. Regulators and owners, in short, are treated as co-owners who exercise parallel agenda-setting authority over resources. But the exercise of a legal power by a regulator to deny permission to an owner to proceed with a project is fundamentally different from a refusal by co-owners to ratify an agenda. It is only the *illegitimate* exercise of discretionary power by regulators that mimics the legitimate use of hold-out power by private owners. Whereas owners may withhold their consent to a proposal for reasons that are opaque and without reference to the public good,[67] regulators would violate established rule of law principles were they to do the same.[68] We would take a very pessimistic view of the state if we were to assume that the illegitimate use of public power is the standard case of regulation. But this is the only basis for treating regulators and owners as horizontally related parties exercising competing veto-powers.

The ordinary relationship between owners and regulators does not produce an anticommons (i.e. a deficiency in the form of private or public authority) because regulators and owners do not ordinarily compete to set the agenda for resources. They are vertically, not horizontally related. Consider for a moment what regulators do when they exercise the second-order (public) power to define the scope of the owner's authority. Legislatures, regulators and courts, in setting a public agenda, exclude certain kinds of private agendas (e.g., harmful, immoral, inefficient ones) and even certain kinds of reasons for action (e.g., a direct intent to harm).[69] They do so in a number of ways: by setting out a detailed schema of permitted and prohibited agendas or reasons *ex ante*; by approving prospective agendas case by case, *ex ante*; by ruling on impermissible agendas or reasons *ex post*; by establishing a system of incentives which favor certain agendas or reasons and discourage others. *But they take it for granted that owners will carry on with the business of agenda-setting within the constraints that they have set.*

I am making a very basic public/private distinction here.[70] The analogy between ownership and sovereignty may be helpful in teasing out what it means for owners

---

if he were a private owner of some portion of the resource, but the ability to force zoning officials to behave … is … trick[y]." *See* GRIDLOCK, *supra* note 4, at 132.

67 I argue elsewhere that there is a principle of abuse of right in common law property systems that regulates an owner's reasons: an owner must actually act on the basis of what she subjectively determines is a worthwhile use of an asset and not just in order to cause harm, either as an end in itself or as leverage. *See* Larissa Katz, *A Jurisdictional Principle of Abuse of Right*, 2009 SSRN, *available at* http://ssrn.com/abstract=1417955 [hereinafter *Abuse of Right*].

68 *See, e.g.*, Jeremy Waldron, *The Rule of Law in Contemporary Liberal Theory*, 2 RATIO JURIS 79, 88 (1989).

69 *See Abuse of Right, supra* note 67.

70 *Exclusion and Exclusivity, supra* note 12, at 293. Ownership and sovereignty or private and public authority are analogous but not identical. Both are preserved as supreme but not absolute positions through a system of rules that ensure the deference of others. The

and regulators to be vertically related. The relationship between regulators and owners is analogous in some respects to the relationship between owners and non-owners. This analogy is not a perfect one if only because owners are members of the public whose interests regulators are meant to serve, whereas owners have no obligation to concern themselves with the interests of non-owners in the agendas that they set and pursue.[71] The important respect in which these relationships are similar is that both are hierarchically ordered rather than competitive and preserved by rules that establish priority and obligations of deference. In the case of owners/non-owners, the owner sets the agenda, which means that she gives the resource its purpose or character (e.g., opening her land to the public as a shopping centre,[72] conserving her land as protected habitat, preserving a sword as an *objet d'art*). Ownership is not in principle undermined where others use the resource to pursue subsidiary ends that are consistent with the agenda that the owner has set. A right to exclude, backed by injunctive force, thus often overprotects owners.[73] By the same token, the ancient principle of "innocent use," which gave non-owners protection against trespass actions where their use was consistent with the owner's agenda, adequately preserved an owner's position.[74] Ownership authority is, however, threatened where others use the resource for ends that are inconsistent with the owner's agenda. Ownership depends on hierarchy—rules that require non-owners to fall in line with the owner's agenda—in order to preserve the possibility of agenda-setting. Owners and non-owners are vertically related because non-owners

---

distinction between public and private authority over land, although long under attack by legal realists, is well-entrenched in the common law tradition. *See* London County Council v. Allen and Others, 3 K.B. 642 (Ct. App. 1914) (distinguishing the Council's power to control land from a property interest in land).

71 *See Abuse of Right*, *supra* note 67. I am grateful to Evan Fox-Decent for pushing me on this point.

72 Harrison v. Carswell, [1976] 2 S.C.R. 200 (Can.); PruneYard Shopping Center v. Robins, 447 U.S. 74 (1980).

73 *See Exclusion and Exclusivity*, *supra* note 12, at 315.

74 Lawrence Becker, *The Moral Basis of Property Rights, in* NOMOS XXII: PROPERTY, 187, 206 (J. Roland Pennock & John W. Chapman eds, 1980) ("In Europe, as late as Grotius, one finds reference to an analogous principle of 'innocent use' with respect to land. (The origin and scope of the principle is somewhat obscure, but it seems to have come down from archaic law and to have prohibited owners from taking legal action against trespassers as long as they were in no way interfering with the owners' use of the land)"). In common law systems, owners are usually only protected with a liability rule or a right to the fair market value of the use in cases where it turns out that a use is consistent with the owner's agenda (rather than property rule protection, which in some cases would require punitive damages. *See, e.g.*, Jacque v. Steenburg Homes, Inc., 563 N.W.2d 154 (Wis. 1997); *Abuse of Right*, *supra* note 67, at 10–11 (citing crane cases); Penarth Dock Engineering Co. v. Pounds, 1 Lloyd's Rep. 359 (Q.B. 1963) (requiring owner of a pontoon to pay fair market value for unauthorized use of a dock).

owe deference to the owner's agenda, even in cases where non-owners are also able to make (subordinate) decisions that affect what happens to a thing.

Just as owners limit and organize the subsidiary ends of non-owners by setting a private agenda, so too do public authorities shape the ends that owners are able to pursue with respect to the asset, by setting a public agenda for assets and activities within their territory. What owners in fact are able to achieve with their property is limited by the requirements of deference to the public agenda. Regulators and owners, like owners and non-owners, are not characteristically in a competitive or a collaborative (horizontal) relationship, but rather in a hierarchical (vertical) one. This does not rule out the possibility that government entities might in fact assume ownership or an ownership stake in a resource, alongside private actors. But this is just to say that the government entity in question wears the hat of private owner, and so, is subject to the same rules, and operates in the same arena as private owners. Their spheres of authority are typically different in kind. Regulators define, rather than block, owners' means and in so doing, block (some of) their ends. In some cases, regulators have a great deal of leverage over the ends that an owner chooses to pursue. But it is the exercise of an owner's means, and not the successful attainment of any particular ends, that an anticommons characteristically threatens. Owners are free to carry on with the business of ownership and to set the agenda for resources within the constraints that the state, through its regulators, has created.

It remains a threshold question whether in a particular case the vertical relationship that ordinarily exists between regulators and owners has been converted in fact into a horizontal one. Heller appears to make this claim in the Moscow storefront case when he says: "Local agencies often find themselves using their rights as if they were owners because they lack indirect mechanisms of governmental control over real estate, such as zoning boards and property taxes."[75] What is left unsaid is the sense in which the entities in question acted like owners and unlike Western regulators. Is Heller referring to the fact that Russian regulators lacked the arm's length procedural mechanisms for determining the scope of owners' authority but rather relied on informal decision-making procedures without proper rule of law protections (such as transparency and judicial review) for owners? This would clearly point to significant (and costly) problems with the exercise of public authority, but without more evidence it does not clearly show how the regulators' authority mimics the *private* authority that the regulators were meant to define. The Moscow storefront case as described suggests that regulators have more than usual leverage over the ends that owners pursue, but there is no basis on the facts as described for concluding that the hierarchy that structures the relationship between regulator and owner had collapsed in that case.

It is ordinary, if cumbersome, relationships between regulators and owners that de Soto describes in his book, *The Mystery of Capital*. And indeed it is a recognizably public/private relationship between regulators and owners that characterizes

75 *Tragedy of the Anticommons*, *supra* note 4, at 637.

the Moscow storefront case and other cases that Heller often calls "anticommons."[76] In the context of these *vertical* relationships, the concept of the anticommons obscures rather than extends the insights de Soto generates from a simple cost-based analysis of regulation in the formal sphere. In cases of vertical relationships, Heller's work on the anticommons does not point to a deeper problem with the form of ownership but rather leaves us with de Soto's basic observation: the personal costs associated with regulation may drive owners to the informal sector.[77]

Complements and Horizontal but Non-overlapping Relationships The concept of the anticommons has also been extended to explain situations where too many regulators or owners with separate but complementary jurisdictions exercise their authority in ways that impede the achievement of a particular project.[78] Heller describes what he calls BANANA republics as jurisdictions where developers are prevented from building anything anywhere because of the difficulty in assembling all the required approvals from multiple agencies or multiple levels of government.[79] In a BANANA republic, agencies with quite separate mandates (e.g. one over environmental standards, another over building codes, another over historical preservation) all have the power to veto a particular project. This, in Heller's view, creates a regulatory anticommons. In the ownership context, separate owners of complementary resources may also find themselves unable to combine their resources to achieve an otherwise valuable goal. Heller documents this problem in the context of patents, where patented technology that is most valuable as an input in a larger project (e.g. the development of a new drug) is

76 In other respects, the Moscow storefront case remains a good example of an anticommons. To the extent that multiple owners in fact wield the "same" right, they may well find themselves locked in a limited anticommons with respect to the kinds of decisions or uses that the particular right controls. *Tragedy of the Anticommons*, *supra* note 4, at 639 (acknowledging that an anticommons requires that multiple owners have the same right. If there are multiple owners who in fact all have the same right to sell the property (rather than a regulator's power to approve or to veto certain sale, which is not the same as the right to sell, or leverage over the sale because of power to regulate pricing, etc.), then we have the indicia of an anticommons).

77 De Soto's analysis in Other Path, *supra* note 2 may lack any further overarching conceptual point. But it does have one clear advantage over applying the concept of an anticommons to explain what about the relationship between people and public authorities drives them informal. De Soto's cost-based approach has the virtue of being open-ended with respect to the kinds of regulation that it draws into the analysis. By contrast the concept of a vertical anticommons draws certain kinds of regulatory costs into the center of the discussion and marginalizes others which, from the perspective of the owner, contribute to the overall costs of formality, e.g., regulatory hurdles at the end of which regulators are bound to say yes, such as building codes; informational obligations, including filing requirements, and so on.

78 *Tragedy of the Anticommons*, *supra* note 4, at 651; Gridlock, *supra* note 4, at 6–9 (discussing assembly problems in spatial "anticommons"), 43 (discussing problems with separately owned complements).

79 Gridlock, *supra* note 4, at 131.

diverted to a less valuable use because the person with the big idea is unable to pull together rights to all the necessary inputs.[80]

Extended thus, the concept of the anticommons would provide another layer of analysis of an important trigger of informality in the developing world. In *The Mystery of Capital*, de Soto chronicles the procedural hurdles created when multiple regulators are required to sign off before an owner gains formal title to land or is able to operate a business within the formal sector. Whereas de Soto would simply identify these problems as red tape and the transaction costs it produces, Heller would suggest that an anticommons is responsible for the gridlock. Both de Soto and Heller draw our attention to the costs that owners bear where they need to collect approvals from multiple agencies or levels of government. What would the concept of the anticommons add? Once again, it would suggest that a diffusion of veto-power is a deficiency built right into the form of authority exercised in the regulatory anticommons, a deficiency symptomized by under-use of formally owned assets or, in other contexts, a flight to the informal sector.

The concept of the anticommons does not fit situations where owners are in full control of their own means but are unable to co-opt the means of others necessary for the success of their projects.[81] In a true anticommons, owners wield independent authority over the same resource and yet owe deference to those in the exact same position. The result is of course gridlock: the inability of any one owner in an anticommons to exercise her authority at all without simultaneous ratification by the others. This deficiency in the form of authority exists no matter what agenda the owner proposes—it is not a project-specific problem.[82] In a true anticommons, hold-out problems are built right into the structure of authority and threaten *any* exercise of agenda-setting authority.[83]

By contrast, in cases where owners and regulators have complementary but non-overlapping authority, the so-called anticommons problem is in fact a distributional problem. In these cases, hold-out problems threaten only particular uses or projects, namely, those requiring the cooperation of others who control inputs necessary for a particular project, but not the exercise of agenda-setting

---

80 Michael A. Heller & Rebecca S. Eisenberg, *Can Patents Deter Innovation? The Anticommons in Biomedical Research*, 280 Sci. 698 (1998).

81 Even if we posit a very tight relationship between liberty and ownership, a person can be free even if she lacks the inputs to successfully achieve all of her ends. Freedom simply requires that she be left in charge of her means. *See Exclusion and Exclusivity*, *supra* note 12, at 313 (citing Arthur Ripstein, *Beyond the Harm Principle*, 34 Phil. & Pub. Aff. 215, 216 (2006)).

82 Whether or not the anticommons turns tragic will indeed depend on the project. Tragedy is avoided only where the owners in an anticommons all ratify a particular agenda, and presumably a decision to get on board or hold out will turn on the desirability of the project.

83 *See supra* note 55 and accompanying text. Because of reciprocal claims of authority and obligations of deference, no one can get on with the business of ownership in an anticommons without ratification of their agenda by others.

authority as such.[84] Where a particular project depends on contributions from neighbors, an owner's authority over her own resource is left intact: it is her project but not the exercise of her authority that is blocked when her neighbors refuse to go along with her.[85] In situations where authority over resources is widely distributed rather than concentrated in the hands of a few, it is more likely that owners will need to cooperate with others to get the requisite inputs for a project.[86] And the greater the number of parties to a transaction, the more likely it is that the project will become mired in transaction costs and hold-out problems.[87] This, however, is simply a problem of external costs that puts pressure on the question of how we distribute property rights and not a problem concerning the form of the owner's authority.

It would thus be a mistake to look to the concept of the anticommons to deepen de Soto's analysis of the relationship between too many regulatory hurdles and the flight to informality.[88] The reason is that Heller's discussion of gridlock where regulators (or owners) have separate but complementary authority simply points to problems with the *distribution*, not the *form*, of authority.[89] The challenge then is to decide which projects are sufficiently important to require the redistribution of authority to a single owner so as to minimize coordination costs.[90]

---

84 *See* Ellickson, *supra* note 33, at 1331 ("practitioners of transaction-cost economics stress avoidance of 'excessive dependence of coordination on large-number transactions'") (citing Michelman, *supra* note 4, at 20).

85 *See* discussion *supra* note 81 and accompanying text, on the importance to the integrity of ownership of protecting means but not ends.

86 *See* GRIDLOCK, *supra* note 4, at 26. *See also* Ellickson, *supra* note 33, at 1354.

87 *See* Ellickson, *supra* note 33, at 1330 (describing the consensus view that transaction costs rise as more people are involved in a project); *Common Interest Tragedies*, *supra* note 35, at 928–929 (pointing out that hold-out problems are often treated as a class of transaction cost).

88 While de Soto is very attentive to what Heller calls gridlock in the regulatory sphere, he does not seem resistant to what Heller might identify as "ownership" gridlock. On the contrary, his famous exhortation to listen to barking dogs in formalizing title acknowledges the value of a diffuse distribution of land among many small landowners. MYSTERY OF CAPITAL, *supra* note 2, at 178. What this points to is the importance of a full normative framework for evaluating when diffuse holdings are appropriate.

89 The distributional claim of gridlock in this context follows from the insight that transaction costs are higher the more people are involved in a project. *See* Ellickson, *supra* note 33, at 1330 (referring to the "consensus position that transaction costs tend to increase with the number of individuals involved").

90 The use of the anticommons in this context looks like an upfront application of Epstein's single owner test. *See* Richard A. Epstein, *Holdouts, Externalities, and the Single Owner: One More Salute to Ronald Coase*, 36 J.L. & ECON. 553, 557 (1993) ("Where resources are under the command of two or more persons, they seek to create that legal arrangement that induces all the parties to behave in the same fashion as would a single owner who owned all the relevant resources").

Distributional Questions

Heller's discussion of gridlock in the context of separate but complementary assets (or mandates) points to problems in the distribution, but not the form, of authority. Thus, Heller's gridlock analysis of regulatory hurdles does not add a new *conceptual* dimension to de Soto's analysis of red tape; rather Heller is advancing a very similar transaction-cost-based argument for streamlining the regulatory process.[91] De Soto's analysis raises but never adequately resolves the question of how we determine whether there is "too much" red tape; that is to say, it lacks an adequate normative basis for evaluating good and bad law.[92] One potential contribution of Heller's gridlock analysis is to set out the normative framework that would provide adequate guidance on how we ought to distribute public authority, in other words a measure of good regulation and valuable regulatory checkpoints as opposed to bad regulation and pointless regulatory hurdles.[93] But Heller does not add a deeper normative dimension to de Soto's approach perhaps because his discussion of regulatory gridlock emerges from his conceptual work on the anticommons rather than squarely from a policy-based review of the distributional issues regulatory gridlock in fact raises. Heller, like de Soto, skirts the central question of explaining what constitutes good and bad law and so what makes for "too many" regulators wielding complementary power.

Distribution of Ownership Authority

But that is not to say that Heller entirely lacks a normative basis for distinguishing between good and bad distributions of authority. In the ownership context, his work on the anticommons suggests that we evaluate a given distribution of rights through the lens of the highest-value use of a resource.[94] Thus, a distribution of patent rights among many separate owners is a poor one if the highest-value use of several technologies is in combination, for example to produce a miracle drug. There is

---

91 *See* Ellickson, *supra* note 33, at 1330–1331 (reducing the number of people).

92 *See Tragedy of the Anticommons*, *supra* note 4, at 644–647 (citing OTHER PATH, *supra* note 2, at 158 (good law is "efficient law")).

93 In fact, Heller simply cites de Soto on this. *Tragedy of the Anticommons*, *supra* note 4, at 644–647.

94 This brings Heller quite close to libertarians like Richard Epstein, who suggest that the object of the law is to develop a set of rules that promotes the closest possible approximation to the world of zero transaction costs. *See* Epstein, *supra* note 90, at 566. Heller's point, that once fragmented, property rights are difficult to reassemble, is similar to Richard Epstein's caveat about correction costs: "The rules of individual ownership therefore should be, and largely are, organized in a fashion that minimizes these correction costs. The usual articulation of the common-law rules—that ownership entails with it possession, use, and disposition—is an effort to overcome the problem of subsequent transactions costs by giving a single person the control over all relevant aspects of a single thing." *Tragedy of the Anticommons*, *supra* note 4, at 644–647, 562.

a striking resemblance between what appears to be Heller's view of ownership and a bundle of rights approach to the idea of ownership.[95] Largely in response to Coase's lessons about the importance of transaction costs, a whole generation of law and economics scholars saw property as a flexible institution that is entirely ends-driven.[96] On this approach, the social value of conflicting uses determines the content of the bundle of rights that an owner has in a particular case.[97] Fragments of the bundle are parceled out to the highest-value user case by case. Heller has been critical of the bundle of rights view on the grounds that it has led courts to treat fragments of property rights as discrete, constitutionally protected property rights.[98] What he rejects about the bundle of rights approach is its willingness to carve up ownership of what he considers to be indivisible rights. But in my view, Heller's view of ownership looks quite a lot like a bundle of rights approach constrained by the *numerus clausus* principle. The reason is that, on Heller's approach, just as on a bundle of rights approach, a notion of ideal (or highest-value) use guides law-makers to a coherent bundle of rights. Indeed, Heller's anticommons analysis relies even more heavily on a notion of ideal use in making the case for consolidating authority.[99] I say it relies more heavily on some prior notion of ideal use because Heller does not appear to want to say that the distribution of property rights should be *directly* responsive to efficiency concerns in particular cases, as it is on a bundle of rights approach. Unlike a bundle of rights approach, where courts engage in *ex post* balancing of interests and values case by case, Heller's approach implies that courts or legislators ought to anticipate an ideal use for resources and then *ex ante*

95 There is some irony in this because Heller has been very critical of a bundle of rights approach on the grounds that it propertizes fragments. *See Boundaries*, *supra* note 4, at 1165–1166. *See also* Michael A. Heller, *Property Rights: A View from the Trenches*, 19 Yale J. Int'l. L. 203 (1994); *Three Faces*, *supra* note 33, at 431.

96 Merrill & Smith, *supra* note 13, at 380–381 (describing a commitment to a bundle of rights approach in law and economics and arguing that efficiency is better served by a boundary approach, given information costs). *See* Fitzpatrick, *supra* note 2, at 1006 (Coase's treatment of a transaction-cost free world reminds us of how important transaction costs are in our world); Armen A. Alchian & Harold Demsetz, *Production, Information Costs, and Economic Organization*, 62 Am. Econ. Rev. 777, 783 (1972) ("Coase's penetrating insight is to make more of the fact that markets do not operate costlessly" in explaining institutions). *See also* Oliver E. Williamson, *The New Institutional Economics: Taking Stock, Looking Ahead*, 38 J. of Econ. Lit. 595, 598 (2000) (first-order choices [e.g., system of property rights] are "unarguably important to the economic productivity of an economy").

97 *Exclusion and Exclusivity*, *supra* note 12, at 275–276.

98 *Boundaries*, *supra* note 4, at 1205–1206 (arguing against constitutionally protecting these fragments as "private property" because of potential anticommons problems).

99 The term "gridlock" is much more prominent in Heller's newest work, *The Gridlock Economy*. This is not surprising and is quite appropriate. Furthermore, projects, not rights, are gridlocked.

distribute property rights so as to facilitate this use.[100] It is only once we know what the project is that we can facilitate market activity by ensuring that there are fewer people at the bargaining table with the ability to block that project. It is not terribly contentious to suggest that the distribution of ownership authority should attend to the potential value of resources—moreover, to today's users, not yesterday's. But there simply is no fixed "ideal" use for a resource that can provide a stable measure of what constitutes a good or bad distribution of authority. Insofar as this approach is not entirely *ex post* facto in operation, it relies too heavily on some notion of ideal use to guide allocation *ex ante*.

Despite these difficulties with evaluating the distribution of property rights from the perspective of a particular project, let us assume that our starting point in identifying gridlock, in other words a poor distribution of property rights, is the suitability of that distribution for the successful achievement of some valuable use of a resource. At the very least, an adequate normative framework for evaluating and resolving gridlock requires more than a simple economic analysis. What it requires, and what Heller's gridlock discussion never makes explicit, is a fuller discussion of the plurality of values that support a conclusion that property rights are too broadly distributed among separate owners.[101]

The Distribution of Regulatory Authority

The bundling of entitlements might be said to follow bargaining costs in the ownership context, but there is no analogous market in the regulatory context that a good bundling of regulatory power facilitates. Absent corruption, administrators do not trade authority the way that owners trade rights, continually moving authority to the public sphere's equivalent of the highest-value user.[102] An account of the optimal distribution or bundling of authority relies directly on some foundational

100 *See* Michelman, *supra* note 4 (distinguishing between *ad hoc* efficiency and market facilitation).

101 *See* Hanoch Dagan, *The Craft of Property*, 91 CAL. L. REV. 1517, 1519 (2003). Dagan imports a fuller pluralistic notion of value right into the analysis of how best to "bundle" use rights. *See also* Gregory S. Alexander, *The Social-Obligation Norm in American Property Law*, 94 CORNELL L. REV. 745 (2009); Eduardo M. Peñalver, *Land Virtues*, 94 CORNELL L. REV. 821 (2009).

102 Of course in practice, it might be that there *is* a highest value user of regulatory authority. Lee Fennell points out (in correspondence with the author) that regulatory decisions may well be the product of negotiations among regulators, who seek to capture the surplus of political capital created by a regulatory decision. To draw out the analogy, the highest-value user, in this context, would be the regulatory body that stands to gain the most political capital from a particular regulatory move. Whether or not this is a realistic description of the incentives that regulators have, such an understanding of "highest-value use" does not carry the same normative punch that the concept has when we are referring to the highest-value uses of owners. This is because no one, to my knowledge, suggests that political capital is itself valuable (whereas wealth-generating transactions arguably are).

notion of good or bad regulation. On Heller's account, the measure of a good distribution of regulatory authority is taken from the perspective of the socially valuable uses or projects that are affected.[103] And there are few projects that will be helped along by more rather than fewer regulatory hurdles.[104] For example, in his discussion of BANANA republics, Heller describes the plight of the developer who is stymied in his attempt to build anything by the regulatory hurdles placed in his way. Looked at through the lens of a presumably valuable development, the elimination of regulatory steps appears always to be better. This approach, with its one-way ratchet in the direction of consolidating authority, delivers an anti-regulatory message without making explicit any substantive political theory to explain and justify it. More specifically, there are two problems from a liberal perspective with evaluating the distribution of regulatory authority through the lens of a particular project. First, regulation in a liberal society does not depend for its legitimacy on maximizing productive uses of land.[105] The kinds of costs that gum up otherwise valuable projects may advance legitimate political aims or community values.[106] Any evaluation of regulation must attend directly to the plurality of interests and values it serves. Second, Heller's approach pushes us into a kind of *ad hoc* analysis of regulatory authorities that converge on a single project but are only very contingently related to one another. For example, the historical preservation board and property standards committees might both have "veto-power" over a proposed development of a Victorian house into an apartment building. But the relationship between regulatory bodies is mediated by the particular project that happens to draw the two together. Without a more robust framework for understanding what makes good or bad regulation, we would have to be prepared to redistribute authority in response to the costs that a given distribution of authority presents for particular projects that are affected.

In some contexts, where informality is a real option, this simple, project-driven normative framework may make sense. If a regulatory scheme imposes sufficiently

---

103 Heller seems to recognize that he needs a notion of good or bad law but then circles back and cites de Soto: good law is cost-effective. *See Tragedy of the Anticommons*, *supra* note 4, at 644–645.

104 The existence of an anticommons, on this approach, is assessed from the perspective of the highest valued use, whether we are talking about the conservationist's project to get a historic designation for a building or a developer's building project. The more regulatory hurdles in the way of that project, the more likely that regulatory thicket is to be classed as an anticommons. This gives Heller's work on the anticommons an anti-regulatory slant, although not necessarily a pro-development slant (however in most of his examples he does indeed take the perspective of the active or intensive user of land).

105 *See* Richard B. Stewart, *Regulation in a Liberal State: The Role of Non-Commodity Values*, 92 Yale L.J. 1537, 1566 (1983).

106 For example, giving residents a say in the kinds of projects that can go ahead might prevent backlash against otherwise efficient uses. *See* Mark J. Roe, *Backlash*, 98 Colum. L. Rev. 217, 220–221 (1998). Of course, a more broadly democratic process may also have intrinsic value.

high personal costs so that people and assets exit to the informal sphere, the aims that might have justified a more complex regulatory scheme are subverted in any case. Perhaps it is defensible to say that, when flight to the informal sector is a real risk, a good regulatory scheme is just one that manages to keep people and assets in the formal sphere. This limited rationale for de Soto's pared-down approach to distinguishing good from bad regulation may also make sense of why de Soto (unlike Heller) does *not* apply the same project-driven framework for evaluating the distribution of property rights. Indeed, while de Soto calls for streamlining the regulatory process to reduce the personal costs to owners of operating formally (thereby calling for solutions to what Heller would see as a regulatory anticommons), he at the same time makes the case for formalizing property rights in ways that Heller would identify as legal or spatial anticommons. By listening to the "barking dogs"[107] in formalizing property rights (by which de Soto means the facts on the ground), we would produce a pattern of diffuse, small-scale ownership[108] and would also in many cases propertize fragmentary use rights.[109] Although de Soto does not offer an explicit account of the measure of distributive justice in advocating for a broad initial distribution of property rights, he implicitly acknowledges the limited reach of a simple projects-driven framework for determining a "good distribution" of property rights.

Even assuming that de Soto's limited normative framework has some value where the survival of the formal sector is at stake, such a project-driven economic analysis is of limited value in the context of the developed world, where exit to the informal sector is not generally practicable. Where exit to the informal sector is contained, a determination that there are "too many owners" or that there is

---

107 Mystery of Capital, *supra* note 2, at 179 (recommending listening to the "barking dogs" to discern who owns what as a guide to formalizing property).

108 *Id.* at 33 (individual holdings are low-value: "Many of these dwellings are not worth much by Western standards"). On the small scale of informal holdings, *see, e.g.*, Winnie V. Mitullah & Kivutha Kibwana, *The Tale of Two Cities: Policy, Law and Illegal Settlements in Kenya*, *in* Illegal Cities: Law and Urban Change in Developing Countries 191, 202 (Edesio Fernandes & Ann Varley, eds, 1998) (reporting that over 1,000 hectares of Nairobi's land is held informally. In informal settlements there are an average of 250 dwellings and 750 persons per hectare. In contrast, in middle and upper income neighborhoods the population density is between 10–30 units and 50–180 persons per hectare. Assuming all land in the hectare was used for housing, the average informal dwelling unit size would be just 40m^2. In contrast, the average size of a formal unit would be at least 120m^2 three times the size). Similarly, a study of rural property rights in Ecuador indicates that the lot size in invaded communities was "considerably" smaller than in formal settlements. *See* Jean O. Lanjouw & Philip I. Levy, *Untitled: A Study of Formal and Informal Property Rights in Urban Ecuador*, 112 Econ. J. 986, 993 (2002) (formal purchasers had an average lot size of 255.7m^2 while untitled squatters' average lot size was 137.1m^2).

109 *See* Mystery of Capital, *supra* note 2, at 178–187 (advocating respect for existing extralegal norms that govern resources).

"too much regulation" is squarely a question of policy and government's role in striking a balance between productivity and other substantive social and political values.[110]

Conclusion

Heller may well be right that streamlining regulatory processes is often desirable. But in casting red tape as gridlock, we do not acquire a new conceptual tool for analyzing the problem of regulatory hurdles. Most of the gridlock problems that Heller identifies as factors triggering informality in the developing world and under-use of resources in the developed world are problems with the distribution of public or private authority. In most cases of gridlock, there is no deficiency in the form of authority that regulators and owners have. In short, most cases of gridlock proceed not from an anticommons but rather the straightforward transaction costs and hold-out problems that de Soto identifies as costs of formality or red tape.

110 *See* Stewart, *supra* note 105.

Chapter 9
Mercantilism, American Style

Nicole Stelle Garnett[1]

The enormity of Hernando de Soto's influence on international economic development policies can hardly be overstated. Importantly, de Soto's conviction about the critical importance of clear titles and stable property rights has led to the proliferation of "titling" programs, which transfer marketable property rights to squatters in informal settlements in developing nations.[2] And, while titling efforts are not without critics, even de Soto's detractors admit that they are the idea *du jour* in economic-development circles.[3] The dominance of the property-law aspects of de Soto's work, however, poses a significant difficulty for those interested in thinking about how his ideas apply on the American scene. After all, in the United States, titles are so clear and recording systems so accurate that the ancient common-law doctrines designed to clear titles—prescription and adverse possession—strike

---

1 I received valuable feedback on the ideas in this chapter at the 2009 American Association of Law Schools Annual Conference, Property Law Section, and especially from Richard Briffault, Eduardo Peñalver, and Carol Rose. Jaclyn Sexton provided excellent research assistance.

2 *See* Hernando de Soto, The Mystery of Capital: Why Capitalism Triumphs in the West and Fails Everywhere Else, 49–62 (2000) [hereinafter Mystery of Capital]; Mystery of Capital, at 182–188; Hernando de Soto, The Other Path: The Economic Answer to Terrorism, 17–59 (1989) [hereinafter The Other Path]; Eduardo Moisés Peñalver and Sonia K. Katyal, *Property Outlaws*, 155 U. Penn. L. Rev. 1095, 1151–1152 (2007) (describing de Soto's argument); Matthew Miller, *The Poor Man's Capitalist*, N.Y. Times, July 1, 2001. *See also*, Jonathan Conning and Partha Deb, *Impact Evaluation for Land Property Rights Reforms* at 1 (draft manuscript, on file with author) (noting that the World Bank alone as committed $1 billion to land administration, land-titling, and other land reform projects in past decade); Sebastian Galiani and Ernesto Schargodsky, *Property Rights for the Poor: The Effect of Land Titling*, at 1 (discussing land titling efforts in Vietnam, Cambodia, Colombia, Mexico, Honduras, Paraguay, Ghana, Egypt, South Africa, Turkey, Brazil, and the Phillipines) (draft manuscript on file with author); Jean O. Lanjouw and Philip I. Levy, *Untitled: A Study of Formal and Informal Property Rights in Urban Ecuador*, 112 The Econ. J. 986 (October 2002) (suggesting that titling programs should be targeted at young disorganized communities).

3 *See* John Gravois, *The De Soto Delusion*, Slate, Jan. 25, 2005, available at http://www.slate.com/id/2112792 (arguing that titling programs do not benefit poor squatters, but rather saddle them with assets that are either worthless or snatched up quickly by developers intent on large-scale property assemblages).

many first-year law students as unnecessary and anachronistic.[4] True, de Soto himself argues that the United States underwent a transition similar in many ways to those convulsing the developing world—and, moreover, that our transition was assisted by our own grand version of "titling," namely, homesteading.[5] But he uses this (contested) historical account to bolster his argument that developing nations can successfully emerge from their transitions, not to assert that we are still in the midst of ours. Modern-day "titling" efforts in the United States, such as "urban homesteading" programs, have been both rare and relatively unsuccessful.[6]

But de Soto's central insight—that third-world poverty results not from a lack of wealth, ingenuity and entrepreneurial spirit, but rather from the inability of the hard-working entrepreneurs in developing nations to harness the wealth generated in the informal economy by transforming it into mainstream capital—is not simply a *property law* insight. De Soto also argues, especially in *The Other Path*, that many millions of hard-working entrepreneurs are forced to operate in the informal economy because of regulatory rules that resemble, and are the remnants of, "mercantilism."[7] On its face, de Soto's concern with mercantilism seems as inapplicable in the United States as his focus on the need for clear titles. After all,

4 In *J.A. Pye (Oxford) v. United Kingdom* (ECHR 2005), the European Court of Human Rights ruled that application of British adverse possession law to deprive record-holders of interest in property violated the property rights guaranteed by the European Convention on Human Rights; the court reasoned that the land records system eliminated the need for prescriptive transfers of property rights. Pye, Application N. 44302/02 (2005) available at http://www.echr.coe.int/Eng/Press/2005/Nov/ChamberjudgmentJAPye(Oxford)LtdvtheUnitedKingdom151105.htm. The decision was reversed by the Grand Chamber of the ECHR two years later. *See J.A. Pye (Oxford) v. United Kingdom*, Application N. 44302/02 (2007) available at http://www.asil.org/pdfs/echr070907.pdf.

5 Mystery of Capital, *supra* note 2, at 105–151. It is worth noting that the extent of the stabilization occasioned by homesteading in the United States may have been overstated. As Michael Heller has noted, many nineteenth-century homesteaders' plots were too small to be economically viable as farms and, because the law required them to occupy the property for a period of years to perfect title, "people either stayed and starved or abandoned their land." Michael A. Heller, *The Boundaries of Private Property*, 108 Yale L. J. 1163, 1172 (1999).

6 On urban homesteading, *see* Eduardo M. Peñalver and Sonia Katyal, *Property Outlaws*, 155 U. Pa. L. Rev. 1095, 1122–1128 (2007); Nicole Stelle Garnett, *Property Inlaws*, 156 U. Pa. L. Rev. Pennumbra 279 (2007), available at http://www.pennumbra.com/responses/12–2007/Garnett.pdf. More recently, Steven Clowney has suggested, intriguingly, that city governments should deregulate and transfer title to properties in their *in rem* portfolios (primarily acquired through tax delinquencies) to inner-city entrepreneurs. *See* Stephen Clowney, *Invisible Businessmen: Undermining Black Enterprise with Land Use Rules*, 2009 Ill. L. Rev. 1061.

7 Mercantilism is that term used to describe highly interventionist, centralized state efforts to control economic activity during the transition from agrarian to industrial societies. *See* Charles Wilson, Mercantilism, 26 (1963); Henry William Spiegel, The Growth of Economic Thought, 98 (1983).

the U.S. economic system is generally considered the mirror image of mercantilism, that is, a system epitomized by free enterprise, not centralized state control. In many American cities, however, the regulations governing the two areas of economic activity most closely described in *The Other Path*—urban transportation and street vending—are characterized by mercantilist qualities akin to those that concern de Soto: "Popular access to private enterprise is difficult or impossible for the popular classes, the legal system is excessive and obstructive, there are massive public and private bureaucracies … and the state intervenes in all areas of activity."[8]

These regulatory realities ought to concern those interested in the urban poor for the same reason that they concern de Soto. As Sudhir Venkatesh describes in his ethnographic account of one Chicago neighborhood, American inner-city communities, like poor urban communities in developing nations, are characterized not by capitalism's absence, but rather by its abundance, most of which is carried out in a vibrant informal economy.[9] Still, Michael Heller reminds us, "[W]e should not mistake a vibrant scene for an optimal one. People create an underground economy because the law drives them to it … [T]he underground economy represents a 'second best solution.' It is the triumph of poor people's ingenuity in the face of bad law."[10] This is certainly the case in many urban neighborhoods in U.S. cities. Not only do transportation services and street vending require little formal training and minimal capital investment, but, because they are demanded by residents of poor city neighborhoods, many poor people with entrepreneurial spirit choose to provide transportation services and to vend in the informal economy. But laws preventing these entrepreneurs from operating legally foreclose, or dramatically curtail the possibility of, entry into the mainstream economy by those at the bottom rungs of the economic ladder. As a Federal Trade Commission report on local transportation regulations concluded, many of these restrictions lack any economic justification and "impose a disproportionate burden on low income people."[11]

This chapter examines the regulation of street vending and urban transportation services in the United States, focusing in particular on the "mercantilist" details that concern de Soto—namely, centralized bureaucratic control and the protection of favored, privileged economic interests from competition, both through the erection of barriers to entry and by the granting of exclusive monopoly franchises. The chapter draws in particular upon two late twentieth century disputes over vending and "jitney" services in New York City. Many aspects of life in New York, our largest and densest city, are *sui generis*, but the city's street vending and transportation regulations are not. Most cities tightly regulate vending; some go so far as to ban

---

8 The Other Path, *supra* note 2, at 235–236.

9 Sudhir Alladi Venkatesh, Off the Books: The Underground Economy of the Urban Poor (2006).

10 Michael Heller, The Gridlock Economy: How Too Much Ownership Wrecks Markets, Stops Innovation, and Costs Lives, 155 (2008).

11 Mark W. Frankena and Paul A. Paulter, *An Economic Analysis of Taxicab Regulation*, 155 (Fed. Trade Comm'n, 1984).

it outright. The same is true of private shared-ride or "jitney" services that serve as the primary means of transportation for the urban poor in developing nations.[12] These regulations privilege economic insiders and impose high costs both on those entrepreneurs who choose to operate illegally and the individuals whom they serve. In other words, the costs of informality, to borrow from de Soto, are high.[13]

This chapter posits two explanations for why these two aspects of economic life prove amenable to mercantilist-style regulations. First, street vendors and jitneys operate in the public commons. As a result, relatively "simple" one-shot private property solutions, like titling, are all but impossible to employ.[14] The government remains in a constant cycle of resource allocation—forced to make repeated determinations about who is entitled to access public spaces, when, and for what purposes. The situation necessarily favors insiders with reputational and historical ties to the allocator of public space. Second, neither street vendors nor jitneys fit the aesthetic image of the "good city" dominating urban development efforts. As the discussion below illustrates, these disputes about the aesthetics of city life are neither new nor unique to the United States The current urban resurgence, however, has resulted, at least in part, from an increased demand for city life among elites. Contemporary disputes involving street vendors and jitneys bring contested ideas of the city into sharp focus.

This chapter concludes with a reflection on the relationship between the presence, on many U.S. city streets, of illegal vendors and de Soto's important insight about the need to pay attention to the costs of *legality*. This insight is particularly important in the United States, precisely because we enjoy well-functioning property markets. Both street vendors and jitney services operate illegally because they have no choice—in most cases, the law precludes them from operating legally. Unlike jitneys, however, vendors, at least theoretically, have the option of moving their activities to a location where the law sanctions them—namely, inside commercial buildings. In the inner-city communities where most street vendors operate, private property is not a scarce commodity. On the contrary, the urban landscape is dotted—or marred, as the case may be—with thousands of vacant and abandoned buildings that city governments would love to see filled with new entrepreneurial ventures. The fact that vendors are *not* moving inside suggests something about the costs of legality in these markets. As De Soto observes, when the costs of legality exceed the costs of informality, entrepreneurs will choose to operate in the informal economy. In contrast to the situation facing vendors in many developing nations, however, in the United States clear titles are not a barrier to entry. But other factors—especially high property taxes and excessive regulation—may well be.

---

12 *Id.* at 25 (finding that "most [American] jurisdictions prohibit shared ride services, including … jitney service").

13 The Other Path, *supra* note 2, at 158.

14 I place "simple" in quotations to reflect my recognition that titling squatter settlements is, in many cases, anything but simple.

Mercantilism in Action: Two Case Studies

New York's Street Vending Wars

New York City, like most local governments, tightly regulates street vending. The city licenses 3,000 food vendors, but prohibits them from operating on many of the city's busiest streets, especially in midtown and downtown Manhattan. Only 850 licenses are available for "peddlers" selling merchandise other than food. As a result of these restrictions, many thousands of street vendors in New York City operate illegally. Most merchandise vendors operate without a license. According to the Urban Justice Center's Street Vendor Project, the waiting list for merchandise licenses is now longer than 25 years, and no new licensees have been added since 1993. As a result, city officials estimate as many as 10,000 unlicensed merchandise vendors operate on any given day. Food vendors are more likely to be licensed, but many operate illegally on streets that are off-limits to them.

These regulations are nothing new. Throughout history, many individuals operating at the economic margins have sold wares on busy streets and sidewalks. (As an observer of the New York scene noted in 1899, "For those who had no handicraft, there was but one resource—peddling.")[15] And urban governments have attempted (often unsuccessfully) to curtail their activities. New York's effort to control street vending is a case in point. Regulatory efforts in the 1990s followed a pattern reflected throughout the city's history: frustration over the proliferation of illegal vendors, formal efforts to control and contain them, and the eventual abandonment of enforcement efforts when the containment efforts failed and vendors returned to the streets. The motivations for the enforcement efforts also sound a familiar theme. In the 1990s, as in the 1890s and before, city officials cracked down on vending under pressure from established merchants, who expressed concerns about "unfair competition" from vendors; and from development interests, who object to vendors on essentially aesthetic grounds.

Regulation of street vending in New York City dates to a 1691 ordinance prohibiting street selling by "hucksters" until two hours after the public markets opened. In 1707, the city prohibited all street hawking. These rules were unquestionably mercantilist ones designed to protect the government-sponsored public market system. As commercial activity increasingly moved inside fixed shops in the nineteenth century, the old regulated public market system disappeared, but the city's interest in protecting preferred commercial outlets from competition did not. During the late nineteenth and early twentieth centuries, thanks in large part to immigration, the number of itinerant peddlers in the city exploded, and informal, semi-permanent street markets began to emerge. Newcomers were poor, familiar with street markets in Europe, and eager to buy cheap goods; the markets provided safe cultural space and, importantly, economic opportunity.

---

15 Daniel M. Bluestone, *"The Pushcart Evil": Peddlers, Merchants, and New York City's Streets, 1890–1940*, 18 J. Urb. Hist. 68, 72 (1991).

To some, pushcart markets were an integral and picturesque part of urban life. Elite opinion, however, strongly disfavored them. As middle- and upper-class residents ceased their patronage of street markets, vending increasingly became viewed as a lesser form of commerce contrasting sharply with the "modern" urbanism exemplified by enclosed shops and skyscrapers. By the turn of the twentieth century, pressure to ban vending intensified. The strongest pressure came from established merchants seeking to limit (or eliminate) competition. Moreover, as immigrants began to move out of the ghettos, the vendors moved with them into wealthier neighborhoods. This phenomenon troubled development interests and property owners, who worried that the pushcart markets drove down property values: Not only were pushcarts associated in the popular imagination with poverty and urban decline, but crowded streets curtailed development opportunities by limiting the space available for intensified land uses. In 1906, a municipal "Pushcart Commission" recommended limiting the number of carts on a block to four. After massive protest by pushcart operators derailed the proposal, the City opted instead to establish official pushcart "markets." But these containment efforts failed, and by the 1930s, the pressure to ban pushcarts outright gained steam. Mayor Fiorello LaGuardia, who viewed vending as "unworthy of the reputation of this great City," closed many pushcart markets, drastically limited the number of peddling licenses, and increased enforcement against vendors operating illegally.[16] By the 1940s, only a vestige of the old pushcart system remained. Mayor Rudy Giuliani inherited it.[17]

For reasons that are not entirely clear—although immigration clearly was a major factor—the number of street vendors in New York City increased dramatically during the early 1990s. Although the trend was city-wide, it was felt acutely along 125th Street, Harlem's main thoroughfare, where as many as 1,000 unlicensed peddlers crowded the sidewalks each day in competition with shop owners. The Harlem experience is hardly unique. Immigrant vendors appeared in large numbers in many American cities during the same time period. And, as Gregg Kettles has observed, most came "from a culture where sidewalk vending is widely accepted … and expressed bewilderment as to why sidewalk vending is illegal."[18] In Harlem, the rise of the busy street marketplace may have helped to kick-start the previously moribund Harlem economy. The vendors attracted thousands of tourists, who arrived daily in tour buses and generated substantial foot traffic along the commercial corridor. Some merchants therefore sided with the vendors, citing the tourism boom. Many merchants and vendors co-existed peacefully, with vendors paying shop owners to store their goods overnight—and, in some cases, even agreeing not to sell the same merchandise as an adjacent store. When the vendors were driven from the street in late 1994, some merchants

16 Bluestone, *supra* note 15, at 88.

17 Bluestone, *supra* note 15, provides an excellent history of New York City's effort to regulate street vendors prior to the 1940s.

18 Gregg W. Kettles, *Regulating Vending in the Sidewalk Commons*, 77 Temple L. Rev. 1, 25 (2004).

worried their businesses would suffer as the tour buses stopped coming. The fact that many at the economic margins—especially poor African immigrants—depend upon street vending for their livelihood also led some observers to worry about the social and economic consequences of displacing them.

Most Harlem merchants, however, demanded that the City crack down on the vendors, making arguments that echoed those made in opposition to early twentieth century pushcart commerce. A 1911 petition submitted by Greenwich Village shopkeepers voiced two complaints: The pushcarts were disorderly ("It is impossible for the ordinary customer to pass by our stores without being molested by the push-cart peddlers as well as hundreds of hawkers")[19] and the pushcarts engaged in unfair competition, "selling practically the same kind of merchandise that we have in our stores thus working great hardship upon us."[20] As with the debate over pushcart commerce a century before, it is difficult to sort through the competing motives for the enforcement efforts. Some of the complaints about the vending-related disorder, especially along 125th Street, undoubtedly were true. As one editorialist observed during the controversy, "Even the vendors concede that 125th Street is out of control."[21] Mitchell Dunier's ethnographic account of street vendors on New York's Lower East Side describes mentally ill individuals who "lay shit out," placing miscellaneous items on pieces of corrugated cardboard or directly on the sidewalk, thus making the "streets feel *less safe* and *less vital.*"[22] Giuliani also cracked down on the practice described in Dunier's work—called by one commentator "Alphabet City's version of a garage sale"—at least in part because some of the peddlers were trafficking in stolen goods.[23] It is difficult, however, to avoid drawing conclusions that many vending opponents had motives other than orderly sidewalks. Clearly, the bulk of opposition came from established businesses upset about competition and developmers who objected to the image conveyed by the vending bazaar.

These latter arguments resonated with Giuliani, who resolved to eliminate the vendors altogether. As had his early twentieth century predecessors', Giuliani's policy incorporated tough law enforcement and official containment efforts: He used the police to clear the vendors from 125th Street and established an official marketplace, several blocks away, as a vending safe haven. Yet vendors viewed the market as a poor substitute for their lucrative 125th Street location; it was set apart from foot traffic and, the vendors argued, poorly lit and dangerous. A new market, operated by a local mosque, achieved modest success, but many vendors found themselves in the red after paying the modest fee to operate there. Similar efforts to relocate vendors to official "marketplaces" in other parts of the city

---

19 Bluestone, *supra* note 15, at 78.

20 *Id.*

21 Editorial, *Street Peddlers in New York*, N.Y. Times, May 28, 1994, §1, at 18.

22 Mitchell Duneier, Sidewalk (2001), 43.

23 Monte Williams, *Neighborhood Report: Lower Manhattan; Crackdown on Ave. C Peddlers*, N.Y. Times, Mar. 12, 1995, §16, at 6.

also floundered. Ultimately, the City's effort to impose order on New York City's sidewalks—or at least to contain vendors in an out-of-the-way location—failed. A 2004 Business Week profile described 125th Street as "street vendor territory with table after table of books, posters, incense, and CDs."[24]

Giuliani also sought to rid most midtown and downtown streets of food vendors. Many of these streets were already officially off-limits, largely as a result of restrictions imposed by former Mayor Ed Koch, who abandoned his enforcement effort in the face of massive protest by vendors and their patrons. (Koch referred to the vendors as "a hydra-headed monster.")[25] In 1994—the same year that he swept vendors from 125th Street—Giuliani established a Sidewalk Vendor Review Panel to consider requests for additional street closures. Over the next several years, city officials—backed by restaurant owners and, as in Harlem, the pro-development Business Improvement Districts—engaged in a tug of war with vendors and their supporters. A New York Times editorialist worried, for example, whether Giuliani had "lost a sense of proportion about his civility campaign," observing:

> There is a difference between making the streets safer and making war on the New Yorkness of New York City. In his zeal for order and obedience, he must not destroy the lively street scene that is part of the city's historic flavor. No one misses the squeegee men, but do we really want to outlaw the corner hot-dog stand? … Any new system will never—and should never—totally eradicate the hurly-burly nature of the city's pushcart trade. There must be a better way for the city to hear the voices of hot-dog vendors and their customers, not just those who sell sandwiches and real estate nearby.[26]

Other New Yorkers expressed alarm that Giuliani had gone too far in his effort to sanitize the city, with some characterizing Giuliani's vending plan as "ridiculous."[27] Giuliani relented, and, in a rare admission of misjudgment, acknowledged that his plan "may have been broader than necessary."[28] Ultimately, the Review Panel passed a compromise plan, restricting vending on 130 blocks and rejecting the requests for 300 additional block closures.[29]

---

24 Robert McNatt, *Harlem On My Mind: Black America's Cultural Capital Is Thriving Again*, Business Week, Sept. 20, 2004, at 109.

25 Mike Allen, *Giuliani to Bar Food Vendors on 144 Blocks*, N.Y. Times, May 24, 1998, §1, at 27.

26 *And Now, the Hot-Dog War*, Editorial, N.Y. Times, Jun. 4, 1998, at A26.

27 *See* Allen, *supra* note 25. *Giuliani to Bar Food Vendors on 144 Blocks*, N.Y. Times, May 24, 1998, §1, at 27.

28 *Giuliani Says a New Plan Will Not Please Vendors*, N.Y. Times, Jun. 19, 1998, at B8.

29 On Street Vending in New York City, see Duneier, *supra* note 22; McNatt, *supra* note 24, at 109; Williams, *supra* note 23, §13, at 6; Robert McNatt, *Council Peddles Plans to Limit Vendors*, Crain's New York Business, Feb. 1, 1993, at 12; Editorial, *supra* note 21, at A18; Jonathan P. Hicks, *Many 125th Street Vendors Say They Will Resist Move*, N.Y. Times, Oct. 17, 1994, at B3; Jonathan P. Hicks, *Vendors Ouster and Boycott Divide Harlem*,

New York's Jitney Wars

Elsewhere in the city, Giuliani was siding with illegal "jitney" services in their ongoing battle with the Metropolitan Transportation Authority, which provides public bus and subway service. In much of the world, especially in developing nations, such low-cost jitneys operated by private entrepreneurs are the preferred method of transportation for the urban poor. Jitney service combines characteristics of bus and taxi service: Like buses, jitneys provide shared-ride transportation service for unrelated passengers; like taxis, they accept street hails and frequently deviate from their usual routes. In general, jitney service is provided in vans or minibuses operated by private entrepreneurs. After studying the operation of jitneys in six cities abroad, one scholar summarized their appeal as follows:

> They charge relatively low fares and provide wide coverage across a city, often serving poor areas that get no other service. Their operations are flexible so they can add service at peak times and quickly cover new neighborhoods. Their small size and cheap labor enables them to profitably provide frequent service in smaller neighborhoods and along narrow streets, as well as work the main thoroughfares. With fewer passengers, they often make fewer stops and faster times.[30]

Although they operate informally in many U.S. cities, especially in neighborhoods with large immigrant populations, jitneys are prohibited in almost every American jurisdiction.[31]

To understand why, a word about the politics and history of U.S. transportation policy is in order. Jitneys briefly flourished in nearly every major American city for a short time a century ago, but they disappeared from urban streets as quickly as they appeared, thanks to a remarkably successful campaign by streetcar providers anxious to regulate their competition out of business. Legend has it that the American jitney phenomenon began in Los Angeles on July 1, 1914, when a man named L.P. Draper picked up a passenger and transported him a short distance for

N.Y. Times, Oct. 23, 1994, at A1; Douglas Martin, *City Begins Enforcement of Food Cart Restrictions*, N.Y. Times, Apr. 21, 1994, at B3; Raymond Hernandez, *City's Right to Bar Vendors from Streets is Upheld*, N.Y. Times, Jun. 18, 1997, at B1; *Giuliani to Bar Food Vendors*, *supra* note 26, at A27; Mike Allen, *Sidewalk Vendors Face a New Set of Critics*, N.Y. Times, May 31, 1998, at A27; Editorial, *supra* note 25, at A26; Mike Allen, *Sidewalk Vendors Rally to Protest Street Restrictions*, N.Y. Times, June 4, 1998 at B3; Mike Allen, *City Pursuing Negotiations with Street Food Vendors*, N.Y. Times, Jun. 15, 1998, at B3; *Giuliani Says a New Plan Will Not Please Vendors*, *supra* note 27, at B8.

30 *See* Isaac K. Takyi, *An Evaluation of Jitney Systems in Developing Countries*, 44 Transp. Q. 163, 170–171(1990) ("The archetypical urban jitney system consists of a constellation of loosely regulated owner-operated collective vehicles following more or less fixed routes with some deviations as custom, traffic, and hours permit").

31 *See* Claire E. McKnight, *Transportation with Women in Mind*, J. Urb. Tech. 1, 12 (Fall 1994).

a nickel (the coin known in contemporary slang as a "jitney"). The practice rapidly gained momentum, and, by early 1915, jitneys began to appear in most American cities. During a two-week period in Kansas City, the number of jitneys jumped from zero to 200 cars carrying nearly 25,000 passengers a day; two weeks later, the number of jitney patrons reached 50,000 per day. At the peak of the phenomenon, in 1915, more than 60,000 jitneys were operating in the United States.

The jitneys' instant popularity reflected public dissatisfaction with the quality of service provided by urban streetcar companies. Jitneys had significant advantages over streetcars. Not only were they 150 to 200 percent faster than streetcars, they ran more frequently and they were much more flexible. Typically, the jitneys picked up passengers every two to six minutes, and many drivers did not choose a destination before picking up their first passenger; they would then post that passenger's destination on the windshield and pick up additional passengers en route. Many drivers also would drop passengers off at their doors for a nominal fee. While reliable figures for jitney-related streetcar losses do not exist, the industry was undoubtedly dealt a severe blow. The Electric Railway Journal referred to the jitneys as "a menace," "a malignant growth," and "this Frankenstein of transportation."[32] The streetcar industry quickly mobilized to launch a nationwide anti-jitney campaign. Municipal governments readily endorsed the industry's (irreconcilable) arguments that jitneys were inefficient and uneconomical and that they could be put down only by regulation. The disorganized jitney operators' efforts to respond came too late. By the end of 1915, less than 18 months after jitneys had first appeared in Los Angeles, anti-jitney ordinances were enacted in 125 of the 175 cities that experienced jitney competition. By the early 1920s, the streetcar industry's victory was complete. The jitneys were regulated out of existence.[33]

Unfortunately, the resulting legal impediments to operating jitney services in the United States make it difficult to learn much systematically about them, beyond the fact that they exist. Indeed, one of the great scholarly feats of de Soto's *The Other Path* was his effort to actually measure the extent of various sectors of the informal economy in Peru, including transportation services. Such a comprehensive study is certainly beyond my capacity, and so I draw instead on one version of jitney service that I became familiar with as a young attorney. For two years after law school, I worked for the Institute for Justice, a small public interest law firm in Washington D.C. that seeks to help low-income entrepreneurs overcome regulatory impediments. In this capacity, I represented four individuals who operated the jitney services in Brooklyn and Queens, New York championed by Giuliani. Thanks to Hector Rickets, Pat Harvey, Vincent Cummins, and Dennis Harry, I was able to spend hours riding in the vans and learning first hand about their services.

---

32 Ross D. Eckert and George W. Hilton, *The Jitneys*, 15 J.L. & Econ. 293, 299–300 (1972).

33 On the U.S. jitney experience, see Eckert and Hilton, *supra* note 32; Carlos A. Schwantes, *The West Adapts to the Automobile: Technology, Unemployment, and the Jitney Phenomenon of 1914–1971*, 16 W. Hist. Q. 307 (1985).

New York City has long had a large and vibrant informal market for transportation services. Millions of New Yorkers, especially those who do not live in lower Manhattan, depend upon illegal transportation services, or legal services that operate in extra-legal ways. These services are vitally important, particularly in peripheral neighborhoods that are underserved by public transportation and ignored by medallion-carrying "yellow cabs." Residents of the neighborhoods served by these services, the majority of whom are low-income minorities, would find it difficult to function without them.[34] Although jitneys have always played a role in this informal transportation market, they gained prominence in the early 1980s during a series of public transportation strikes. Seemingly overnight, hundreds of industrious New Yorkers, primarily Caribbean immigrants who were accustomed to using jitneys in their native countries, stepped forward to fill the void by providing inexpensive van service. Many commuters found that they preferred the jitneys to public bus service, and the vans quickly developed a loyal customer base. Therefore, much to the consternation of transit officials, when the strike ended neither the entrepreneurial van drivers, nor their customers, showed any inclination of returning to the status quo ante. During the 1980s and 1990s, the van industry continued to grow, despite persistent efforts by the authorities to suppress its operations. Estimates of the extent of the industry vary widely, but none of them are insubstantial. A decade ago, the Interborough Alliance of Community Transportation, an informal van industry association, estimated that the vans carry as many as 60,000 people each day. More modest estimates range from 20,000 to 40,000 people per day. In 1992, the New York's Metropolitan Transportation Authority, which operates public transportation in the city, estimated that competition from van services cost it $30 million each year.

Van services serve two niche markets in New York City. First, one popular form of van service essentially replicates the express public bus service that links New York's outer boroughs and downtown Manhattan. A second type of service, known popularly as "dollar van" service, operates exclusively in the outer boroughs. (Like the term "jitney" itself, the popular name for the "dollar vans" reflects their usual fare—$1 per ride.) Most of the dollar vans' customers rely on them as a substitute for public "feeder" bus services that link more remote residential neighborhoods and subway stations. While the vast majority of van services operate without any official authorization whatsoever, a few services have limited operating authority to operate a "commuter van service." Even authorized van services, however, operate in clear derogation of the law. Commuter vans may neither accept street hails nor operate on bus routes. Even a casual observer of the vans in action quickly will realize that authorized "commuter van services" routinely defy both prohibitions.

Like the jitneys of the early twentieth century, the dollar vans normally operate along informal, semi-fixed routes. Drivers accept street hails and are generally

34 *See*, *e.g.*, Sigurd Grava, *We're Not Yellow, We Go Anywhere*, 42 Transp. Q. 349 (1988).

willing, for a nominal fee, to provide door-to-door service upon a customer's request. It also is not unusual for drivers to make specialized arrangements to serve particular passengers' needs. Riders also told me that they prefer the vans because they are faster, more reliable, and more comfortable (every passenger is guaranteed a seat) than public buses. Because the vans are considerably smaller than buses, and do not pick up passengers after all of their seats have been filled, they make far fewer stops than public buses. Many operate late into the night, ensuring that vans arrive at frequent intervals and that customers need not wait long for service, even during off-peak hours. When asked to compare van to bus service, passengers complained that the buses are slow and unreliable and asserted that they can cut their commuting time in half—saving as much as two hours each day—by relying on vans rather than public bus service.

Even the vans' most ardent opponents grudgingly acknowledge their advantages. For example, in 1992, the New York Metropolitan Transportation Authority, which operates public bus service in New York City, commissioned a study that was designed to determine how to respond to the competitive threat posed by illegal car and van services operating in the City. Ultimately, the study recommended increased enforcement efforts against the illegal operations. Before reaching this conclusion, however, the MTA was forced to admit that "[f]eeder vans are strong competitors with the Transit Authority's local bus routes. They appeal to riders because they often offer more frequent service, are faster, charge less, and provide a seated ride, even in rush hour periods."[35] The MTA further acknowledged that "commuter vans have the advantage of being more flexible than buses" and that "many van riders perceive transit as a poor alternative."[36] Not surprisingly, sporadic enforcement sweeps targeting illegal van operations have done little to curb customer loyalty. If anything, enforcement efforts contribute to the sense of solidarity between van drivers and passengers.[37]

Mercantilism in the Modern City

Both the regulations of jitneys and vendors have mercantilist qualities. The mercantilist roots of New York's street-vending regulations are uncontestable: After all, the 1691 anti-"huckster" regulation was straight out of the pre-industrial mercantilist playbook—it protected a state-sponsored marketplace from entrepreneurial competition. The anti-jitney regulations are of more recent vintage

35 N.Y. City Metropolitan Transp. Authority, Van and Car Service Issues Affecting NYCTA Surface Operations (1992) [hereinafter Mta Study], 8.

36 *Id.*

37 Howard Husock, *Enterprising Van Drivers Collide with Regulation*, City J., Winter 1996, at 60; Mta Study, *supra* note 35, at 8; N.Y. City Dep't of City Planning, Commuter Van Service Policy Study, 5–22 (1997) (reviewing literature and summarizing study findings) [hereinafter Van Study].

but similarly aim to protect a state-sponsored service from competition. This section explores two possible explanations for why these mercantilist regulations remain in our modern market economy. The first is the inherent difficulty of allocating rights to a public commons. City government strategies for public-space allocation, including ones billed as "market-based" reforms, almost always privilege economic insiders and tend to push marginal economic actors into the informal economy. The second is the conflict between elite aesthetic preferences and the aesthetics of poverty. Complaints about the inherent "disorder" of street vending and jitney services concern not simply the externalities generated by vendors, but also their appearance. Street vendors and jitneys, especially those operating at the economic margins, are viewed unfavorably by those who pin urban development hopes on catering to elite aesthetic and cultural tastes.

The Problem of the Commons

It is axiomatic that, absent regulation, a commons is likely to become tragic. And, while Carol Rose, in my view, correctly emphasizes that commons properties serve important "comic" functions as well[38] (and perhaps especially in cities, where open space is at a premium) the comedy only exists when public spaces are governed well enough to permit people to enjoy them. The regulations need not be formal legal rules. Most of the time, informal social norms do the work of commons allocation satisfactorily. Indeed, in healthy communities, the norms of public space allocation and the social interactions that they enable likely have important feedback effects upon one another. That is, the norms enable the interactions, and, in turn, the interactions enable the norms. Not all communities, of course, enjoy healthy norms of public space allocation. For example, in some poor urban communities, public spaces are governed by individuals who use intimidation and criminal behaviors to enforce deviant norms. In others, economic circumstances cause competition for scarce urban public spaces.

The fact that a commons appears unregulated, of course, does not necessarily mean that it is. One of de Soto's most important insights is that the informal economy is governed by a complex set of rules, albeit extra-legal ones. Even the apparent chaos of a third-world marketplace—or Harlem's 125th Street bazaar—frequently masks the intricate system of informal norms of public space allocation: vendors respect one another's claims, enter into mutually advantageous contractual arrangements with established merchants, etc. And my own observations suggest that the apparently chaotic scene at busy subway stops served by vans was actually quite orderly. The vans arranged themselves, informally, by anticipated destination, and customers exiting the subways quickly made their way to the appropriate service without any confusion. De Soto also reminds urban policymakers that legal rules restricting access to the formal market feed the informal one and urges

38 Carol M. Rose, *The Comedy of the Commons: Commerce, Custom and Inherently Public Property*, 53 U. Chi. L. Rev. 711 (1986).

them to remain attentive to the risk that the wrong kinds of legal intervention into informal markets may well make a suboptimal situation worse. The reality is, however, that when public spaces become contested—as with disputes over street vending and jitneys—government intervention is inevitable. Frequently, as de Soto predicts, it makes things worse.

In the vending and jitney contexts, even regulators amenable to market solutions (and many are not) face an obvious difficulty. The classic solution to the tragedy of the commons—privatization—does not work well with public streets and sidewalks. As a result, regulators become locked into a repeated cycle of allocating rights to urban public spaces. It should come as no surprise to anyone with a passing familiarity of public choice theory that *all* of the options in the regulators' tool kit tend to favor economic insiders. The most popular regulatory strategy—prohibition (either complete or partial)—privileges, respectively, established merchants and the providers of public bus services. For example, while Giuliani himself may have viewed the vendors as disorderly, there is significant evidence that vending opponents' primary motivation was a desire to eliminate competitors selling similar products for less money. As deputy mayor Rudy Washington noted at the time, "When I hear people yelling, 'They're putting us out of business,' that gets my ears up and I pay attention."[39] After admitting that his food-vending proposal "may have gone too far," Giuliani himself reflected on the "ongoing need to trying to balance the need for the street vendors to make a living and the need for the businesses that are affected by the street vendors also to make a living."[40] Even the divergence between the hard-line stance in Harlem (favoring a total prohibition) and the food-vending compromise (favoring partial prohibition) can be explained by public choice theory: While unlicensed vendors on 125th Street were primarily immigrants (some of them undocumented aliens) who operated independently, a single company with the resources to threaten legal action owned a majority of available food-vending permits.

Similarly, like their early twentieth century antecedents, today's jitney laws have as their intent and effect the protection of economic insiders—primarily the providers of public transportation, whether operated by governmental or private entities—from competition by those operating at the economic margins. Even where some private group transportation services are allowed, regulatory approvals are exceedingly difficult to secure. Providers frequently are subject to "public convenience and necessity" requirements that give public transportation providers virtual veto power over potential competitors. In order to secure the required certificate, a would-be provider must prove that the proposed service is something that the public as a whole "requires" and not something that a portion of it "desires." The applicant thus bears the burden of rebutting evidence, usually submitted by existing public transportation providers who are entitled to intervene

39 *See* Allen, *City Pursuing Negotiations With Street Food Vendors*, *supra* note 28, at B3.

40 *See Giuliani Says a New Plan Will Not Please Vendors*, *supra* note 29, at B8.

in the proceedings, that the existing providers not only do not serve the public need, but also that they *could not be made to satisfy that need.*

The certificate of public convenience and necessity requirement is a classic regulatory barrier to entry; its practical (and intended) effect is to protect existing providers from competition. Indeed, one long-accepted justification for the requirement is the need to prevent "ruinous competition" among providers.[41] Because, as public choice theory teaches, repeat players in the regulation game tend to "capture" the regulators, even the best efforts and most fervent arguments of a would-be entrant tend to fall on deaf ears, regardless of their validity: "[T]he entrepreneur seeking entry generally must back his judgment with substantial resources, whereas the regulatory body risks nothing by denying entry and may indeed protect itself against troublesome problems of administration by protecting a familiar (if obsolete) incumbent."[42]

In New York City, for example, the law does not specify how an applicant might go about making a "public convenience and necessity" showing, but it does give opponents of the service the opportunity to rebut an applicant's effort. Not only is the City's Department of Transportation required to provide for public notice and comment on the application, it must directly notify the MTA when an application is filed. If an application is "protested by a bus line operating in the City," then the Department of Transportation must also consider "the adequacy of existing mass transportation facilities" and "the impact that the proposed operation may have on any existing mass transit or mass transportation facilities."[43] In one case, an applicant submitted 938 support statements indicating that the proposed service was desperately needed to augment inadequate bus service; the application was denied. Since the City assumed regulatory responsibility in 1994, virtually all applications for the limited "commuter van service" licenses described above have been denied. In a number of cases, the applicant successfully negotiated the administrative process, convincing the Department of Transportation that the proposed service was "necessary" and that mass transportation was "inadequate." Under pressure from unions representing public transportation workers, however, the City Council vetoed approval of the application.[44] It is also worth noting that

---

41 William K. Jones, *Origins of the Certificate of Public Convenience and Necessity: Developments in the State, 1876–1920*, 79 COLUM. L. REV. 426, 428 (1979).

42 *Id.* at 515.

43 N.Y., N.Y., ADMIN. CODE §19–504.2(e)(3) (1993).

44 On vans in New York, *see generally* Nicole Stelle Garnett, *The Road from Welfare to Work: Informal Transportation and the Urban Poor*, 38 HARV. J. ON LEGIS. 173 (2001). *See also Council on Road to Vandalism*, Editorial, N.Y. DAILY NEWS, Aug. 4, 1997, at 26; *Dream On*, Editorial, WALL ST. J., July 21, 1997, at A22; *Transit Union Roadblock*, Editorial, N.Y. POST, July 27, 1997. On public convenience and necessity requirements, *see* William B. Tye, *The Economics of Public Convenience and Necessity for Regulated Industries*, 60 TRANSP. PRACT. J. 143 (1992); Jones, *supra* note 41, at 427; Ford P. Hall, *Certificates of Convenience and Necessity*, 28 MICH. L. REV. 107, 108 (1929). *See also generally* 13 AM. JUR. 2d *Carriers* §§125–130 (2000).

Giuliani's support for the van services during these political battles undoubtedly was influenced by his negative feelings about the union representing public transportation workers—which rabidly opposed jitneys.

Unfortunately, the "market based" alternatives to these prohibitory strategies also favor dominant interests over marginalized ones. For example, the vending "markets" established in New York City, at both ends of the twentieth century, had the intent and effect of containing vendors in locations set away from busy public thoroughfares where they posed a competitive threat to established merchants. Other market-based regulatory strategies—for example, auctioning sidewalk rights—also favor those with financial means. For example, in 1995, the New York City Council passed a "one-vendor-one-permit" law in response to a concern that the corporations holding the vast majority of available food-vending permits exploited the vendors operating under their authority. The city exempted vendors in public parks from complying with the rule, however, and instead instituted a (lucrative) bidding system for park access. More recently, city officials have floated the idea of using a similar bidding system to allocate vending rights on public streets. The proposal has generated screams of protest from vendors, who argue that bidding would force hundreds of hard-working entrepreneurs out of business.

In the transportation context, even those jurisdictions that permit shared-ride services restrict them so as to protect established taxi and bus services. For example, some, including New York, permit limited "commuter van" or "van pool" services, but limit their attractiveness by mandating that customers prearrange pick-up and drop-off times. Those few jurisdictions that recognize a class of private transportation called "jitneys" generally require providers to operate along fixed, franchised routes or in specified zones, thereby depriving them of the flexibility that gives jitneys much of their competitive advantage. The privatization of mass transportation services usually involves the granting of long-term monopoly franchises, which quickly turn private providers into economic insiders. And, as former Indianapolis Mayor Stephen Goldsmith learned when he proposed competitively auctioning off local bus routes, significant political impediments exist to taking even that step.[45]

The Elite Aesthetics of Urban Life

New York's vending and jitney disputes also hint at another explanation for the mercantilist qualities of vending and transportation regulation. Namely, third-world services conflict with elite ideals of first-world cities. To abstract from the early twentieth century pushcart debates, vendors and jitneys usually are not picturesque. They often are downright junky. This is one reason why development

45 Anthony Jewel, *Free Enterprise: Indianapolis Mayor Calls on Private Sector to Get the Job Done*, Nat'l Cities Weekly, Jan. 22, 1996, at 8. On public transportation generally, see José A. Gómez-Ibáñez and John R. Meyer, Going Private: The International Experience with Transport Privatization, 62–83 (1993).

interests, in both early and late twentieth century New York City, opposed the street vendors: They conflicted with image of the city that development interests wanted to sell. There is a perceived tension, in other words, between enabling poor entrepreneurs to operate and fostering the kind of economic and social life in cities that will attract desired residents, namely elites with pro-urban aesthetic tastes. Interestingly, the economic development literature suggests that the tension is not unique to the United States; many developing nations struggle to strike a balance between incubating "microcapital" enterprises like vending and overhauling the economic climate of cities to promote large-scale development.[46]

In the United States, Washington, D.C.'s proposal to completely overhaul the rules governing street vending in the nation's capital illustrates how elite aesthetics influence policymakers' public-space allocation decisions. The District's regulatory regime was for years one of the most generous in the United States Historically, the District did not cap the number of available vending permits, and the result was evident in the number of vendors on city sidewalks. Concern over the excessive congestion and competition for sidewalk space led the District to place a moratorium on new licenses beginning in 1996, which was lifted in 2007. At that point, the District distributed 400 new licenses by lottery, but required that license-holders apply for a "public space permit" for a specific vending location, with a preference for vendors seeking to work in business improvement districts. The District coupled the new permits with proposed regulations that purportedly seek to "modernize" the vending program. The regulations eliminate the requirement that holders must operate as sole proprietors, as well as rules designed to prevent the concentration of vendors in a single spot.

Municipal officials encourage the vendors to work with development interests, including business improvement districts, on innovative food cart initiatives, including sidewalk food courts. Historically, the business improvement districts have opposed street vending on aesthetic grounds, but the regulations address this concern by phasing in design standards. The result is hoped to be more-attractive vending stands selling a greater diversity of food. The current one-vendor-one-permit rule democratizes the distribution of vending permits, but also discourages innovation and prevents vendors from expanding their businesses. The District anticipates that the new rules will attract more entrepreneurs like Gabe Klein, one of the brains behind the shared "zipcar" system. Klein's "On the Fly" serves food, ranging from sushi to barbecue, from eco-friendly vehicles. (The carts exceed the current vending size restrictions, but Klein is operating in two "demonstration zones.")[47] Perhaps unsurprisingly, the District, which historically has had relatively

46 *See, e.g.*, Hans Illy, *Regulation and Evasion: Street Vendors in Manila*, 19 Policy Sciences 61 (2005); I.M. Jimu, *An Exploration of Street Vending's Contribution Towards Botswana's Vision of Prosperity for All by 2016*, 18 Botswana J. of African Stud. 19 (2004).

47 *See* Mayor of the District of Columbia, Notice of Proposed Rulemaking, available at http://www.dcra.dc.gov/dcra/lib/dcra/proposed_rulemaking_vending_regulati

liberal taxi regulations, imposed additional aesthetic rules on both cabs and their drivers a decade ago. The rules mandate relatively new, air conditioned cabs and impose a dress code for cabbies.[48]

The municipal focus on aesthetics is not irrational. As Robert Bruegmann argues in his recent history of suburban sprawl, the very economic changes lamented by many scholars of urban life—including the decline in the urban industrial base—ultimately may save our cities. Freed from congestion, pollution, and disease, cities will become more attractive to elites who previously chose to live in the suburbs. Bruegmann hypothesizes, "[i]t is quite possible that sprawl could recede everywhere as more citizens become affluent enough to live like the residents of the Upper East Side," because "as individuals pass from affluent to extraordinarily affluent they are better able to enjoy the benefits of density without the negative side effects."[49] Edward Glaeser and Joshua Gottlieb's recent study of the apparent "urban resurgence" experienced over the past two decades provides some empirical support for Bruegmann's predictions. As Glaeser and Gottlieb observe, "one plausible hypothesis is that the urban resurgence can be understood as reflecting the rising demand for urban amenities caused by rising income and education levels nationwide."[50] Glaeser and Gottlieb further argue that elite demand for the informal social interactions enabled by city densities and mixed-land-use patterns has been fueled by the dramatic decreases in urban crime and disorder, both factors that made it difficult to enjoy city life. Efforts to cater to elite aesthetic preferences (and to alter the aesthetics of vending to fit them) also are reflected in the growing popularity of the so-called "new urbanism" among city planners. The "new urbanists" strongly prefer urban landscapes over suburban ones, but they also promote detailed design standards as an alternative to traditional land-use-based zoning. These design standards, like the ones to be implemented for street vendors in D.C., may succeed at their appointed task of forming the aesthetics of city life to match elite preferences. But they also impose economic barriers to entry that will price many operating on the economic margins out of the formal economy.[51]

---

ons_100108.pdf. *See also* Tim Carman, *New Freedoms to Go: D.C. Street Vendors Try Out Laxer Rules*, Wash. Post, Oct. 1, 2008, at F1; Karen Leigh, *In D.C. Street-Food Wars, Hot Dogs Face Competition from Hummus*, Bloomberg News, June 11, 2008; Missy Frederick, *Taking it to the Street: D.C. Struggles to Breathe New Life into a Stale Outdoor Food Cart Scene*, Wash. Business J., Sept. 12, 2008.

48 Hamil R. Harris and Victoria Benning, *D.C. Cabbies to Suspend Service Today: 12-Hour Protest Aimed at New Regulations*, Wash. Post, April 22, 1997 at B1; *New Taxi Rules Too Taxing?*, Editorial, Wash. Post, April 24, 1997, at A24.

49 Robert Bruegmann, Sprawl: A Compact History, 221 (2005).

50 Edward L. Glaeser and Joshua D. Gottlieb, *Urban Resurgence and the Consumer City*, 43 Urb. Stud. 1275, 1277 (2006)

51 *Id.* Nicole Stelle Garnett, *Save the Cities, Stop the Suburbs?*, 116 Yale L. J. 598, 625–629 (2006).

Conclusion: The Costs of Illegality, the Costs of Legality

De Soto documents and emphasizes the tremendous costs of informality, that is, the costs incurred by those forced to operate in the informal economy. He notes, for example, that informals spend a great deal of time and energy avoiding detection, penalties, and taxation; informals must rely on reputation (and occasional involvement with corruption) to enforce agreements because they cannot avail themselves of contract law; and informals' lack of access to property rights prevents them from leveraging the wealth that they generate into capital.[52] These realities are illustrated by an exchange Michael Heller recalls having with a kiosk operator in Moscow: "As one kiosk owner told me, 'It is easy to bribe the prefect officials, but hard to keep them bribed.' More important, you can't borrow against your illegal kiosk to finance another location, get a building permit to expand …. Illegal capital can't be easily leveraged to create new wealth."[53] As a result, a legal store generates an "economic multiplier" but an illegal kiosk a "flatline of service."[54]

The "flatline of service" also has important consequences for the individuals—usually those at the economic margins—that informals serve. Faced with a constant threat of enforcement and lack of access to mainstream sources of capital, informals likely will under-invest in the amenities that ensure high-quality, safe, products and services. (Some important consumer protections, such as insurance, are likely off-limits to informals as well.) As detailed above in the New York City example, authorized commuter van services that operate as jitneys do so in clear derogation of rules restricting them from accepting street hails and picking up and discharging passengers on bus routes. By operating in this fashion, they incite the wrath of public transportation officials and their political allies, as well as expose themselves to regular traffic citations and vehicle impoundments. Still, in my experience, the legal authorization made a difference in the quality of the service provided. Van companies operating pursuant to a valid authorization were more likely to be insured and were perceived by their customers to be safer, cleaner, and more reliable than those that operated without any authorization at all.

De Soto also urged attention to the costs of *legality*—that is, the burdens that the law imposes on those who wish to operate legally. As de Soto observes, when the costs of legality exceed the costs of informality, entrepreneurs will choose to operate in the informal economy. The costs of legality are especially important to consider in a market economy. This insight is particularly important in the United States, precisely because we enjoy well-functioning property markets. Most street vendors and jitney services operate illegally in U.S. cities because the law precludes them from operating legally. Unlike jitneys, however, vendors,

---

52 The Other Path *supra* note 2, at 152–172; Mystery of Capital, *supra* note 1, at 47–67.

53 Heller, *supra* note 10, at 156.

54 *Id.*

at least theoretically, have an alternative to vending. They could move inside. De Soto sees in a busy third world marketplace would-be store owners deprived of access to private property by unclear titles and uncertain contract rights. Similarly, Michael Heller influentially argued that the proliferation of kiosks in post-Soviet Russia resulted from a "tragedy of the anticommons"—that is, because too many individuals held exclusion rights to storefronts, the costs of assembling those rights kept storefronts empty.[55] In the United States, we, by and large, do not have these problems. On the contrary, our urban landscapes—especially in inner-city communities where street vendors are most likely to operate—are replete with vacant and abandoned buildings that city governments would love to see filled with new entrepreneurial ventures.

The fact that vendors are *not* moving inside, in other words, suggests something about the costs of legality in these markets. However, other legal factors may well be in play. In a recent article, for example, Stephen Clowney set forth an intriguing proposal to reverse the troubling economic decline of many inner-city communities, which he calls the Vacant and Abandoned Land Transfer program, or VALT. Clowney suggests that local governments might eliminate land-use restrictions on vacant and abandoned buildings and then transfer title to inner-city entrepreneurs. As Clowney notes, many cities already have voluminous *in rem* portfolios of buildings seized as a result of tax delinquencies; some have been quite aggressive in acquiring title to abandoned buildings through public nuisance actions and tax foreclosures. Clowney intuits that neighbors would prefer to have these building utilized for commercial activity than to remain vacant, and, moreover, that this desire might overcome public-choice impediments to implementing his proposal. While the VALT proposal is, in my view, both ingenious and promising, it also brings to the surface two other impediments to the regeneration of poor urban communities that relate to the costs of legality. First, some economist argue that the tax delinquencies that enable cities to acquire title to abandoned buildings are themselves a significant contributing factor to urban decline. Excessive property taxes, according to this view, lead property owners to abandon buildings in inner-city communities. Vendors seeking to transition from informal to formal economies would not be well situated to absorb the tax burden. Second, the new owners of abandoned buildings in poor neighborhoods would face very high renovation costs—deferred maintenance being an inevitable result of abandonment. But while the VALT proposal would reduce the costs of legality by freeing the abandoned buildings from zoning restrictions on land use, other property regulations drive up the cost of renovations. For example, building codes may require rewiring and replumbing, and the Americans with Disabilities Act may impose expensive accommodation requirements. These fiscal and regulatory impediments, which are significant enough to lead some cities to consider rehabilitation-specific building codes, may also have contributed to the relative lack of success in our modern

55 Michael A. Heller, *The Tragedy of the Anticommons: Property in the Transition from Marx to Markets*, 111 Harv. L. Rev. 621 (2009).

urban titling efforts, such as "urban homesteading" programs. They certainly are an obstacle to vendors' relocation.[56]

In both the developing and the developed world, hard-working, but poor, individuals find their efforts to enter the mainstream economy stymied by legal rules designed to protect economic insiders from competition. Policy makers concerned about economic development, both at home and abroad, should pay heed to Hernando de Soto's warning about the risk of creeping mercantilism and seek to address regulatory barriers to entry that force poor entrepreneurs to operate in the informal economy.

56 Clowney, *supra* note 6.

Chapter 10
Hernando de Soto, Formal Property Systems, and the Intangible Asset Paradox

Juliet M. Moringiello[1]

With *The Mystery of Capital: Why Capitalism Triumphs in the West and Fails Everywhere Else*, Hernando de Soto made a terrific contribution to property law literature. De Soto does not write from a legal perspective (he is an economist, not a lawyer); rather, he examines property systems from a perspective that he describes as "extralegal," or outside of the formal property system.[2] Although de Soto wrote the book to explain the slow or non-existent economic development in countries without a Western property rights system, his ideas have tremendous relevance even in developed economies as they move from systems in which tangible assets are of paramount importance to systems in which intangible assets become more valuable.

De Soto's major contribution to property law is his explanation of how a system of well-defined property rights, supported by statutes, judicial decisions, and recording systems, enables the holders of assets to use those assets productively. The ability to use assets productively flows from both the benefits and burdens of formal property ownership. As de Soto explains, property makes people accountable. Without property to lose, potential participants in the economy "cannot make contracts with strangers [and] cannot get credit."[3] Thus, a stable system of secured credit, in which easily discernable and transferable property interests can be granted as security for loans, is a key component of a modern economy.

According to de Soto, capitalism is successful in the West because Western property systems successfully convert tangible assets into intangible concepts. The example used throughout the book is a house: the American real property recording system successfully converts an object (the house) into a concept (the title to the house). In a Western system, a person wishing to buy a house can easily determine the ownership of that house because Western systems, such as that of the United States, have recording systems containing information about ownership. This recorded information is useful not only because it is publicly available, but also because it is in a standard form. As a result, anyone seeing a deed stating that

1 Many thanks to Jim Smith for helpful comments on a draft of this chapter.

2 Hernando de Soto, The Mystery of Capital: Why Capitalism Triumphs in the West and Fails Everywhere Else, 48 (2000) [hereinafter Mystery of Capital].

3 Mystery of Capital, *supra* note 2, at 56.

John and Mary own a house as tenants by the entirety knows that neither John nor Mary has a separate transferable interest in the house. The recording system works because it is supported by statutes and judicial decisions that define interests in real property and set forth rules governing the transfer of these interests.

De Soto's description of the American property system is accurate insofar as it describes the real-estate system. It falls apart, however, as we move across the asset spectrum from tangible assets in a fixed location (real estate) to intangible assets. Intangible assets are particularly relevant in a modern economy for two reasons. First, the development of the World Wide Web as a business tool has led to the emergence of new intangible assets, such as Internet domain names, and the increased importance of others, such as computer software. Second, as financing becomes more sophisticated, assets representing packages of loans are sold from lenders to investors worldwide. While the underlying, or first, loan is often secured by a familiar asset such as real estate or equipment, the intangible assets representing those loan packages take less familiar forms. To fully develop the potential of Internet transactions and other transactions involving intangible assets, potential investors must have confidence in those transactions. In order to encourage such confidence, our property system must convey accurate information about the extent and ownership of property rights in all assets, tangible and intangible. We have long recognized several categories of intangibles, such as payment rights and intellectual property, but many emerging intangible assets do not fit into these known categories.

I will draw on Chapter 3 of the *Mystery of Capital*, which shares its title with that of the larger book, to critique some failings in the U.S. legal system's treatment of intangible assets. In that chapter, de Soto explains the conversion process that allows physical assets to "lead a parallel life as capital outside the physical world."[4] To do so, de Soto identifies six "property effects" that formal property systems produce that allow participants in those systems to generate capital. While he focuses on physical assets, by using the real-estate system as an example, de Soto is really describing a system in which immovable assets can be "moved" by moving a representation of those assets. In credit systems, even movable assets are "moved" by some form of representation, as businesses routinely use assets used in their operations, such as equipment and inventory, as collateral for loans.

In my discussion, I will identify an important paradox of American property law. While our property system does, as de Soto recognizes, transform real property into uniform and comprehensible intangible concepts that enable the productive use of such property, it does not always transform intangible rights into those same comprehensible concepts. To support this contention, I will focus on three of de Soto's property effects: "Fixing the Economic Potential of Assets," "Integrating Dispersed Information into One System," and "Making Assets Fungible," and the extent to which those property effects are incorporated into Article 9 of the Uniform Commercial Code (U.C.C.).

---

4 Mystery of Capital, *supra* note 2, at 39.

Fixing the Economic Potential of Assets

De Soto calls his first property effect "Fixing the Economic Potential of Assets." This effect enables the "potential value locked up in a house"[5] to be "revealed and transformed into active capital."[6] As de Soto describes the process, "capital is born by representing in writing … the most economically and socially useful qualities *about* the asset as opposed to the visually more striking aspects *of* the asset."[7] De Soto gives three examples of such a writing: a title, a security, and a contract.[8]

It is interesting that de Soto focuses on the importance of a writing given that the writing is evidence not of something physical, but of an "economic and social concept."[9] Like legal academics, de Soto defines property conceptually, explaining that property is "not the house itself, but an economic concept *about* the house."[10] His definition is similar to the typical legal definition of property, commonly stated as the "legal relations between persons with respect to a thing."[11] Legal relationships among persons are, of course, important to economic relations, and a formal property system as described by de Soto defines those relationships both by revealing the identity of the person entitled to transfer the house, by sale, lease, security interest, or any other method and by identifying the extent of the economic interest in the house that said person can transfer. De Soto's formal representations do two things: they "secure the interest of other parties" and "provide all of the information, references, rules and enforcement mechanisms required" to secure those interests.[12]

De Soto's description of the process by which the economic potential of assets is fixed is accurate insofar as it applies to real estate in the United States. In order to make this process useful in fixing the economic qualities of intangible assets, it is important to examine the key components of this process. Comprehensive written property representations, as de Soto describes them, exist in only a handful of sectors in the American property system. As de Soto explains, land is represented in the United States by deeds. The requirement that a conveyance of land be accomplished by delivery of a deed is a descendant of the medieval method of transferring a possessory freehold interest in land by feoffment with livery of seisin. In this medieval ceremony, the grantor handed over a twig or clod of dirt to the grantee to symbolize the conveyance. Because this ceremony could

---

5 Mystery of Capital, *supra* note 2, at 49.

6 *Id.*

7 *Id.* at 49–50 (emphasis in original).

8 *Id.* at 49.

9 *Id.* at 50.

10 *Id.*

11 Restatement of Property, Introductory Note (1936). The drafters of the Restatement recognized that the thing need not be tangible, adding that "[t]he thing may be an object having physical existence or it may be any kind of intangible such as a patent right or a chose in action."

12 Mystery of Capital, *supra* note 2, at 51.

be inconvenient, as it required travel to the land, conveyancers developed methods of transfer that did not require livery of seisin.[13] The Statute of Uses, enacted in England in 1536, enabled several new types of conveyances that did not require livery of seisin. Because Parliament feared that the Statute of Uses would facilitate secret conveyances, it passed the Statute of Enrollments, which required that all freehold conveyances be recorded in a public place.[14]

Today in the United States, ownership interests in real property are conveyed by delivery of a deed. In order to be effective as a conveyance, the deed must be delivered, and delivery usually involves the physical delivery of the deed.[15] Only a handful of other property interests are transferred by the use of a paper document. A transfer of ownership in an automobile to an end-user is also evidenced by paper, the certificate of title.[16] Several other types of personal property, such as boats,[17] are covered by certificates of title but for the most part ownership in tangible personal property is transferred by the manual transfer of the item itself, not a representation of the item. The absence of a representational system for ownership interests in tangible personal property is generally not a problem; manual possession of an item sends a message to the world that the person in possession is the owner.[18] In situations in which the tangible item cannot be manually delivered, because it is large or because the transferor and transferee are located in different places, the law has recognized a variety of methods of constructive delivery. We see these substitutes for manual delivery in many places: the law of gifts has long recognized constructive and symbolic methods of delivery,[19] and the law of creditors' rights recognizes constructive methods of seizure when large items of collateral cannot be manually repossessed.[20]

Transfer of ownership in intangible assets is more difficult to summarize. Some intangible assets, such as payment rights, are transferred by the transfer of a physical representation of those rights, such as a check or a promissory

---

13 William B. Stoebuck and Dale A. Whitman, The Law of Property §11.1 (3rd ed., 2000).

14 Stoebuck and Whitman, *supra* note 13.

15 *Id.*

16 *See* Uniform Motor Vehicle Certificate of Title and Anti-Theft Act §9 (stating that a certificate of title is *prima facie* evidence of the facts appearing on it, which include the name of the owner). I use the term "end-user" because no certificate of title need be issued for automobiles held by a dealer for sale. Uniform Motor Vehicle Certificate of Title and Anti-Theft Act §2 (a)(2).

17 *See* 30 Pa. Cons Stat. §5321 (1996) (requiring certificates of title for boats).

18 *See generally* Carol M. Rose, *Possession as the Origin of Property*, 52 U. Chi. L. Rev. 73 (1985).

19 *See, e.g., Coke & Reardon v. Ikard*, 87 S.W. 869 (Tex. Civ. App 1905) (recognizing delivery of cattle when the donor branded the cattle with separate marks and recorded those marks, as required by statute, in the name of the donees).

20 *See, e.g.* U.C.C. §9–609 (a)(2) (allowing a secured party to disable equipment collateral upon the debtor's default).

note.[21] Likewise, ownership of an interest in a business entity is sometimes (and was historically) transferred by the transfer of a paper certificate and there is a well-developed indirect holding system in which stock in most large corporations is held. In that system, paper shares are held by a securities depositary and transfers of those shares are recorded on the depositary's books.[22] More recently developed intangible assets, such as Internet domain names and computer software, are transferred by contracts that purport to define the extent of the transferee's property rights in the asset.[23] While methods for delivering rights reified in paper are well-developed and recognized, methods for transferring newer intangible assets are not.[24]

To identify the important characteristics of de Soto's paradigmatic Western property regime, it is useful to examine the role of property representation. De Soto writes that "[p]roperty representations enabled people to think about assets not only through physical acquaintance but also through the description of their latent economic and social qualities."[25] In a sense, de Soto is saying that the representation itself, be it the deed, the promissory note, or the share of stock, communicates valuable information to the world. While this is certainly desirable, the representation can only do so if supported by a legal system that clearly defines property rights.

A deed plays several roles. First, as described above, because a deed must be delivered in order for a transfer of real estate to be effective, it stands in for the immovable real property in the transfer ceremony. Therefore, it symbolizes the land. If this symbol is recorded in the land records, it gives notice of the ownership in the land and thus priority to the transferee over anyone else who might claim an interest in the land. A deed generally also contains a set of promises from the grantor to the grantee, warranting that the grantor owns the land and has the right to convey it, that the land is free from encumbrances, and that the grantor will execute any additional documents necessary to perfect title, as well as defend against any legal challenge to the grantee's title.[26] While it is unlikely that a buyer would rely on deed covenants alone to assure herself that she is receiving good title to real estate, these deed covenants are part of the overall system that makes land titles in the United States reliable. De Soto recognizes the role of title insurance

21 *See* U.C.C. §§3–104 (defining "negotiable instrument"); 3–203(b) (granting the transferee of an instrument the right to enforce the instrument).

22 *See* James Steven Rogers, *Policy Perspectives on Revised Article 8*, 43 UCLA. L. Rev. 1431, 1441–1446 (1996) (explaining the history and mechanics of the indirect holding system).

23 *See, e.g.*, Register.com Master Services Agreement §29, available at http://www.register.com/policy/servicesagreement.rcmx#29 (limiting the right of a domain name registrant to transfer the name, and stating that the name will be cancelled if a creditor attempts to reach the domain name to satisfy a judgment).

24 I explore this issue in more detail in Juliet M. Moringiello, *False Categories in Commercial Law: The (Ir)relevance of (In)tangibility*, 35 Fla. St. U. L. Rev. 119, 156–164 (2007).

25 Mystery of Capital, *supra* note 2, at 51.

26 Stoebuck and Whitman, *supra* note 13, at §11.13.

and the recording system as the other building blocks of stable land titles in his description of the sixth property effect, "Protecting Transactions."[27]

A negotiable instrument performs some of the same functions as a deed. Because a debt cannot be manually transferred, the paper instrument stands in for the obligation. The U.C.C. dictates the content of a negotiable instrument, and the required content notifies those interested in the instrument of the identity of the person entitled to transfer the instrument.[28] Article 3 of the U.C.C., which defines negotiable instruments and sets forth the rules for transfer of those instruments, provides the necessary legal structure for a stable system of transferring property interests in payment rights that have been reified in negotiable instruments.

Representational systems are necessary when the asset in question either *cannot* be moved or *will not* be moved. Land, of course, can never be physically moved, so a representational system that reflects all transfers, full and partial, is necessary to encourage confidence in land transfers. Tangible personal property, on the other hand, can be moved, and our laws support the generally held view that possession gives notice of ownership.[29] A representational system that records all ownership transfers is therefore not necessary for such property, as ownership in such assets is generally conveyed by a transfer of possession, and conveyances that are not accompanied by a transfer of possession are often considered suspect.[30] A security interest, however, is a partial interest, and a representational system facilitates the transfer of partial interests. Although a secured party can perfect an interest in tangible personal property by taking possession of the property,[31] doing so is not feasible when the debtor needs the asset to conduct its business. Article 9 of the U.C.C. was designed to provide a representational system for security interests in personal property.

A system under which an owner can grant a security interest in assets without transferring possession of those assets is essential to economic development. Non-possessory security interests in business assets such as inventory are necessary for business financing, but in the 1800s such security interests were considered fraudulent if the borrower was permitted to sell the inventory without being required to account to the lender for the proceeds of sale.[32] Similar objections were raised when receivables financing came into being, and in *Benedict v. Ratner* the U.S. Supreme

27 MYSTERY OF CAPITAL, *supra* note 2, at 61–62.

28 U.C.C. §§3–106 and 3–110.

29 For example, *inter vivos* gifts are deemed invalid unless there is some transfer of possession. JOSEPH WILLIAM SINGER, INTRODUCTION TO PROPERTY §16.2.3 (2nd ed., 2005) ("the law of gifts requires (1) *intent* to transfer title, (2) *delivery* of the property, and (3) *acceptance* by the donee").

30 *See, e.g.*, UNIFORM FRAUDULENT TRANSFER ACT §4(b) (providing that a transfer of property without a transfer of possession is evidence of actual intent to defraud creditors).

31 U.C.C. §9–313.

32 *See* Grant Gilmore, *Article 9: What it Does for the Past*, 26 LA. L. REV. 285, 289 (1966) (describing cases that held non-possessory security interests in inventory to be fraudulent).

Court held that a transfer of accounts receivable as security was fraudulent as to creditors if the debtor was allowed to collect the accounts and apply the proceeds to its own purposes.[33] In 1925, when *Benedict v. Ratner* was decided, there was no law that provided a notice-filing system for interests in accounts receivable.[34]

Article 9, by providing a system of notice filing for security interests in personal property, ideally helps to fix the economic potential of assets. Under Article 9, a person interested in learning of the existence of a security interest in another person's property can do so by consulting a defined set of public records, the records of the Secretary of State's office in the property owner's state.[35] The paper[36] notice, a U.C.C. Financing Statement, does not convey the extensive information conveyed by a deed to real property, but in theory it provides enough information to put a searcher on notice that a secured party has an interest in defined personal property owned by an identified debtor.[37] Arguably, the Article 9 filing system performs this function for all types of personal property, tangible and intangible. All property of a debtor can be subject to a security interest, and Article 9 provides a catch-all category, general intangibles, which covers assets such as intellectual property and software.[38]

To be an effective system, however, a modern property system must do other things: it needs to integrate dispersed information into one system and it must make assets fungible. In those respects, the American property system as a whole often does not convey adequate information about intangible assets. I turn to the ways in which the American system fails below.

Integrating Dispersed Information into One System

DeSoto credits Western property regimes with integrating most assets into "one formal representational system."[39] By one system, de Soto is not referring to one centralized recording system; rather, he is referring to the general respect in Western countries for "one law—the official one."[40]

---

33 *Benedict v. Ratner*, 268 U.S. 353 (1925).

34 *See Benedict v. Ratner*, 268 U.S. 353, 362 ("the statutes which embody the doctrine [of ostensible ownership] and provide for recording as a substitute for delivery do not include accounts").

35 *See infra* notes 44–49 and accompanying text.

36 This notice no longer need be in paper form. *See* U.C.C. §9–102(a)(39) (defining financing statement as a "record") and 9–102(a)(69) (defining record as "information that is inscribed on a tangible medium or which is stored in an electronic or other medium and is retrievable in perceivable form").

37 *See* U.C.C. §9–502(a) (setting forth information that is necessary in order for a financing statement to be effective).

38 U.C.C. §9–102(a)(42).

39 Mystery of Capital, *supra* note 2, at 52.

40 *Id.* at 53.

A recording system can define both the person entitled to transfer an asset and the extent of that person's property rights in the asset. The automobile title system also conveys this information. The title certificate is *prima facie* proof of ownership,[41] and no one buying or financing the purchase of a car would do so without seeing this certificate. This certificate is essential to financing transactions; all states require a person with a security interest in a car to note that interest on the car's certificate of title.[42]

Certainly, de Soto is correct on this point; a stable property system in which buyers know what they are buying is an important engine of economic growth. In several areas, the U.S. property system incorporates this idea. Although there are thousands of offices in which real property documents are recorded, the American law of real property is uniform in its most important respects. Deeds and other conveyances are recorded in the county in which the subject land is located and whether the land is in Anchorage, Alaska or Philadelphia, Pennsylvania, a potential buyer or lender knows that she will have to search the local land records. Likewise, while recording statutes affecting priority differ somewhat from state to state, every state has a statute defining priorities among those claiming an interest in the land.

Not surprisingly, given de Soto's focus on well-developed Western property systems, the real-estate recording system provides the best support for his overall thesis. The history of Article 9 of the U.C.C., governing secured transactions in personal property, also provides excellent support for his thesis. Before Article 9 was drafted, there were many diverse systems for granting security interests in personal property. The purpose of the original Article 9 was to pull these diverse systems, such as those for chattel mortgages and trust receipts, into one comprehensive code.[43]

On its face, today's Article 9 succeeds in providing an authoritative filing system for security interests in personal property. Today, most notices of security interests are filed in the Secretary of State's office in the state in which the debtor is located.[44] Under the earlier version of Article 9, some financing statements were filed in the Secretary of State's office, some were filed at the county level, and some were filed in both offices.[45] In addition, some financing statements were filed at the location of the debtor and others were filed at the location of the collateral.[46] Further complicating things, the debtor's location was defined, in the case of an

41 Uniform Motor Vehicle Certificate of Title and Anti-Theft Act §9.

42 Uniform Motor Vehicle Certificate of Title and Anti-Theft Act §21.

43 1 Grant Gilmore, Security Interests in Personal Property §9.1 (1965) ("Gilmore, Treatise").

44 U.C.C. §9–301(1) (stating that the law of the debtor's jurisdiction governs perfection of a security interest) and 9–501 (stating that all financing statements, except for financing statements covering certain types of real estate-related collateral, must be filed in the Secretary of State's office).

45 U.C.C. §9–401(1) (1995).

46 U.C.C. §9–103 (1995).

entity, as its "chief executive office,"[47] a location that is increasingly elusive given modern communications. Today, all registered entities—such as corporations, limited partnerships, and limited liability companies—are located in their states of registration.[48] This location is easy to verify by doing a simple Internet search, as many, if not most states have their corporate records online.[49]

The personal property security system is not completely integrated, as there are valid filing systems outside of Article 9. Yet the law supports and clarifies this separation, and in most cases provides that there is *one* system for publicizing personal property security interests. In the case of motor vehicles, this is explicit in Article 9.[50] There are also federal systems, such as those for aircraft and for some types of intellectual property, but courts make clear that lenders do not have a choice of filing systems. If the law mandates a federal system, as it does for copyrights, the lender must file in the office mandated by the federal statute.[51] Courts recognize the need for certainty in filing systems. In one case, the court, rejecting the creditor's argument that either a copyright office or a Secretary of State's office filing should suffice to perfect a security interest in a copyright, stressed that "[a] recording system works by virtue of the fact that interested parties have a specific place to look in order to discover with certainty whether a particular interest has been transferred or encumbered."[52]

The various filing systems, however, are only part of the overall system that fosters confidence in the certainty of property transfers. A property system must not only publicize the transfer of property rights; it must also adequately define those property rights. Definitions are a crucial part of a representational system. In order to fully integrate intangible assets into our property system, we need to have a common understanding of the meaning of property definitions. In the intangible rights arena, much of this information is private and therefore not integrated into a property system that depends on notice. Grantors of intangible assets such as software and Internet domain names attempt to define the extent of those assets in contracts known as end user license agreements and courts tend to uphold these agreements. As a result, software is almost universally licensed, not sold,[53] and

47 U.C.C. §9–103(3)(d) (1995).

48 U.C.C. §9–307.

49 *See, e.g.,* Pennsylvania Department of State, available at http://www.dos.state.pa.us/dos/site/default.asp.

50 *See* U.C.C. §9–311(a)(2) (stating that the filing of a financing statement is not necessary or effective to perfect a security interest in property subject to a certificate of title statute).

51 *See National Peregrine, Inc. v. Capitol Federal Savings & Loan Ass'n* (*In re* Peregrine Entertainment, Ltd.), 116 B.R. 194 (C.D. Cal. 1990).

52 *Id.* at 200.

53 *See generally* John A. Rothchild, *The Incredible Shrinking First-Sale Rule: Are Software Resale Limits Lawful?* 57 Rutgers L. Rev. 1 (2004) (arguing that attempts by software vendors to limit the ownership rights of transferees should be legally ineffective); Elizabeth I. Winston, *Why Sell What You Can License: Contracting Around Statutory*

at least one court has held that an Internet domain name is a contract for services rather than an asset available to creditors.[54] In order to accommodate modern financing transactions, our property system, comprised of defined property forms and an authoritative recording apparatus, needs to better incorporate emerging intangible rights. In the next section, I will explain why clear property definitions are a necessary part of another one of de Soto's property effects.

Making Assets Fungible

When property rights are not visible, it is important that the law develop a language in which to describe those rights. As de Soto explains, Western property systems do so successfully when they describe estates in real property. According to de Soto, one of the most valuable functions of a formal property system is that such a system makes assets fungible. A formal property system "transform[s] assets from a less accessible condition to a more accessible condition, so that they can do additional work."[55] In explaining this property effect, de Soto argues that a formal property system must have standard categories so that an asset's attributes can be measured.[56] Here, de Soto appears to echo some of the thoughts of legal scholars who have written on the *numerus clausus* principle.[57]

Like de Soto, Henry Hansmann and Reiner Kraakman identify verification mechanisms as essential components of a viable property system. While de Soto focuses on recording systems and their supporting laws as verification mechanisms, Hansmann and Kraakman provide more detail on what verification mechanisms should do. Not only should such mechanisms identify the owner of the rights at issue, they should also identify the extent, or boundaries, of the rights at issue.[58]

One place to look for property definitions is Article 9. The Article 9 system, however, is designed to provide only two types of important information. The Article 9 system provides information about the owners of and lenders against the assets, but it provides often minimal information about the boundaries of the rights described.[59] While the U.C.C. provides property categories, courts, as I will

---

Protection of Intellectual Property, 14 GEO. MASON L. REV. 93 (2006) (arguing that "private legislation," in the form of end user license agreements, is increasingly being used to circumvent the balance of property rights embodied in federal copyright laws).

54 *Network Solutions, Inc. v. Umbro Int'l, Inc.*, 529 S.E. 2d 80 (Va. 2000).

55 MYSTERY OF CAPITAL, *supra* note 2, at 56.

56 *Id.* at 58.

57 *See, e.g.*, Henry Hansmann and Reiner Kraakman, *Property, Contract and Verification: The* Numerus Clausus *Problem and the Divisibility of Rights*, 31 J. LEGAL STUD. 373 (2002); Thomas W. Merrill and Henry E. Smith, *Optimal Standardization in the Law of Property: The* Numerus Clausus *Principle*, 110 YALE L.J. 1 (2000).

58 *See generally* Hansmann and Kraakman, *supra* note 57.

59 Article 9 today allows a creditor to file a financing statement describing the collateral as "all the debtor's property." U.C.C. §9–504(2). Even before the 2001 revision

explain below, do not always honor them. Both software and domain names are classified as "general intangibles,"[60] and a creditor can perfect a security interest in both by filing a financing statement covering "general intangibles." That financing statement, however, will communicate only that *if* the debtor has a property right in the asset, then the creditor is claiming a security interest in it.[61]

Generic definitions of real estate and tangible personal property do not cause many problems because both the real estate and personal property filing systems require the searcher to do more than simply search the public records to learn about the asset in question. A searcher interested in a house will not know the value of a house simply by viewing a deed that gives the address of the house. That searcher can, however, visit the property to learn important facts about the house such as the number of bedrooms and bathrooms and the physical condition of the house. The same applies to a car. A certificate of title might describe a car as a 2006 Saab 9-3 and give the vehicle identification number, but a person interested in the car will not know how to value the car without seeing it and ascertaining its condition. We can take these extra steps to evaluate real estate and tangible personal property, however, because we can see these items.

When the extent of a property right is defined by a contract and courts uphold the property definitions in those contracts regardless of whether such definitions conform to known property forms, integration of property information into one system is incomplete. The two examples of intangible property that I have used so far, Internet domain names and software, might appear at first to be forms of intellectual property. While software incorporates intellectual property and a domain name *may* incorporate intellectual property, both assets also incorporate "traditional" property rights. When software was commonly delivered on a tangible disk, it was easy to see the distinction between the creator's intellectual property rights in the software and the transferee's property rights in the disk. As software is increasingly delivered electronically, however, it becomes harder to see the distinct rights in the copy. Likewise, while the domain name "cocacola.com" is protected by trademark law, the generic name "wine.com" is not. The generic name "wine.com," however, has many property attributes: it is rivalrous, meaning that only one person can control it any time, and it can be sold for a large amount

---

to Article 9, the public notice could be very minimal, and the U.C.C. allows property descriptions by Article 9 type, such as "inventory," or "accounts." U.C.C. §9–108; U.C.C. §9–110 (1995).

60 U.C.C. §9–102(42).

61 In order for an asset to be collateral for a loan, it first must be property. *See* U.C.C. §9–203 (stating that a security interest becomes enforceable when the debtor has rights in the collateral). Despite the drafters' best efforts to transform anything of value into property usable as collateral, *see* U.C.C. §9-408 (invalidating certain statutory and contractual transfer restrictions to the extent that those restrictions would impair the granting of a security interest), some valuable rights have been held to be not property and therefore not collateral. *See N.J. Div. of Taxation v. United Trust Bank*, 367 F. Supp. 2d 696 (D. N.J. 2005).

of money. Therefore, the language of intellectual property law can only help us to understand *some* of the rights embodied in software and domain names.

As noted in the introduction of this chapter, de Soto's description of the ideal Western property system might not apply to a system in which interests in tangible and real-estate assets are packaged into securities and sold to investors around the world. Real property is made fungible so that it can be sold and mortgaged, but those mortgages are then transferred, transformed into securities, and transferred again. Equipment loans are sold the same way. In a case that provides a good view of the complexity of the financial crisis that began in 2008, we can see the problems that arise when our legal system has not fully integrated property rights into a representational system. One of the more controversial cases decided under Revised Article 9 of the U.C.C. is *NetBank FSA v. Kipperman (*In re *Commercial Money Center)*.[62] At issue in that case was a practice described by the plaintiff as "a bedrock principle of the securitization industry"[63]—the stripping of the right to payment from the underlying chattel paper. *Commercial Money Center* illustrates the importance of certainty in the classification of assets.

The debtor in *Commercial Money Center* leased equipment to companies with subprime credit. After entering into these leases, it packaged groups of leases together and assigned its rights to payment to different entities, including the plaintiff, NetBank. In addition to assigning the payment streams to NetBank, the debtor assigned the underlying leases to NetBank. NetBank never took possession of the leases and no financing statements were filed.[64]

Under Article 9 of the U.C.C., most security interests must be perfected by either filing or possession.[65] In that sense, Article 9 embodies de Soto's ideal legal regime—one in which persons interested in property can ascertain the extent of the property right and the persons able to transfer that right. Both filing and possession give public notice of a security interest: filing because everyone acquiring an asset should know to search the public records for possible interests in that asset and possession because a potential purchaser should view its collateral before purchasing.

But not all Article 9 interests must be publicized.[66] One interest that need not be publicized is the purchase-money security interest in consumer goods.[67] This

62 *NetBank, FSB v. Kipperman* (*In re* Commercial Money Center), 350 B.R. 465 (B.A.P. 9th Cir. 2006).

63 *Id.* at 479.

64 NetBank itself was never in possession of the leases and at the outset of the deal, the debtor was in possession of them. Later, one of the sureties in the deal took possession of the leases, and one of NetBank's arguments was that it had possession of the leases through the surety. In re *Commercial Money Center*, 350 B.R. at 471–473.

65 U.C.C. §9–310.

66 I use "interests" here rather than "security interests" because some sales are subject to Article 9, specifically the sales of accounts, chattel paper, promissory notes and payment intangibles. U.C.C. §9–109(a)(3). Another issue in *Commercial Money Center* was whether the debtor had sold or granted a security interest in the payment streams.

67 U.C.C. §9–309 (1).

exception is not troubling because it is rare that consumer goods are used twice as collateral.[68] Revised Article 9 added several other security interests that can be perfected without any type of public notice, such as security interests in deposit accounts,[69] and sales of payment intangibles and promissory notes.[70]

In *Commercial Money Center*, NetBank claimed that its interest in the payment streams arising from the chattel paper was perfected despite the absence of a filed financing statement and the failure of NetBank to take possession of the chattel paper. NetBank argued successfully that the payment streams arising from the chattel paper were not part of the chattel paper but instead payment intangibles. The court agreed that the payment streams were payment intangibles, so if NetBank had acquired its interest in them by sale, its interest would have been automatically perfected, that is, perfected without notice.[71] Because the court found that the transactions were loan transactions, not sales, NetBank was unperfected.

Commercial Money Center illustrates the divergence of Article 9 from the de Soto ideal. In its earliest form, Article 9 was designed to eliminate nonsensical distinctions among intangible assets and unify the law of secured transactions in personal property.[72] The writings of Grant Gilmore, one of Article 9's original drafters, are rife with suggestions that preview de Soto's contention that a clear method of determining rights in property is essential to economic growth. For instance, Gilmore identified the "sudden and enormous increase of industrial production dictated by the [World War II] effort" as the catalyst for financing secured by contract rights.[73] He describes contract rights financing as necessary to entrepreneurship. A corporation expanding into a new area of business is likely to organize a subsidiary to do so; that subsidiary's only valuable asset is likely to be its contract rights.[74] Likewise, new financing devices were necessary to allow small businesses to borrow money. Although Gilmore labels these businesses as "marginal borrowers," a term that would seem to make Article 9 a catalyst for the credit crisis of 2008–2009, Gilmore's marginal borrowers were the new

---

68 Non-purchase-money security interests in many consumer goods are considered unfair trade practices. 16 C.F.R. 444 (2005). Also, buyers of consumer goods need not worry about this exception, as buyers of consumer goods from consumers take free of security interests that are automatically perfected. §9–320(b).

69 A security interest in a deposit account is perfected by control (U.C.C. §9–312(b)(1)). Article 9 prescribes several methods of control, one of which, an agreement among the debtor, the secured party, and the depositary bank under which the bank agrees to follow the secured party's instructions regarding disposition of the funds in the account, gives no public notice. *See* U.C.C. §9–104 (listing requirements for control of a deposit account).

70 U.C.C. §9–309.

71 In re *Commercial Money Center*, 350 B.R. at 481.

72 Gilmore, Treatise, *supra* note 43, at §12.5.

73 Gilmore, *The Assignee of Contract Rights and his Precarious Security*, 74 Yale L.J. 217, 218 (1964).

74 Gilmore, *supra* note 73.

businesses that could not offer "the traditional types of collateral: real estate, industrial equipment, or securities to be left in pledge."[75]

As new borrowers and new types of collateral emerged, a plethora of new lending devices were developed. These new lending devices spawned new statutes and a multiplicity of filing systems. Article 9 was designed to simplify the business of financing so that the financing system could provide better information to prospective financiers.[76] Again, this makes Article 9, at least in its earlier incarnations, a statute that supports de Soto's thesis. The drafters recognized that a multiplicity of filing systems made credit information "more difficult and expensive to find," and therefore potentially useless.[77]

Revised Article 9, as interpreted by *Commercial Money Center*, upsets this plan in several ways. First, as noted above, it allows for unpublicized security interests in transactions in which the failure to publicize can wreak great havoc. Revised Article 9 also created a new collateral category, "payment intangibles." A payment intangible is defined as a "general intangible under which the account debtor's principal obligation is a monetary obligation."[78] To the non-expert, this looks like a fairly broad definition, but it was in fact designed to be very narrow. A payment intangible must first be a general intangible, and a general intangible cannot be, among other things, an account.[79] The definition of account encompasses most payment rights that are not embodied in paper, and that definition was expanded in Revised Article 9 to facilitate securitization.[80] The payment intangible category was added to respond to concerns from the banking industry that even the sale of loan participations could fall under Article 9 and that imposing a filing requirement on the banks selling loan participations would be wasteful.

Many are disturbed by *Commercial Money Center*. Some commentators believe that courts should not recognize payment rights stripped from chattel paper as a separate category of collateral, while others argue that payment stripping is a sound commercial practice but not effectively governed by Article 9. While the nature of the concerns may differ, both types of concern illustrate why our laws governing intangibles might not conform to de Soto's ideal Western capitalist system.

One criticism of *Commercial Money Center* is that the court disregarded what should be a clear collateral category under Article 9: chattel paper. Article 9 was designed to govern all types of secured financing transactions, thus replacing the existing scheme of different financing transactions being governed by different laws. According to Gilmore, the "only residue from the original plan" to have

---

75 Gilmore, *The Secured Transactions Article of the Commercial Code*, 16 Law & Contemp. Probs. 27, 29 (1951).

76 Gilmore, *supra* note 75, at 32.

77 Gilmore, *supra* note 75, at 32.

78 U.C.C. §9–102(a)(61).

79 U.C.C. §9–102(a)(42).

80 *See generally* Paul M. Shupack, *Making Revised Article 9 Safe for Securitizations: A Brief History*, 73 Am. Bankr. L.J. 167 (1999).

different parts of Article 9 for different types of transactions was the retention of collateral categories.[81] There are three broad categories of collateral under Article 9: goods, which is the category encompassing various types of tangible personal property, and then two types of intangible collateral, described by Gilmore as "pledgeable intangibles" and pure, or "non-pledgeable" intangibles.[82] While Gilmore himself suggested that Article 9 contained too many categories (in its earlier form, it contained a separate category called "contract rights"),[83] there is no evidence that anyone thought that the categories of pledgeable and non-pledgeable intangibles should be merged.

As noted several times in this chapter, de Soto's desired certainty in property rights includes not just a definite and easy-to-use filing or recording system, but also a set of clearly defined property rights. Without this clear definition of property rights, it is nearly impossible to determine the holders of the right (including those who have extended credit against it) and the method by which the right can be transferred. This is the danger of the *Commercial Money Center* case. While the court recognized that the policy behind the U.C.C. is to "provide certainty in financial transactions and some means for third parties to discover competing interests in property,"[84] it came to a decision that does neither.

Chattel paper is defined in the U.C.C. as "a record or records that *evidence* both a monetary obligation and a security interest in specific goods … [or] a lease of specific goods."[85] The *Commercial Money Center* court, in interpreting this definition, found that the U.C.C. "distinguishes between the monetary obligation *evidenced* by the chattel paper and the chattel paper itself," allowing it to hold that "[p]ayment streams stripped from underlying leases are not records that evidence monetary obligations, they *are* monetary obligations."[86] This interpretation seems counter, however, to the whole idea of chattel paper as a pledgeable intangible.

Perhaps the use of the word "evidence" in the chattel paper definition is misleading. As Julian McDonnell has pointed out, chattel paper does not *evidence* a payment right, it *embodies* a payment right.[87] Although this reading might at first appear counter to the U.C.C.'s clear language, one must consider the fact that the U.C.C. allows—in fact, prefers in many instances—perfection of a security interest in chattel paper by possession.[88] If one sees the chattel paper as an embodiment of

---

81 Gilmore, *supra* note 32, at 295.

82 Gilmore, *supra* note 32, at 295.

83 *See* GILMORE, TREATISE, *supra* note 43, at §12.5 (1965).

84 In re *Commercial Money Center*, 350 B.R. at 477.

85 U.C.C. §9–102(a)(11) (emphasis added).

86 In re *Commercial Money Center*, 350 B.R. at 475–476 (emphasis in original).

87 PETER F. COOGAN, WILLIAM E. HOGAN, DETLEV F. VAGTS AND JULIAN B. MCDONNELL, 1 SECURED TRANSACTIONS UNDER THE UNIFORM COMMERCIAL CODE §28.02 [1](a) (2008).

88 U.C.C. §9–313(a) (allowing perfection by possession for chattel paper); 9–330(a), (b) (granting priority in chattel paper to certain purchasers (including secured parties) who take possession of the chattel paper).

a payment right, is should be impossible to strip that right from the remainder of the chattel paper.[89]

One argument advanced by the bankruptcy trustee in *Commercial Money Center* was that the provision allowing automatic perfection of sales of payment intangibles was intended to address only loan participations.[90] While the official comments to Article 9 merely include the loan participation as an example of a payment intangible,[91] much commentary on Revised Article 9 supports the trustee's contention.[92] The lack of clear statutory guidance is dangerous in that the collateral categories were designed to provide useful information. To de Soto, clear property definitions are essential, in that they allow transfers and combinations of assets.

Even those commentators who agree that payment stripping is a necessary component of securitization transactions have argued that the automatic perfection regime allowed by Article 9 is faulty. Tom Plank, recognizing that "any legal system regulating the transfer of property should reflect the nature of both the property item and transactions involving the property item,"[93] argues for a different statute, separate from Article 9, to govern the sale of receivables. Steven Schwarcz would like to see a filing requirement included in Article 9 for all transfers of payment intangibles.[94] There are many ways to alleviate the problem of faculty communication about intangibles in our secured credit system, but there seems to be agreement on one point: the system needs to be repaired.

Conclusion

Turning back to de Soto's ideal property system, the American system works in that it supports lending on a basic level very well. The systems for transferring and publicizing interests in real property and tangible personal property are well-established. As de Soto recognizes, such well-established systems are important

89 LexisNexis Expert Commentaries, Julian McDonnell on Stripping Payment Streams from Chattel Paper (2007).

90 In re *Commercial Money Center*, 350 B.R. at 478.

91 U.C.C. §9–109, Official Comment 5.

92 *See* Steven L. Schwarcz, *Automatic Perfection of Sales of Payment Intangibles: A Trap for the Unwary*, 68 Ohio St. L.J. 273, 274 (2007) (explaining that the provision allowing the automatic perfection of the sale of a payment intangible was the result of "a political compromise between the drafters of Article 9 and the banking lobby," because the banks were concerned that Revised Article 9 would force them to file financing statements for the sale of loan participations, which was contrary to well-established practice); Shupack, *supra* note 79, at 174–176 (explaining the various proposals that would exempt banks selling loan participations from an Article 9 filing requirement).

93 Thomas E. Plank, *Assignment of Receivables Under Article 9: Structural Incoherence and Wasteful Filing*, 68 Ohio St. L.J. 231, 232–233 (2007).

94 Schwarcz, *supra* note 92, at 275–276 (noting that banks "may routinely regard rights to payment under leases as payment intangibles").

engines of economic development. As economies become more sophisticated, however, with intangible assets taking on greater economic importance, a property system must clearly define the menu of available rights in a variety of intangible assets.

It would also be negligent not to mention, especially in light of the 2008–2009 financial crisis, that a system that notifies the world that a property right exists is useless unless participants in that system can determine the monetary value of those rights.[95] As intangible assets grow in importance, it is crucial to both keep de Soto's description of a well-developed property system in mind and implement the components of that system in our secured credit laws.

---

95 Anna Schwartz, the co-author, with Milton Friedman, of *A Monetary History of the United States*, described the 2008 credit crisis as a crisis of information rather than a liquidity crisis. She described "toxic securities" as the root of the problem, explaining that the securities are "toxic because you cannot sell them, you don't know what they're worth, your balance sheet is not credible and the whole market freezes up" (Brian M. Carney, *The Weekend Interview with Anna Schwartz*, Wall St. Journal, October 18–19, 2008 at A11).

Chapter 11
The Economics of Welfare: Of Hernando de Soto and Susette Kelo

Denis J. Brion

In 2005, the U.S. Supreme Court announced its controversial decision in *Kelo v. City of New London*.[1] This case involved a large-scale redevelopment project on a substantial tract of land along the Thames riverfront in New London, Connecticut. The project plan was developed by a public corporation, the New London Development Corporation (NLDC), in order to convert the riverfront land from a mix of economically modest residential and light commercial uses divided among a large number of small-scale private owners to a different mix of primarily intensive commercial and high-end residential uses, also in private ownership.

When NLDC began to encounter resistance in the process of assembling the development tract by negotiation with the individual owners, the municipal government of New London agreed to exercise its power of eminent domain to assist in the assemblage of the development tract. This would remove a barrier (a holdout) to the market reallocation of the land in the development tract to an economically more intensive use, a reallocation that would increase the aggregate wealth of the community, thereby serving the general economic welfare.

Several of the modest property owners in the development tract who were subjected to the eminent domain taking of their property resorted to the Connecticut courts to challenge the legitimacy of the taking, a challenge based on two grounds. First, the constitutional basis for the eminent domain power, embodied in the Taking Clause ("nor shall private property be taken for public use without just compensation")[2] limits textually the purposes for its exercise to public uses. The uses proposed for the redevelopment, however, would be for the most part private. Second, in any event, there had not been an adequate showing that this redevelopment would actually serve the general economic welfare.

In its *Kelo* decision, the Supreme Court rejected these challenges. Ratifying its 1954 decision in *Berman v. Parker*,[3] a case substantially similar analytically

---

1 545 U.S. 469 (2005). Detailed accounts of the controversy over the decision are set out in Jeff Benedict, Little Pink House: A True Story of Defiance and Courage, 310–336 (2009); Carla T. Main, Bulldozed: "Kelo," Eminent Domain, and the American Lust for Land, 171–194 (2007).

2 U.S. Const., amend. V.

3 348 U.S. 26 (1954).

to *Kelo*, the Court held that a private use with a substantial benefit to the public economic welfare satisfies the *public use* criterion of the Taking Clause. As to the adequacy of the public benefit justification offered for the redevelopment project, the Court held that this was a legislative finding of government, to which the judiciary is to accord substantial deference. The Court thus declined to review the public benefit justification offered for the redevelopment project.

The Preamble to the U.S. Constitution provides, "We the People of the United States, in Order to … promote the general Welfare … ."[4] The subject of this chapter is economic welfare. The context is the matter of the assemblage of tracts of land by private actors in the land market for redevelopment to more economically intensive uses—uses that strongly tend to generate an increase in the aggregate wealth of society. The focus is a problem of market breakdown, that the holdout phenomenon acts as a substantial barrier to assemblage and thus to the enhancement of the aggregate wealth of society.

Market breakdown is a significant matter in a polity based on market capitalism. Assemblage is a significant matter as well. Benjamin Franklin memorably asserted, "But in this world nothing can be said to be certain, except death and taxes."[5] A history of the United States can be written as an ongoing pattern of migrations, each necessitating new patterns of land use. To Franklin's short list of certainties can be added the ongoing demand for the redevelopment of land, for which assemblage often is an enabling step.

The argument offered in this chapter is as follows. Assume that it can be shown conclusively that a redevelopment project will create substantial wealth, which can be captured in part through the system of taxation and devoted to public purposes. Despite this anticipated enhancement to the aggregate wealth of society, however, it cannot be shown that, if the power of eminent domain is exercised in order to make this redevelopment possible, carrying out the redevelopment will actually lead to an increase in the aggregate welfare of society. Moreover, a widespread use of eminent domain assemblage is likely to result in a systematic erosion of aggregate welfare. Thus, the consequences of the application of the *Kelo* Doctrine, justified for its purpose of smoothing the path for private entrepreneurial activity that will increase aggregate welfare, are perverse.

This argument sounds deeply in the seminal book by Hernando de Soto[6] that provides the touchstone for the chapters in this book. In Third World countries, de Soto argues, mature market systems of capitalist production have not emerged because a considerable portion of their productive resources are not, in a legal sense, formally owned by those who actually hold those resources; and there is no formal ownership because of the considerable administrative barriers to

---

4 U.S. Const., pmbl.

5 *Letter to Jean Baptiste Le Roy*, Nov. 13, 1789, *in* OXFORD DICTIONARY OF QUOTATIONS, 293 (Angela Partington, ed., rev. 4th ed., 1996).

6 HERNANDO DE SOTO, THE MYSTERY OF CAPITAL: WHY CAPITALISM TRIUMPHS IN THE WEST AND FAILS EVERYWHERE ELSE [hereinafter MYSTERY OF CAPITAL] (2000).

establishing that ownership. The consequence is that those resources are not, in an economic sense, capital. Underlying de Soto's argument is the proposition that the economic welfare of a society is maximized when all productive resources have become capital so that, in response to the forces of market action, these resources will be allocated efficiently—that is, to those uses that are the most productive of wealth.

We have, then, two apparently inconsistent assertions about the consequences of allocation of land to more economically productive uses. On the one hand, consistent with de Soto's position, the market reallocation of productive resources to economically more intensive private uses advances the aggregate economic welfare of society. On the other hand, the systematic reallocation of land to economically more intensive private uses through eminent domain assemblage, in order to escape the effects of market breakdown, erodes the aggregate economic welfare of society.

The purpose of this chapter is, in particular, to argue that these assertions about the welfare consequences of the reallocation of land to economically more intensive uses are actually not inconsistent. Indeed, it is to show that the perverse welfare consequences of the *Kelo* Doctrine are actually entailed by de Soto's conclusions. Thus, the purpose is to explore the link between de Soto's concept of full capitalization of productive resources and the economic welfare of society.

Assemblage

The history of the United States can be understood as a history of recurring migrations,[7] beginning in the early seventeenth century with the migration of immigrant Europeans, from the Atlantic Coast to the Pacific, in the process reallocating the land to a pattern of land use in nearly all instances more intensive than the uses by the displaced native population. Other migrations of varying scope and direction arose and took place both during and after the major migration from East to West that substantially had ended by the 1890s.[8]

In the early nineteenth century, as the Industrial Revolution proceeded, the burgeoning mill towns of the Northeast attracted an influx of young people from the surrounding rural areas to work in the new mills.[9] New waves of European immigration provided workers for the heavy industries and the railroads, and the coal mines that fed them,[10] that developed in the aftermath of the Civil War.

---

7 FREDERICK JACKSON TURNER, THE FRONTIER IN AMERICAN HISTORY (1920); Lewis Mumford, *The Fourth Migration*, 7 Survey Graphic 130 (May 1925).

8 TURNER, *supra* note 7.

9 LOUIS HUNTER, A HISTORY OF INDUSTRIAL POWER IN THE UNITED STATES, 1780–1930, vol. I: WATER POWER IN THE CENTURY OF THE STEAM ENGINE (1979).

10 RONALD D ELLER, MINERS, MILLHANDS, AND MOUNTAINEERS: INDUSTRIALIZATION OF THE APPALACHIAN SOUTH, 1880–1930 (1982).

The early twentieth century saw the rise of streetcar[11] and railroad[12] suburbs, the beginning of an outmigration from the central cities that would become massive in scope in later years. In the 1930s, considerable numbers fled the Dust Bowl for the more hospitable climate of Southern California.[13] In the 1940s through 1960s, large numbers of African Americans migrated from the cotton fields of the deep South to the industrial areas of the upper Midwest, particularly to Chicago.[14]

Soon after the end of the Second World War, the massive suburbanization of the major cities began. At the same time, people began to leave the colder climate of the upper Midwest for the far sunnier climate of California and the economic opportunities in its growing aerospace industries. In the later twentieth century, however, a reverse migration from the dispersed suburbs back to the urban core began as people, particularly empty-nesters, sought the amenities not found in the monotonous tract-house and strip-mall landscapes of the traffic-choked suburbs. This migration has become coupled with a new migration from the breadbasket areas of the heartland to urban areas as family farming has been displaced by large-scale industrial farming that requires far fewer workers. These two migrations have resulted in the more intensive development of the inner rings the original suburbs, giving rise, in some of the larger urban areas, to the phenomenon of edge cities, typically located at the exits of beltways that ring such places as Atlanta and Washington, D.C.[15] And, beginning with the first generation to retire with full Social Security benefits, there has been a considerable ongoing migration of retirees from the northern areas to such warm areas as Florida and Arizona.

As the current epicycles of migration play out, it is perhaps not entirely possible to predict what particular patterns of inner migrations might occur in the near future. As enterprise in the United States continues to shift from heavy manufacturing to the manipulation of information and ideas,[16] however, it is possible that the increasing capability to move information electronically long distances at continually decreasing cost might continue to result in the dispersal of routine information-handling tasks from high-wage, high-real-estate-cost areas to areas of substantially lower costs, smaller towns and cities far from the large population centers. On the other hand, a commentator considering what changes might come about in the aftermath of the global economic crisis that began in 2008, foresaw a

11 Henry C. Binford, The First Suburbs: Residential Communities on the Boston Periphery, 1815–1860 (1988).

12 *E.g.*, Carl W. Condit, The Port of New York: A History of the Rail and Terminal System from the Beginnings to Pennsylvania Station (1980); Harold M. Mayer and Richard C. Wade, Chicago: Growth of a Metropolis (1969).

13 An intimate, though fictional, portrait is presented in John Steinbeck, The Grapes of Wrath (1939).

14 Nicholas Lemann, The Promised Land: The Great Black Migration and How it Changed America (1991).

15 Joel Garreau, Edge City: Life on the New Frontier (1988).

16 Robert B. Reich, The Work of Nations: Preparing Ourselves for 21st Century Capitalism (1991).

concentration of the better educated and more creative in the small number of large metropolitan areas that are centers of a diversity of creative industries making up an innovative economy.[17] Or, if even the most cautious predictions of the effects of global warming come to pass, there will be a massive shift of the population northward.[18] Whatever might come to pass, it would seem to involve little risk to predict a continuing pattern of inner migration in the United States.

At the same time, there is occurring a steady immigration to the United States literally from around the globe. A quick perusal of the restaurant listings in the telephone directory of any even medium-sized city will demonstrate how polyglot the United States is becoming. With this continual flow of immigration and the ongoing epicycles of inner migrations, there is a continual demand for the redevelopment of land.

Moreover, beginning in the latter half of the twentieth century, land developers have increasingly turned to carrying out land redevelopment through the vehicle of large-scale, integrated projects involving a mix of uses. Thus, there has been, and most likely will continue to be, a substantial demand for the assemblage of extensive development tracts from existing patterns of fragmented land ownership. Assemblage, then, is a significant matter in economic activity in the United States.

The economic problem that accompanies this ongoing demand for land assemblage is market breakdown. As the assembler purchases a substantial number of parcels in the target area by voluntary sale by parcel owners, the holders of the remaining parcels are now in a position to ask for a payment far above a remunerative amount, the upper limit being an amount slightly less than the developer's opportunity cost. This is the problem of holdout.

It is possible to assemble a substantial development tract if this is carried out in secret. A noteworthy example is the assemblage for Columbia, Maryland, a new town located between Baltimore and Washington, D.C. on a 15,000-acre rural tract in Howard County in the 1960s.[19] The assemblage was carried out through an elaborate structure of dummy corporations and purchasing agents that enabled the individual parcels making up the tract to be purchased without the public generally, and the landowners in the target area in particular, becoming aware that an assemblage was

17 Richard Florida, *How the Crash Will Reshape America*, THE ATLANTIC, March 2009, at 44, 49. Jane Jacobs graphically describes these urban economies as thriving on the synergism engendered by the spatial concentration of diversely creative people. JANE JACOBS, CITIES AND THE WEALTH OF NATIONS: PRINCIPLES OF ECONOMIC LIFE (1984). These areas include, in North America: "the Boston-New York-Washington Corridor, … Sun Belt centers like the Char-Lanta Corridor, Northern and Southern California, the Texas Triangle of Houston-San Antonio-Dallas, and Southern Florida's Tampa-Orlando-Miami area; the Pacific Northwest's Cascadia, stretching from Portland through Seattle to Vancouver; and both Greater Chicago and Tor-Buff-Chester in the Old Rust Belt" (Florida, *supra*, at 50).

18 Perhaps it is not too early to be thinking about acquiring a vacation home on the balmy shores of Hudson's Bay.

19 The conceptual approach to, and the planning, financing, and development of Columbia are described in GURNEY BRECKENFELD, COLUMBIA AND THE NEW CITIES (1971).

being carried out by a single entity. In this way, the holdout problem was avoided and the tract was assembled at an average per-acre cost that was within the target amount that the developer determined would be financially viable.[20]

Secrecy, however, cannot always be maintained. A far more typical large-scale land development project is the redevelopment of a substantial, economically down-scale part of an urban area. Particularly when the impetus for redevelopment comes from local or state government, the matter will quickly enter the arena of public attention and debate. Once that occurs, there will be strong potential for holdout as the development tract is assembled from the inevitably fragmented pattern of current land ownership. The problem can be eliminated only through some mechanism that forces the resisting target area property owner to yield ownership to the developer.

The exercise of the public power of eminent domain is just such a mechanism, a power reflected in the Taking Clause of the Fifth Amendment to the U.S. Constitution, "nor shall private property be taken for public use without just compensation." Under the traditional interpretation of this language, government may take private property, forcing an unwilling property owner to yield title, provided that the property is put to a public use and provided that the former property owner is given just compensation. The just-compensation requirement is typically treated judicially as meaning market value.[21]

For the developer unable to avoid the potential for holdout in assembling a development tract, the eminent domain power is an altogether attractive vehicle for carrying out the assemblage. For a municipal corporation, exercising the eminent domain power in order to assist a developer in assembling a development tract makes possible the carrying out of a project that will enhance the proceeds from the real property tax, a principal source of local government revenue. Moreover, the redevelopment project itself can address a matter of public concern, such as the elimination of a physically blighted area or the provision of substantial opportunities for employment in circumstances of a high rate of unemployment. There is, then, a synergy in the redevelopment of land between the pursuit of profit by private developers and the exercise of public functions by local government. It was in the undertaking of large-scale urban renewal that the legal controversy over public assistance of assemblage for private land development projects arose. The landmark decision of the U.S. Supreme Court in 1954 in *Berman v. Parker*[22] rejected a challenge to a redevelopment plan for a physically blighted area of the District of Columbia under which the eminent domain power would be used for assembling a development tract that would be put to largely private use.

In 1950, the National Capital Planning Commission, pursuant to the District of Columbia Redevelopment Act of 1945,[23] developed a comprehensive plan that

20 The elaborate precautions taken to maintain secrecy are described in Breckenfeld, *supra* note 19, at 224–243.

21 *United States v. Miller*, 317 U.S. 369 (1943).

22 348 U.S. 26 (1954).

23 60 Stat. 790 (1946), D.C. Code §§5-701–5-719 (1951).

provided for the redevelopment of a substantial area in the Southwest quadrant of the District, occupied predominantly by low-income African Americans, that was physically blighted. Under the plan, the District of Columbia Redevelopment Land Agency was to acquire the land in the designated area by eminent domain; clear it of its existing structures; establish a new pattern of infrastructure; transfer to the appropriate "public agencies the land to be devoted to such public purposes as streets, utilities, recreational facilities, and schools;"[24] and transfer the remainder of the land to private entities to be developed according to the pattern of uses provided in the plan drawn up by the Planning Commission.[25]

The owner of a going business in the redevelopment area, Schneider's Department Store, challenged the proposed eminent domain taking of his property, on the grounds that it was not in any way physically blighted, and thus was not an element of the conditions that the redevelopment project was designed to eliminate; and that the result of including it in the project would amount to a taking of private property for a private use, inconsistent with the express provisions of the Taking Clause.[26] The U.S. District Court upheld the constitutionality of the Redevelopment Act,[27] and the U.S. Supreme Court affirmed. The Court observed that the redevelopment project dealt with what traditionally has been known as the police power, "[s]ubject to specific constitutional limitations, when the legislature has spoken, the public interest has been declared in terms well-nigh conclusive. In such cases the legislature, not the judiciary, is the main guardian of the public needs to be served by social legislation …. The role of the judiciary in determining whether that power is being exercised for a public purpose is an extremely narrow one."[28]

Thus:

> The concept of the public welfare is broad and inclusive. … It is within the power of the legislature to determine that the community should be beautiful as well as healthy, spacious as well as clean, well-balanced as well as carefully patrolled. In the present case, the Congress and its authorized agencies have made determinations that take into account a wide variety of values. It is not for us to reappraise them.[29]

As to the eminent domain power:

> Once the object is within the authority of Congress, the right to realize it through the exercise of eminent domain is clear. For the power of eminent domain is merely

24 *Berman v. Parker*, 348 U.S. at 30.

25 *Id.* at 28–30.

26 *Id.* at 26.

27 *Schneider v. District of Columbia*, 117 F. Supp. 705 (D. D.C. 1953). Schneider passed away during the litigation process; his executor, Berman, was substituted as the named plaintiff.

28 *Berman v. Parker*, 348 U.S., at 32.

29 *Id.* at 33.

> the means to an end. … [T]he means of executing the project are for Congress and Congress alone to determine, once the public purpose has been established.[30]

Schneider, however, had challenged the means of the project—a complete clearing of the area, taking property in good condition as well as blighted property—instead of addressing only blighted property. This the Court also disposed of:

> In the present case, Congress and its authorized agencies attack the problem of blighted parts of the community on an area rather than on a structure-by-structure basis. That, too, is opposed by appellants. The experts concluded that … [i]t was important to redesign the whole area so as to eliminate the conditions that cause slums …. It was believed that the piecemeal approach, the removal of individual structures that were offensive would only be a palliative. … Property may of course be taken for this redevelopment which, standing by itself, is innocuous and unoffending.[31]

The Court concluded, "The rights of these property owners are satisfied when they receive that just compensation which the Fifth Amendment exacts as the price of the taking."[32]

The *Berman* Court thus set out the contours of the validity of large-scale urban renewal projects. It is permissible to take private property for a private use in the process of carrying out a redevelopment project that will advance the public welfare. And it is for the legislative arm of government to determine, with substantial deference by the judicial branch, what ends will serve the public welfare and what means are to be chosen for attaining those ends.

A state court approach to these issues was developed in the 1981 decision of the Michigan Supreme Court in *Poletown Neighborhood Council v. City of Detroit*.[33] This case involved another large-scale redevelopment project the taking by eminent domain of an identified ethnic neighborhood, the Poletown area that straddled the line between Hamtramk and Detroit, in order to assemble it into a single development tract; clearing it of all existing structures; installing a new system of infrastructure to the specifications of the automobile manufacturer General Motors; and transferring ownership of the tract to General Motors for its use for establishing an automobile assembly plant.[34]

In the justification that the City of Detroit offered for the project, "the city presented substantial evidence of the severe economic conditions facing the

---

30 *Berman v. Parker*, at 34.

31 *Id.* at 35–36.

32 *Id.* at 36.

33 304 N.W.2d 455 (Mich. 1981).

34 The acquisition and preparation costs to be incurred by the public for the tract was estimated to be $200.45 million; once it was prepared, the tract was to be sold to General Motors for $8 million. *Berman v. Parker*, at 469 and n. 7 (Ryan, J. dissenting).

residents of the city and state, the need for new industrial development to revitalize local industries, the economic boost the proposed project would provide, and the lack of other adequate sites to implement the project."[35] In particular, the assembly plant would provide some 6,000 jobs.[36]

A coalition of residents of the Poletown neighborhood, the Poletown Neighborhood Council, challenged "the constitutionality of using the power of eminent domain to condemn one person's property to convey it to another private person in order to bolster the economy."[37] The gist of its challenge was that "whatever incidental benefit may accrue to the public, assembling land to General Motors' specifications for conveyance to General Motors for its uncontrolled use in profit making is really a taking for private use and not a public use because General Motors is the primary beneficiary of the condemnation."[38]

In rejecting the Neighborhood Council's challenge, the Michigan Supreme Court held that the "power of eminent domain is to be used in this instance primarily to accomplish the essential public purposes of alleviating unemployment and revitalizing the economic base of the community. The benefit to a private interest is merely incidental."[39] The Court did not, however, express the strong deference to the findings of an administrative body as the U.S. Supreme Court had expressed to the legislature in *Berman v. Parker*:

> The power of eminent domain is restricted to furthering public uses and purposes and is not to be exercised without substantial proof that the public is primarily to be benefitted. Where, as here, the condemnation power is exercised in a way that benefits specific and identifiable private interests, a court inspects with heightened scrutiny the claim that the public interest is the predominant interest being advanced. Such benefit cannot be speculative or marginal but must be clear and significant. … We hold that this project is warranted on the basis that its significance for the people of Detroit and the state has been demonstrated.[40]

In *Berman v. Parker*, the U.S. Supreme Court had held, in effect, that the eminent domain power can validly be exercised to assemble a development tract for private uses if there will be a substantial consequential public benefit. The Michigan Supreme Court held, somewhat differently, that the eminent domain power can validly be exercised to assemble a development tract for private uses if the predominant interest being advanced is public rather than private. The U.S. Supreme Court described the public benefit in the case of the District of Columbia redevelopment in the somewhat softer terms of aesthetics and order rather than

35 *Berman v. Parker*, at 459.
36 *Id.* at 468, n. 6 (Ryan, J. dissenting).
37 *Id.* at 458.
38 *Id.* at 458.
39 *Id.* at 459.
40 *Id.* at 459–460.

in the more easily quantifiable terms of economic gain. The Michigan Supreme Court described the public benefit in the case of the Detroit redevelopment in predominantly economic terms.[41]

Berman v. Parker and *Poletown Neighborhood Council* exemplify two models of large-scale land redevelopment projects for which local government has exercised the eminent domain power to carry out the assemblage of the redevelopment tract. In *Berman v. Parker*, a publicly established planning agency, acting on a public mandate to address a perceived problem in the quality of a portion of the built environment, develops a plan for a new, economically more intensive pattern of uses in that area.[42] In *Poletown*, an entrepreneur determines that a portion of the built environment, currently in an economically modest pattern of use, would be a suitable location for an economically more intensive entrepreneurial use. In the *Berman v. Parker* model, the demand for the more intensive use is determined by an entity with expertise in urban planning, in accordance with professional planning principles. In the *Poletown* model, the demand for more intensive use is determined by an entrepreneur.

In *Kelo v. City of New London*,[43] the U.S. Supreme Court turned to the consequential public benefit of eminent domain assemblage stated in predominantly economic terms. By the late 1990s, New London was in economic decline.[44] In 1996, the Naval Undersea Warfare Center, located in the Fort Trumbull area, a peninsula that extended into the Thames River, was closed, contributing to the economic decline. The State government had become interested in supporting the economic revitalization of New London. To this end, respondent New London Development Corporation (NLDC), a private non-profit entity established some years earlier to assist the City in planning economic development, was reactivated.[45] As a result of the efforts of NLDC, the Pfizer pharmaceutical company decided to establish a research facility on a vacant tract adjacent to the Fort Trumbull area. The City

41 In *County of Wayne v. Hathcock*, 684 N.W.2d 765 (2004), the Michigan Supreme Court overruled the holding in *Poletown* that equated a private use that provides a public economic benefit to a public use.

42 This is the problem of "blight." The assumption is that, if a portion of the urban fabric is in a physically degraded pattern of use, then there is a misallocation of resources, and a consequent inefficiency. Otto A. Davis and Andrew B. Whinston, in *The Economics of Urban Renewal*, 26 Law & Contemp. Probs. 105 (1961), demonstrated, however, that the fact that there is physical blight according to some exogenous aesthetic standard or other, does not mean that there is economic blight, in the form of an inefficient allocation of resources, and the current supply of physical structures in that area may well be meeting a current demand. To put the matter bluntly, poor people live in crummy housing because they do not have any money to afford better.

43 545 U.S. 469 (2005).

44 The relevant facts are set out in 545 U.S. 469 (2005), at 473–475. Extensive accounts of the course of the New London redevelopment are set out in *Kelo v. City of New London*, 843 A.2d 500 (Conn. 2004); Benedict, *supra* note 1.

45 *Kelo*, 545 U.S., at 473.

then charged NLDC to draw up plans for the redevelopment of a 90-acre tract in the Fort Trumbull area. NLDC formulated an extensive redevelopment plan calling for a conference hotel, restaurant and retail establishments, office space, and residences on the tract:

> The NLDC intended the development plan to capitalize on the arrival of the Pfizer facility and the new commerce it was expected to attract. In addition to creating jobs, generating tax revenue, and helping to "build momentum for the revitalization of downtown New London," the plan was also designed to make the City more attractive and to create leisure and recreational opportunities on the waterfront and in the park.[46]

The City approved the plan in 2000 and authorized NLDC to assemble the redevelopment tract by purchase or by eminent domain.

Nine individuals, including named party Susette Kelo, owning 15 parcels in the redevelopment area, resisted the acquisition of their properties by purchase. When NLDC initiated eminent domain proceedings against these properties, these nine individuals brought an action against the City and NLDC in New London Superior Court challenging the taking of their property as a violation of the *public use* criterion of the Taking Clause. The Superior Court granted a permanent restraining order prohibiting the taking of the properties located in parcel 4A (park or marina support). It, however, denied petitioners relief as to properties located in parcel 3 (office space).[47] On appeal, the Connecticut Supreme Court held that all of the proposed takings were constitutionally valid.[48]

The U.S. Supreme Court affirmed the judgment of the Connecticut Supreme Court. In doing so, the Court ratified the import of long-standing precedent that the Taking Clause term *public use* is to be understood expansively, a principle that embraces several distinct but related propositions. First, public use includes a direct private use that will serve a derivative public purpose: "[W]hen this Court began applying the Fifth Amendment to the States at the close of the 19th century, it embraced the broader and more natural interpretation of public use as 'public purpose.'"[49]

The Court then cited with approval[50] *Berman v. Parker*,[51] *Hawaii Housing Auth. v. Midkiff*,[52] and *Ruckleshaus v. Monsanto Co.*,[53] which embraced the proposition that public purpose includes a private use that will provide a derivative public

46 *Kelo*, 545 U.S., at 474–475.

47 *Id.* at 475–476.

48 *Kelo v. City of New London*, 843 A.2d 500 (Conn. 2004).

49 *Kelo*, 545 U.S., at 480 (*citing Strickley v. Highland Boy Gold Mining Co.*, 200 U.S. 527, 531 (1906); *Fallbrook Irrigation Dist. v. Bradley*, 164 U.S. 112, 158–164 (1896)).

50 *Kelo*, 545 U.S., at 480–482.

51 348 U.S. 26 (1954).

52 467 U.S. 229 (1984).

53 467 U.S. 986 (1984).

benefit. The public benefit in *Berman v. Parker* was the elimination of an urban area marked by substantial physical blight: "If those who govern the District of Columbia decide that the Nation's Capital should be beautiful as well as sanitary, there is nothing in the Fifth Amendment that stands in the way."[54] In *Midkiff*, "the State's purpose of eliminating the 'social and economic evils of a land oligopoly' qualified as a valid public use."[55] The public benefit in *Ruckleshaus v. Monsanto Co.* was that taking private proprietary information for the use of a competitor "eliminated a significant barrier to entry in the pesticide market and thereby enhanced competition."[56]

With this expansive concept of the public benefit that would constitute a public purpose, it remained for the *Kelo* Court only to include in this concept the economically more intensive redevelopment of non-blighted land[57] for private use that will provide employment and the enhanced flow of tax revenues to the locality. The *Kelo* plaintiffs argued for "a new bright-line rule that economic development does not qualify as a public use."[58] This the Court declined to do:

> The City has carefully formulated an economic development plan that it believes will provide appreciable benefits to the community, including but by no means limited to new jobs and increased tax revenue. ... Because that plan unquestionably serves a public purpose, the takings challenged here satisfy the public use requirement of the Fifth Amendment.[59]

The *Kelo* plaintiffs, however, argued for a heightened form of review in circumstances of the exercise of the eminent domain power for economic development.[60] In *Berman v. Parker*, the Court had held that, "[s]ubject to specific constitutional limitations, when the legislature has spoken, the public interest has been declared in terms well-nigh conclusive."[61] Thus, "[o]nce the object is within the authority of Congress, the right to realize it through the exercise of eminent domain is clear. For the power of eminent domain is merely the means to the end."[62] The *Kelo* Court rejected the argument for a heightened form of review by quoting *Midkiff*:

> When the legislature's purpose is legitimate and its means are not irrational, our cases make clear that empirical debates over the wisdom of takings no less than

54 467 U.S. 986 (1984), at 481 (*quoting Berman v. Parker*, 348 U.S., at 33).

55 *Kelo*, 545 U.S., at 482 (*quoting Midkiff*, 467 U.S., at 241–242).

56 *Id.* at 482 (*citing Ruckleshaus v. Monsanto Co.*, 467 U.S., at 1015).

57 "There is no allegation that any of these properties is blighted or otherwise in poor condition; rather, they were condemned only because they happen to be located in the development area." *Id.* at 475.

58 *Id.* at 484.

59 *Id.* at 483–484.

60 *Id.* at 487.

61 *Berman v. Parker*, 348 U.S., at 32.

62 *Id.* at 33.

> debates over the wisdom of other kinds of socioeconomic legislation are not to be carried out in the federal courts.[63]

Thus, as to the New London redevelopment plan, attaining the public benefit of new jobs and enhanced tax revenue is a legitimate end; exercising the eminent domain power for direct private uses is a reasonable means.

Finally, the *Kelo* Court addressed the matter of the *just compensation* standard of the Taking Clause: "In affirming the City's authority to take petitioners' properties, we do not minimize the hardship that condemnations may entail, notwithstanding the payment of just compensation."[64] The Court noted, however: "The *amici* raise questions about the fairness of the measure of just compensation. … While important, these questions are not before us in this litigation."[65] Thus, the *Kelo* litigation left intact the long-standing doctrine that the standard for measuring just compensation is fair market value, defined as "what a willing buyer would pay in cash to a willing seller."[66] Just compensation does not include any subjective value that the owner might have in the property.[67] Nor does it include consequential damages, such as moving expenses or loss of business good will.[68] Thus, the Supreme Court's interpretation of the just compensation criterion of the Taking Clause provides limited actual compensation, falling far short of the economic measure of full compensation, the amount of money the utility value of which, to the property owner, would equal her utility value in the property.

Emerging from the *Kelo* decision is a reading of the Taking Clause that finds no constitutional barriers to the exercise of the public power of eminent domain to assist a private developer in assembling the several properties needed for the development tract. The *public use* criterion of the Taking Clause includes a direct private use for a derivative public purpose. *Public purpose* includes a direct private use with a consequential public benefit. *Public benefit* includes the added employment opportunities and enhancement of tax revenues consequent on the more economically intensive private use of the redeveloped land. The determination of the local legislature that a public benefit will result from the private redevelopment of land is "well-nigh conclusive" under the substantially deferential ends-means test. The use of the public power of eminent domain is a reasonable means for achieving this public benefit. Add to this the corollary principle that the measure of the *just compensation* criterion is the limited standard of fair market value. Although not all of the elements of this reading of the Taking

63 *Kelo*, 545 U.S., at 488 (*quoting Hawaii Housing Auth. v. Midkiff*, 467 U.S., at 242–243).

64 *Id.* at 489.

65 *Id.* at 489 n.21.

66 *United States v. Miller*, 317 U.S. 369, 374 (1943).

67 *United States v. 50 Acres of Land*, 469 U.S. 24, 35 (1984); *Kimball Laundry Co. v. United States*, 338 U.S. 1, 5 (1949).

68 *United States v. Miller*, 317 U.S., at 376.

Clause are specific holdings in *Kelo*, for convenience of discussion this reading will be referred to as the *Kelo* Doctrine.

The Economics of Welfare

Under the *Kelo* Doctrine, the public power of eminent domain can validly be exercised to carry out an assemblage for the redevelopment of land for private uses. This exercise of the eminent domain power is justified when the redevelopment provides a consequential public benefit. It is this public benefit that satisfies the *public use* criterion of the Taking Clause.

In the understanding of the *Kelo* Court, the justifying public benefit of the New London redevelopment project was that it would provide substantial employment opportunities and an enhanced flow of local tax revenues for a city with a high unemployment rate and a generally depressed economy. This justification thus is about wealth—the New London riverfront land will be redeveloped to an economically more intensive use, and some portion of this newly-created wealth will accrue to the City and its inhabitants.

What clearly seems to underlie this justification is the commonsense proposition that a net increase in the aggregate wealth of society will enhance the aggregate economic welfare. The justification offered for the Court's interpretation of the *public use* criterion thereby lies in the realm of welfare economics. Thus, an understanding of the historical development and principal propositions of welfare economics will be altogether relevant to engaging in a critical analysis of the *Kelo* Doctrine.

In application, welfare economics consists of the economic analysis of proposals submitted to a public decision-maker for adoption. The decision-maker might be a legislature, a member of the judiciary, an official of the executive, or an administrative agency. The proposal might relate to a change in policy, a change in legal doctrine, or a discrete entrepreneurial project. The question of relevance is what impact will the adoption of the proposal have on the aggregate economic welfare.

A useful place to begin is with the work of the Italian economist Vilfredo Pareto. In the *Manual of Political Economy*,[69] he developed a test for the welfare consequences of the implementation of a proposal. There is a welfare improvement if at least one person is made better off and no one is made worse off. The economy is at a welfare optimum if there are no proposals available that meet the criteria for a welfare improvement.[70] Implicit in this formulation is a compensation principle, that, in the implementation of a proposal, anyone who will suffer a loss will be fully compensated for that loss by those who will gain.

---

69 Vilfredo Pareto, Manual of Political Economy (Ann S. Schwier trans., A.M. Kelley 1971) (1906).

70 *Id.* at 251–279.

The English economist A.C. Pigou developed a detailed analytical framework for welfare economics in *Wealth and Welfare*[71] and *The Economics of Welfare*.[72] Pigou divided welfare economics into two principal parts, production and distribution. Production relates to the matter of the size of the national dividend, the ongoing production of wealth, which is maximized when the values of the marginal social net products across all productive activities are equal.[73] Distribution relates to the pattern by which societal wealth is distributed among all its members, and the effect of different patterns of distribution on the magnitude of the national dividend.[74]

Lying at the core of Pigou's theories is the proposition that economic welfare is properly measured in terms of utility and not wealth. The problem with this approach is that it is not possible either to measure the utility position of an individual directly or to make interpersonal comparisons of utility. Thus, to Pigou's critics, there were considerable difficulties in applying his approach in practice. Pigovian welfare economics, that is, was prescriptive and "soft" rather than objectively scientific and "hard."

In the late 1930s, the English economists Nicholas Kaldor and John R. Hicks undertook to re-establish welfare economics on a scientific basis. They set out on this endeavor through two relatively short papers, published in 1939, which, in retrospect, have come to be regarded, at least in the general discourse of public policy, as seminal. The result was what came to be called the New Welfare Economics.

Nicholas Kaldor's "Welfare Propositions of Economics and Inter-Personal Comparisons of Utility"[75] addresses the problem that, in the mainstream discourse on welfare economics, the status of prescriptions necessarily depends on the status of the comparisons.[76] That is, the economist's recommendation as to whether a proposal ought to be adopted is based on interpersonal comparisons of utility. Such comparisons, however, cannot be made in practice.

In Pigou's division of welfare economics into matters of production and matters of distribution, Kaldor therefore asserts that production is by far the most important part.[77] Thus, Kaldor argues:

---

71 A.C. Pigou, Wealth and Welfare (1912).

72 A.C. Pigou, The Economics of Welfare (4th ed., 1932).

73 *Id.* at 131–141.

74 *Id.* at 645–693. Something of Pigou's position on the matter of wealth distribution may be gleaned from this statement in the preface to the third edition: "The complicated analyses which economists endeavour to carry through are not mere gymnastic. They are instruments for bettering of human life. The misery and squalor that surround us, the injurious luxury of some wealthy families, the terrible uncertainty overshadowing many families of the poor: these are evils too plain to be ignored. By the knowledge that our science seeks it is possibly that they may be restrained." *Id.* at vii.

75 Nicholas Kaldor, *Welfare Propositions of Economics and Inter-Personal Comparisons of Utility*, 49 Econ. J. 549 (1939). This is a quite short essay, slightly more than three pages in length.

76 *Id.* at 551.

77 *Id.*

> In all cases, therefore, where a certain policy leads to an increase in physical productivity, and thus of aggregate real income, the economist's case for the policy is quite unaffected by the question of the comparability of individual satisfactions; since in all such cases it is possible to make everybody better off than before, or at any rate to make some people better off without making anybody worse off. There is no need for the economist to prove as indeed he never could prove that as a result of the adoption of a certain measure nobody in the community is going to suffer. In order to establish his case, it is quite sufficient for him to show that even if all those who suffer as a result are fully compensated for their loss, the rest of the community will still be better off than before.[78]

Kaldor discusses the matter of satisfaction as it relates to the criteria "better off" and "worse off." It is not limited to the money value of income. It also includes such non-pecuniary losses as the loss of satisfaction from engaging in a particular kind of work and the interference with individual freedom consequent on the fact of governmental implementation of a policy.[79] Kaldor thus is defining satisfaction in terms of utility, although his ultimate proposition is expressed in terms of wealth.

Kaldor gives specific attention to the matter of wealth distribution:

> For it is quite impossible to decide on economic grounds what particular pattern of income-distribution maximizes social welfare. If the postulate of equal capacity for satisfaction is employed as a criterion, the conclusion inescapably follows that welfare is necessarily greatest when there is complete equality; yet one certainly cannot exclude the possibility of everybody being happier when there is some degree of inequality than under a régime of necessary and complete equality. (Here I am not thinking so much of differences in the capacity for satisfactions between different individuals, but of the satisfactions that are derived from the prospect of improving one's income by one's own efforts a prospect which is necessarily excluded when a régime of complete equality prevails.) And short of complete equality, how can the economist decide precisely how much inequality is desirable i.e., how much secures the maximum total satisfaction?[80]

Here, Kaldor is proceeding from the principle of declining marginal utility. On a static basis, given the postulate of equal capacity for satisfaction, aggregate utility will be maximized at an equal distribution of wealth across society. On a dynamic basis, however, giving a greater than equal share of efficiency gains to the more inventive and energetic, those who are more productive, provides them with an incentive to produce. The consequential increase in production, and thus in aggregate wealth, of itself increases aggregate welfare. If this welfare increase more than offsets the decrease in aggregate welfare caused by the departure

78 Kaldor, *supra* note 75, at 550.
79 *Id.* at 551 n.1.
80 *Id.* at 551–552.

from equal wealth distribution, then, as Kaldor asserts, a departure from equal distribution can lead to an increase in aggregate welfare.

The problem lies in the application of this concept of aggregate welfare in practice. It is possible, at least in concept, to measure the effect on aggregate productivity of giving an income incentive to the more productive. It is not possible to measure this effect in practice because it is not possible to hold constant all the other factors in the economy that affect productivity while, for example, the progressivity of the income tax is varied over time. Because utility cannot be measured directly, it is not possible either to measure the increase in aggregate utility resulting from an increase in aggregate wealth that is equally distributed or to measure the decrease in aggregate utility resulting from a departure from equality in wealth distribution. It is clear, however, that the implementation of a wealth-increasing measure that has the effect of increasing the spread in the distribution of wealth will erode aggregate economic welfare unless the measure has the effect of creating a productivity incentive.[81] Thus, as Kaldor asserts, "it is quite impossible to decide on economic grounds what particular pattern of income-distribution maximizes social welfare."[82]

This is not to say, however, that it is not possible to describe the general shape of a curve that plots aggregate utility against the degree of inequality in wealth distribution. It is just not possible to assign numerical values to the points on such a curve. It seems to be clear that a curve depicting aggregate welfare will rise from a point of wealth-distributional equality as the income incentive effect comes into play, reach a maximum point, and then, as the income incentive effect reaches a plateau and no longer offsets the now increasing distributional equality effect, aggregate welfare will erode, increasingly substantially.[83]

---

81 And, even then, if a productivity-incentive measure is implemented in circumstances in which the productivity incentive has already been fully exploited, this additional measure will have the effect of eroding aggregate welfare.

82 Kaldor, *supra* note 75, at 551.

83 This erosion is a consequence of declining population quality. *See* THEODORE W. SCHULTZ, INVESTING IN PEOPLE: THE ECONOMICS OF POPULATION QUALITY (1981). Nearly all members of a society are capable of being productive to a greater or lesser degree. As the spread in the distribution of wealth increases, the greater part of the population becomes increasingly ill-housed, ill-nourished, ill-clothed, poorly educated, and with inadequate access to preventive and acute health care. Such a population, as a whole, thereby becomes increasingly less productive. A detailed empirical study that demonstrates the correlation between the degree of inequality in the distribution of wealth across a society and such factors as lower life expectancy, illiteracy rates, infant mortality, homicide rate, imprisonment, teenage births, obesity, mental illness, low social mobility, and low rate of innovation is set out in KATE PICKETT & RICHARD WILKINSON, THE SPIRIT LEVEL: WHY GREATER EQUALITY MAKES SOCIETIES STRONGER (2009). These same factors do not correlate, in relatively wealthy societies, to average income, indicating that the stronger determinant of the level of aggregate social welfare is the magnitude of the spread in the distribution of wealth across society rather than the magnitude of the aggregate wealth of society.

Because of the practical problem of numerical determination, Kaldor asserts that whether those who are worse off because of the implementation of a proposal "should in fact be given compensation or not, is a political question on which the economist, *qua* economist, could hardly pronounce an opinion."[84] Thus, as to matters of distribution, Kaldor concludes, "All that economics can, and should, do in this field, is to show, given the pattern of income-distribution desired [that is, determined on political grounds], which is the most convenient way of bringing it about."[85]

Kaldor thus brackets the question of the pattern of wealth distribution from the advice that the economist gives to the decision-maker. Because of the insurmountable problem of utility measurement, the matter of the pattern of wealth distribution can be decided only on political grounds and not on scientific grounds.

Kaldor thus offers a hypothetical compensation form of the Pareto Test: there is a welfare improvement if those who gain by the implementation of a proposal could compensate those who lose and still be better off; compensation, however, need not actually be given in order for the improvement in aggregate welfare to accrue. And, although Kaldor defined "better off" and "worse off" in terms of satisfaction, which depends on utility rather than on wealth, he defines his hypothetical compensation concept in terms of wealth: the proposal ought to be adopted if the wealth gains of those who are better off would exceed the wealth losses of those who are worse off. Kaldor thereby avoids the problem of measuring utility, and offers a test that, according to his criteria, is scientific rather than soft.

John R. Hicks's *The Foundations of Welfare Economics*[86] is based on a presentation to the Economic Society of Stockholm in May 1939. His stated purpose, similar to that of Nicholas Kaldor, is "to put welfare economics on a secure basis, and to render it immune from positivist criticism."[87] His approach, he asserts, is to present a synthesis of the recent work of R.F. Harrod, Nicholas Kaldor, and Harold Hotelling.[88]

Hicks addresses two principal matters: the criterion for a welfare improvement and the distributional question. He begins with the proposition that optimum organization obtains when "the marginal rate of substitution between any two commodities must be the same for every individual (who consumes them both) and for every producing unit (which produces them both) in the whole economy."[89] Hicks then states a criterion for a welfare improvement that draws strongly on the criterion that Kaldor offered: "A 'permitted reorganisation' must thus be taken

84 Kaldor, *supra* note 75, at 550.

85 *Id.* at 552.

86 J.R. Hicks, *The Foundations of Welfare Economics*, 49 Econ. J. 696 (1939).

87 *Id.* at 711.

88 Hicks, *supra* note 86, at 698 (*citing* R.F. Harrod, *Scope and Method of Economics*, 48 Econ. J. 389 (1938); Kaldor, *supra* note 74; and Harold Hotelling, *The General Welfare in Relation to Problems of Taxation and of Railway and Utility Rates*, 6 Econometrica 242 (1938)).

89 Hicks, *supra* note 86, at 704.

from now on to mean a reorganisation which will allow of compensation being paid, and which will yet show a net advantage."[90]

Turning to the matter of wealth distribution, Hicks observes, "Every simple economic reform inflicts a loss on some people."[91] He addresses the compensation issue somewhat differently from Kaldor's approach. Kaldor carefully stated that the economist has nothing to offer in scientific terms to the decision-maker on the matter of compensation; thus, this is a political matter for the decision maker to determine. Hicks asserts:

> I do not contend that there is any ground for saying that compensation ought always be given; whether or not compensation should be given in any particular case is a question of distribution, upon which there cannot be identity of interest, and so there cannot be any generally acceptable principle.[92]

Because there "cannot be any generally acceptable principle"[93] by which a determination of whether to compensate can be made, Hicks is in agreement with Kaldor that the matter of compensation is one on which the economist cannot provide scientific advice to the decision-maker.

Hicks goes on, however, to assert:

> Nevertheless we must expect that there will be many other cases where the redistribution, resulting from a sound measure carried through without compensation, would be regarded by [the economist] as deplorable; and then, if he considers the measure in isolation from the question of compensation, he will pay no more than lip-service to its productive efficiency, and probably reject it in practice. From this, it is only a step to the state of mind which judges measures solely by reference to their distributive justice, without reference to their bearing on efficiency. If measures making for efficiency are to have a fair chance, it is extremely desirable that they should be freed from distributive complications as much as possible.
>
> We can make this separation in our own minds if we accustom ourselves, whenever we can, to thinking of every economic reform in close conjunction with some measure of compensation, designed to render it approximately innocuous from the distributive point of view.[94]

Hicks does not expressly state what distributive effect of a sound measure carried through would count as deplorable.[95] It is clear, however, that, in agreement

90 Hicks, *supra* note 86, at 706.

91 *Id.* at 711.

92 *Id.* at 711.

93 *Id.*

94 *Id.* at 712.

95 Perhaps it would be one that reduced some people to penury. Or perhaps one by which wealth is redistributed upwards in the economic scale, from the poor to the rich.

with Pigou's position,[96] an increase in the spread of the distribution of wealth is undesirable. What concerns Hicks, however, is not the occurrence of deplorable distributional consequences; instead, it is the psychological effect that the prospect of a deplorable distributional consequence might have on an economist in formulating advice to a decision-maker. Thus, consistently with Kaldor, Hicks treats the matter of distributional consequences as entirely separate from the matter of a welfare improvement. Also consistently with Kaldor, who asserts that wealth production is by far the most important part, Hicks defines a welfare improvement in terms of greater efficiency in resource allocation, which has the consequence of increasing the production of wealth. Thus as well, Kaldor and Hicks define efficiency in terms of a net increase in wealth production, inconsistently with Pareto, who defined an efficient move as one that results in a net increase in wealth production but that leaves no one worse off.[97]

These two papers had considerable influence, establishing the basis for the new welfare economics. What has come to be called the Kaldor-Hicks test amounts to a form of benefit-cost analysis and has come to dominate public policy analysis.[98] It is clear that this form of analysis has advantages over the Pareto test. First, it is straightforward. And it is imbued with abundant common sense: first, an increase in aggregate wealth necessarily increases aggregate welfare; thus, implement a proposal if the gains exceed the losses. Second, it avoids the problem that utility cannot be measured by instead focusing on what can be measured in concrete terms, wealth. And third, it avoids the deadweight loss that the administrative costs of a compensation system would entail.

Although benefit-cost analysis does have its attractive features, it nevertheless is somewhat anomalous that it has come to dominate public policy analysis, given the considerable responsive discussion of the 1939 Kaldor and Hicks papers. One particularly telling response is the paper by Tibor de Scitovsky, "A Note on Welfare Propositions in Economics."[99]

Kaldor and Hicks take the position that the issues of welfare improvement and wealth distribution are separable.[100] De Scitovsky's principal point is that the matters of welfare improvement and of distribution are in fact not separable.

---

96 *See* Pigou (1932), *supra* note 74.

97 It is interesting that, given Hicks' separation between the pattern of wealth distribution and aggregate economic welfare, he does not make clear what it is about a particular distributional consequence that renders it deplorable.

98 For example, any new rule or regulation promulgated by the federal government must be justified with a benefit-cost analysis. 5 U.S.C. §801(a)(1)(B) (2004).

99 Tibor de Scitovsky, *A Note on Welfare Propositions in Economics*, 9 Rev. Econ. Stud. 77 (1941).

100 Interestingly, Kaldor himself, in proposing a welfare test by which compensation need not be given, recognized the connection between aggregate welfare and the pattern of wealth distribution: "If the postulate of equal capacity for satisfaction is employed as a criterion, the conclusion inescapably follows that welfare is necessarily greatest when there is complete equality" Kaldor, *supra* note 75, at 551.

De Scitovsky argues that the implementation of a proposal typically will change the price of particular goods and resources. This can have two distinct effects on any particular individual.[101] Her wealth position might change because of a change in price of a resource that she holds. And her utility position might change because of a change in the price of goods that she consumes.

These income effects necessarily will change her utility schedule, sometimes quite substantially. This can lead to paradox in the application of the Kaldor-Hicks single welfare criterion. Assume a circumstance in which a particular batch of goods is distributed at a particular point, X, on the utility frontier with a corresponding level of aggregate welfare. A proposal is adopted that results in a new batch of goods, distributed at Y on the new utility frontier, such that, from the point of view of position X, the corresponding level of aggregate welfare is greater at position Y than at position X. De Scitovsky demonstrated that, because of income effects, it is entirely possible that, from the point of view of the new position, Y, an improvement in aggregate welfare can be achieved by a move back to position X on the old utility frontier.[102]

Thus, to determine that there will be a net advantage, in wealth terms, from the implementation of a proposal reveals little about the consequences of this implementation in terms of aggregate economic welfare:

> [O]btaining a positive change in aggregate consumers' and producers' surplus is neither a necessary nor a sufficient condition for the satisfaction of a compensation test which involves the hypothetical payment of monetary compensation from the gainers to the losers. ... [I]f some persons gain and others lose, we cannot interpret a positive surplus as an indication that the gainers could compensate the losers and a negative surplus that they could not.[103]

The scope of the hypothetical compensation test proposed by Kaldor and Hicks thus is extremely limited. The only circumstance in which aggregate surplus changes are valid indicators of welfare change would be the fortuitous one in which the marginal social utility of income is identical for all.[104]

In subsequent discussion, I.M.D. Little demonstrated that the paradox revealed by Tibor de Scitovsky can be avoided by adopting two criteria for determining that the adoption of a proposal will result in an increase in aggregate economic

---

101 *See* DAVID A. ALHADEFF, MICROECONOMICS AND HUMAN BEHAVIOR: TOWARD A NEW SYNTHESIS OF ECONOMICS AND PSYCHOLOGY, 114–120 (1982); E.J. MISHAN, WELFARE ECONOMICS: AN ASSESSMENT, 44 (1969); PAUL A. SAMUELSON, ECONOMICS, 437 (10th ed., 1976); DONALD STEVENSON WATSON, PRICE THEORY AND ITS USES, 88–90 (1963).

102 This is demonstrated graphically in de Scitovsky, *supra* note 99, at 85–86; and MISHAN, *supra* note 101, at 40–44.

103 Robin W. Boardway, *The Welfare Foundations of Cost-Benefit Analysis*, 84 ECON. J. 926, 938 (1974).

104 Boardway, *supra* note 103.

welfare. First, the new output must be preferred to the old; second, the pattern of distribution of the new output must be better, that is, more equal, than that of the old.[105] The Kaldor-Hicks test, and benefit-cost analysis itself, founder on the radical separation between aggregate welfare and distribution proposed by Kaldor and Hicks.[106]

Both Kaldor and Hicks set out their purpose as putting welfare economics on a scientific basis. In effect, this amounts to eschewing the attempt to measure the unmeasurable, utility, and instead to measure the measurable, wealth. The problem with this move is a rather fundamental economic postulate, declining marginal utility. The scientific basis for welfare economics that Kaldor and Hicks seek to develop goes forward on the principle that a dollar is a dollar, and thus can be measured objectively. What is being measured, however, are dollar gains to one person or group and dollar losses to another person or group. Necessarily, then, a dollar isn't just a dollar. The value in utility, the proper measure of welfare, of the gain or loss of a dollar to an individual depends strongly on the wealth position of the individual.

Consider the implementation of a proposal that has the consequence of a redistribution of a dollar from a poor person to a rich person. Under the principle of equal capacity for satisfaction, a principle espoused by Kaldor himself,[107] the utility loss to the poor person will substantially outweigh the utility gain to the rich person. This, in fact, is the principle underlying the Pareto test, which requires actual compensation in utility terms. You do not know whether you have a net welfare gain unless you give full utility compensation to all who lose. That is, you cannot simply compare gains and losses in dollar terms. This, however, is exactly the starting point of the attempts by Kaldor and Hicks to put the advice of economists concerning proposals for resource allocation on a scientific basis: you cannot make interpersonal comparisons of utility. And comparing losses and gains, in whatever terms these are stated, whether dollars or utils, necessarily involves interpersonal comparisons of utility.

---

105 I.M.D. Little, A Critique of Welfare Economics (1950).

106 The particular way in which the distributional element of Little's dual welfare criteria is stated accounts for a considerable flaw in the Pareto test. According to Pareto, an economy is at a Pareto optimum if there are no proposals available that will make at least one person better off and leave no one worse off. Amartya Sen has shown, however, that an economy can be at a Pareto optimum and yet be at a low level of aggregate welfare (Amartya K. Sen, Collective Choice and Social Welfare (1970)). This circumstance can obtain when, for example, there is a substantial spread in the pattern of wealth distribution, with the greater part of societal wealth held by a small elite class. This has been shown empirically in Pickett and Wilkinson, note 83 *supra*. In such a circumstance, a considerable improvement in aggregate welfare can be gained by the introduction of a strongly progressive income tax. This proposal, however, would violate the test for a Pareto improvement because, although many people (the poor) would be made better off, some people (the elite) would be made worse off.

107 *See* text accompanying Kaldor, *supra* note 79.

As a consequence, under the form of benefit-cost analysis embedded in the Kaldor-Hicks test, wealth is just as unmeasurable as utility. And the reasoning underlying this test breaks down in a fundamental way. Benefit-cost analysis is altogether rational for an individual deciding whether to take a course of action. After all, what could be more logical for, say, a corporate entity, or, for that matter, an individual, in making a decision about a proposed course of action that involves the expenditure of scarce resources, to calculate the anticipated benefits and expected costs and proceed only if benefits exceed costs? Benefit-cost analysis breaks down, however, when the costs fall on A and the benefits accrue to B. Thus, measuring the prospective wealth gains from the implementation of a proposal bears little relation to the prospective welfare gains because aggregate welfare is strongly sensitive to the pattern of wealth distribution, and whether actual compensation is given is determinative of the pattern of wealth distribution.

We are left with the counterintuitive, though inescapable, conclusion that an attempt to increase the aggregate wealth of society can, except in strictly defined circumstances, actually erode the aggregate economic welfare of society. And we are left as well with the inescapable conclusion that benefit-cost analysis is fatally flawed as a means of engaging in public policy analysis. Because the *Kelo* Doctrine rests strongly on the appropriateness of benefit-cost analysis, we are now in a position to engage in a critical analysis of eminent domain assemblage for private development from the standpoint of aggregate economic welfare.

Eminent Domain Assemblage and Welfare

Holdouts

The New London redevelopment project at issue in *Kelo v. City of New London* and the Detroit automobile assembly plant development project at issue in *Poletown Neighborhood Council v. City of Detroit* together typify the undertaking of urban redevelopment projects in the United States. The *Poletown* project follows an entrepreneurial model, by which an entrepreneur determines that there is a demand for a particular kind of development, designs a project that will meet that demand at a profit, and seeks the assistance of the local government in assembling, through the eminent domain power, the development tract on which the project will be established. The *Kelo* project follows an urban renewal model, by which a publicly chartered entity designs a project that will meet a public objective in economic revitalization of some portion of the urban fabric.

Under either model, the development tract will consist of land currently in uses of low economic intensity. There is, after all, little profit opportunity in redeveloping land already developed at a high level of economic intensity. Ownership of this land typically will be fragmented among a number of private owners, requiring assemblage of the land into single ownership. If this assemblage is not carried out in secret, then, all but inevitably, as the assemblage proceeds, the developer-assembler will encounter the holdout phenomenon: the remaining land owners will begin to ask for more than the developer-assembler is willing to pay.[108]

The consequence of this resistance to market acquisition of the parcels in the development tract is that project acquisition costs now threaten to become excessive—under the entrepreneurial model, excessive in terms of obtaining an adequate profit; under the urban renewal model, excessive in terms of whatever budget of public funds that has been established for the project. It is in the circumstance of holdout that the assembler will seek the assistance of the public power of eminent domain, on the grounds that holdout symptomizes a breakdown in the market, preventing assemblage of the development tract.

Is the occurrence of holdout, however, a symptom of market breakdown? Consider the matter of market exchange itself. An individual engages in exchange in order to increase her utility. Assuming rationality on the part of the parties to a potential exchange, this will occur when Seller's utility in the price offered by Buyer is greater than her utility in her land, and B's utility in S's land is greater than his utility in his money that he is offering for the land. Thus, although nothing can be determined in terms of quantitative measures of the utility positions of the parties, the fact than an exchange has occurred does reveal the relative utility positions of the two parties in the subjects of the exchange.

Typically as well, when the respective utility positions of the two parties are such that a utility-increasing exchange opportunity is present for both parties, this will occur not at a single particular price but instead over a range of prices, a bargaining range, leaving the parties to negotiate over the split of the exchange surplus within that range. In such circumstances, exchange ought to occur. Each party will see an increase in utility, thereby increasing aggregate welfare. And, tautologically, the subject of exchange, the land, will now be more efficiently allocated. In terms of aggregate economic welfare, exchange in a well-functioning market thereby serves the public interest.

When holdout occurs in an assemblage, however, this can have two different causes. The first is what might be called the "utility holdout." This is when the landowner, in response to a monetary offer that is not remunerative on a utility basis, seeking a price for her land that compensates her for her utility value in the land. That is, the utility holdout is seeking a price that puts her in a bargaining range.

The second is the strategic holdout. This is the landowner who has been given a utility-compensating offer, an offer that will, if accepted, increase the landowner's utility position and that is, therefore, in a bargaining range. The strategic holdout,

108 In New London, the New London Development Corporation had successfully purchased a considerable portion of the development tract by direct negotiation with, and purchase from, many of the landowners in the tract. When Susette Kelo and a small number of other remaining landowners rejected the offers made for their property, the City of New London agreed to take, on behalf of NLDC, the remaining parcels by eminent domain. Benedict, *supra* note 1, at 190–191.

however, believes that the offer is at her end of the bargaining range, and is seeking to capture the greater share of the exchange surplus.

The utility holdout, by rejecting the current offer, is testing whether it is efficient for an exchange to take place. Thus, she is a symptom of the market functioning well. The strategic holdout is acting in circumstances in which the proposed exchange will be efficient. She can, however, incorrectly assess the size of the bargaining range, hold out for an offer that will put the assembler out of the range, and, in so doing, prevent an efficient exchange from occurring. The strategic holdout thus is a symptom of market breakdown.

In terms of efficient resource allocation, the utility holdout should be encouraged and the strategic holdout should be frustrated. The problem is that utility cannot be measured directly and interpersonal comparisons of utility cannot be made. Thus, it is difficult to determine, from the position of an objective observer, whether a holdout is a utility holdout or a strategic holdout. The mere fact that holdout is occurring does not demonstrate that there is a breakdown in the market.

The Process of Eminent Domain Assemblage

The process of eminent domain assemblage follows a typical pattern. In the first step, the developer-assembler asks the officials of local government for eminent domain assistance in assembling the development tract, citing the occurrence of holdout, and asserting that this threatens to escalate acquisition costs beyond developer's willingness to pay. Thus, when the assembler requests the assistance of the eminent domain power, neither the assembler nor local government officials know, nor can they know, whether this assistance will facilitate an efficient exchange or an inefficient exchange.

In the second step, local government offers a justification for the exercise of a public power in aid of private development. The developer will then demonstrate that the project presents a profit or public welfare (slum clearance, etc.) opportunity that will put the development tract to a more economically intensive use and provide opportunities for employment. The local government will find that there will be an increased flow of tax revenue to the public treasury and employment opportunities will increase in a circumstance of a high rate of unemployment, thereby providing a consequent public benefit. This justification is arrived at through benefit-cost analysis and will be stated, at a fundamental level, in terms of wealth creation.

The problem with the process of justification is the matter of demand. In the entrepreneurial model, demand is determined by an entrepreneur, who, as an entrepreneur, is a risk-taker best skilled at assessing demand. The entrepreneur determines his opportunity for profit, however, in terms of a certain level of costs, including land acquisition costs. The occurrence of holdout can threaten to escalate costs beyond a level that will allow for a sufficient profit, and the developer will seek the assistance of eminent domain in order to contain land acquisition costs.

What, however, is the basis for the holdout that is taking place? If the price that the developer is willing to pay offers less in utility value to the holdout landowners than their utility in their land, then in fact there is no demand for the developer's project; the land is efficiently allocated in its current use in the hands of the holdout landowners. Only if the basis for the holdout is strategic action by the holdout landowners will it be the case that there is sufficient demand for the developer's project. Thus, the mere occurrence of holdout of itself does not justify providing the assistance of eminent domain. The property of the holdout landowners might well be taken for a use for which there is no efficiency justification and thus for which there is no public purpose.

In the urban-renewal model, demand is determined by an urban planner who, as a planner, is not an experienced entrepreneur and thus is not skilled at determining demand. Instead, the planner designs a project that accords with "sound planning principles"—in effect, a laundry list of "wouldn't it be nice?" uses.[109] Thus, there may be no demand whatsoever for the project. In the New London project, this turned out to be exactly the case. When the developer chosen to carry out the plan attempted to obtain financing, it failed, indicating that commercial lenders, also experienced at estimating demand, concluded that the risk that carrying out the plan would not be profitable was too high, and their construction loans would not be repaid.[110] The development tract, which was assembled and cleared by NLDC, is now a brownfield.[111]

The third step is the actual taking of title by local government. This is accomplished through the typical quick-take legislation, by which the governmental entity takes title to the target property by filing a declaration with the local court of general jurisdiction.[112] It is then left to the former property owner either to accept the offer of an eminent domain award or to litigate to try to obtain an acceptable offer. The former property owner is left in a highly disadvantageous bargaining and litigating position.

In the fourth step, eminent domain compensation is determined. Under the judicial interpretation of the Taking Clause, the measure of the *just compensation* criterion is fair market value,[113] functionally defined as what a willing buyer and a willing seller would agree on. In terms of aggregate economic welfare, however, the proper measure of just compensation is implicit in the Pareto criterion, by which a proposal is efficient if, by its implementation, at least one person is better off and no one is worse off. If the proper measure of *better off* and *worse off* welfare is utility, then full economic welfare compensation is the amount of

---

109 Much of the asserted demand by NLDC for the New London project was based on a wish list, offered by Pfizer, of facilities that would complement its newly-established research facility. BENEDICT, *supra* note 1, at 236–237. There was no offer by Pfizer either to contribute to the construction of these facilities or to acquire any of them once they were built.

110 BENEDICT, *supra* note 1, at 377.

111 Kathleen Edgecomb, *NL Officials Regret Relinquishing Power of Eminent Domain*, THE DAY (New London), Mar. 5, 2009, at 1.

112 Conn. Gen. Stat. Ann. §§8-124–8-139, 48-1–48-25 (West 2006).

113 *United States v. Miller*, 317 U.S. 369 (1943).

money with which the owner subject to an eminent domain-taking will be able to acquire property the utility value of which to that owner is equal to the utility value of the taken property. Only then will she not be worse off in Pareto terms by the implementation of the proposal.

The fair market value standard falls far short of full utility compensation for several reasons. Take, as an example, the homeowner displaced from her single-family residence by an urban redevelopment project. The fair market value standard excludes any consequential costs.[114] These can include the cost of finding a satisfactory replacement residence, the costs associated with negotiating its purchase, the transaction costs associated with obtaining financing, the transaction costs associated with the exchange of purchase price and deed of title, and the subsequent costs of physical relocation. These costs, because in utility terms they will include not only monetary outlays but also expenditures of time and emotion, are quite real and can be quite substantial.

In addition, it is seldom the case that the displaced property owner will be able to find a replacement property that is physically and locationally substantially similar to the current property. Thus, in order not to incur a decrease in welfare, she will have to find a new residence that is the utility equivalent of her current residence but with a different complement of physical and locational attributes. And it is more than possible that this utility equivalent residence will command a market price greater than the fair market value of her current residence. This difference between market value and utility value, termed the sentimental or idiosyncratic value, represents the psychological attachment that the owner has in her current property.

The resistance to the eminent domain-takings in the New London and Poletown redevelopment projects provides clear examples of this value. In the New London redevelopment, the view from Susette Kelo's modest house overlooking the Thames River as it flows into Long Island Sound was the reason that she purchased a house that had been on the market for several years.[115] As an indication of her utility value in this residence, she purchased it in the summer of 1997 for $53,500.[116] In early March 1998, she refused an offer of $78,000 from NLDC,[117] an increase of 46 percent over the purchase price about seven months earlier. That she simply did not want to move from that house is demonstrated by her embarking on a daunting course of resistance to increasing public pressure to accept the NLDC offer and litigation in the New London trial court and on up to the U.S. Supreme Court, a course that extended over a period of eight years.

Others of the group of Kelo's New London neighbors who resisted the eminent domain-taking also manifested a considerable psychological investment in their properties. Elderly Erica Blescus, upon learning of the planned taking, wrote this letter to the mayor and city council of New London:

---

114 *United States v. Miller*, 317 U.S. 369 (1943).

115 Benedict, *supra* note 1, at 12–14.

116 *Id.* at 16.

117 *Id.* at 67.

> I am 91 years of age. Live with my daughter in separate quarters who takes care of me. Have lived here for 27 years and cannot bear the thought of moving. We put so much time, effort & work into this house & the thought that the house could be razed is too much for me to take.[118]

Wilhelmina Dery had been born in 1918 in her house in the development tract, in the same room she still called her bedroom. She planned to die there.[119] Helen Ballestine, Walter and Ces Pasqualini, and Nora Pasqualini expressed similar sentiments.[120]

After the course of litigation was complete and NLDC now had formal title to the land in the development tract, because of the controversy that had arisen over the redevelopment project, the political will forcibly to remove the last of the holdouts did not exist. The state government sought to settle with these individuals.[121] Pasquale and Margherita Cristofaro, who, with Susette Kelo, were the last to settle, expressed their attachment to the neighborhood by offering to leave if they were given the right to purchase at a stated price and occupy one of the upscale residences planned for the development tract.[122] Kelo herself agreed to settle only on condition that her house would not be destroyed; instead she was given sufficient funds to have it dismantled and reassembled, on another plot of land that had been donated, to serve as a memorial to the controversy.[123]

In the Poletown redevelopment, Walter Jakabowski expressed his utility position in this way:

> My parents lived in this house. Two of my children were born upstairs because we couldn't afford hospitals during the war. I went to that [Immaculate Conception] church as a boy. I was married there. My children were baptized there. And now they want to tear it all down. I'll fight that. It's just too hard to take. I want to live here. If I didn't I could have moved a long time ago. … We're not interested in how much they'll give us for our homes. A house can be replaced. But you can't replace memories. A neighborhood is your life and a church the hub of your social and religious life. If they destroy all that, what do you have left?[124]

The Immaculate Conception Church, an ethnic Polish Roman Catholic Church parish in the redevelopment area, was a center of community life, the venue for many of the salient events in the family lives of Poletown residents' christenings, weddings, and funerals. When the redevelopment project and the planned use

118 Benedict, *supra* note 1, at 87.
119 *Id.* at 88, 255–256.
120 *Id.* at 85–86.
121 *Id.* at 356–375.
122 *Id.* at 371–374.
123 *Id.*
124 Jeanie Wylie, Poletown: Community Betrayed (1989), 64–65.

of eminent domain to facilitate it became known, the organized resistance that quickly formed used this church as its headquarters.[125] Even after title had been taken by the City of Detroit to all the properties in the redevelopment area and demolition of the Poletown neighborhood had begun, church members began a series of vigils in an effort to reverse the suppression by the Archdiocese of Detroit of the Immaculate Conception parish and prevent demolition of the church building itself. Eventually, a Detroit Police SWAT team forcibly removed the people holding vigil so that the demolition could proceed.[126]

It is in the nature of individuals to invest elements of the physical environment with meaning, from cultural elements, such as the Gettysburg or Antietam battlefields, to personal elements such as the places where family events, particularly over more than one generation, have occurred.[127] These places occupy a salient position in the cognitive world of the individual, and, as prominent elements of that cognitive world, are necessarily invested with meaning. This meaning necessarily forms a substantial element of the *utility* value of those places to the individual. To the extent that the individual has a property interest in such a place—a meaningful place to that individual—if that property interest is taken away, then the transfer cannot be efficient and economic justice as economic welfare maximization cannot be achieved if that meaning-value is not fully compensated.

In addition to the substantially non-remunerative consequence of the fair market value standard, the way in which governmental entities go about exercising the eminent domain power can result in even greater compensation shortfall. The practical purpose of resorting to the eminent domain power is to minimize land acquisition costs. As a way of minimizing these costs, it is not an infrequent practice for the condemning authority to make a lowball offer, an offer of compensation below fair market value, particularly to condemnees of more modest means. The condemnee now faces a difficult choice: accept a substantially non-remunerative offer of compensation or litigate. Litigation, however, is expensive, in particular because it will require the services of a real-estate valuation expert witness. And whatever recovery that is obtained over the initial offer will be eroded by the contingent fee.

The consequence is that eminent domain awards are systematically inadequate on a utility basis. The eminent domain process, deployed in support of assemblage for private redevelopment, systematically destroys utility and transfers wealth up the economic scale.

---

125 Wylie, *supra* note 124, at 114.

126 The vigils and eventual demolition are described in Wylie (1989) at 153–191. Several of those forcibly removed from the church were elderly woman parishioners whose modest monetary contributions made with considerable sacrifice helped finance the construction of the church in 1935 (Wylie, *supra* note 124, at 16). Formal title to the church had been held, however, by the Archdiocese of Detroit, which settled with the City for $1.3 million. None of this money was given to the parishioners for their loss occasioned by the suppression of the parish and the demolition of the church (Wylie, *supra* note 123, at 117).

127 E.V. Walter, Placeways: A Theory of the Human Environment (1988).

Analysis

The justification offered in the political process for eminent domain assemblage for private development is the benefit to the public that it makes possible; in particular, economic benefit. What, however, is the nature of this public benefit? Consider the dual welfare criteria of welfare economics theory, by which an unambiguous improvement in aggregate economic welfare is demonstrated if the implementation of a proposal will result in wealth creation and a more equal pattern of wealth distribution.

Under the entrepreneurial model, the developer demonstrates his belief that there is a demand for the particular project that he proposes. This demand, however, necessarily exists only at a particular price. And that price is determined by the cost of carrying out the project.

By invoking the eminent domain process, the developer necessarily admits that the cost of the project threatens to price the project out of the market. Unless this threat arises from strategic action by the owners of the land in the development tract, however, there is in fact no demand for the project. Because the eminent domain process has the inevitable effect of suppressing land acquisition costs—indeed, it is deployed for the purpose of suppressing land acquisition costs—then it tends to facilitate carrying out redevelopment projects for which there is no demand when true costs are taken into account. In such cases, there is no net gain in wealth; the prospect of profit to the developer does not correlate with the net creation of wealth for society. The first of the dual welfare criteria thus is not satisfied.

Under the urban renewal model, there actually is no determination of demand, only the assertion, "Build it and (we hope that) they will come."[128] Under this model as well, the eminent domain process suppresses costs. Thus, it cannot be shown that there will be a net gain in wealth by carrying out the project. Here, as well, the first of the dual welfare criteria is not satisfied.

Moreover, it is not unusual for there to be a considerable public subsidy of the redevelopment project, further distorting the benefit-cost assessment. In the *Poletown* project, there was a public subsidy of approximately $192 million.[129] In the New London project, there was a public subsidy of approximately $1 billion.[130]

The second of the dual welfare criteria relates to the pattern of wealth distribution. It is clear that the eminent domain process as it actually is carried out systematically destroys utility and transfers wealth up the economic scale. Thus, this criterion as well is not satisfied. The conclusion is inescapable—eminent domain assemblage for private development systematically erodes aggregate economic welfare.

128 *Cf.* "Field of Dreams" (motion picture, Universal Studios, 1989).

129 *Poletown Neighborhood Council*, 304 N.W.2d at 469.

130 Benedict, *supra* note 1, at 57.

Given the perverse consequences for aggregate economic welfare of eminent domain assemblage for private development, the *Kelo* Doctrine is subject to criticism. The first element of the doctrine includes, under the criterion *public use*, a private redevelopment with a consequential public benefit. The *Kelo* Doctrine expressly defines public benefit, in concept, as the creation of wealth. The proper concept of public benefit, however, is an advance in aggregate economic welfare. Even if the creation of wealth itself would be to the public benefit, the eminent domain process, by suppressing eminent domain awards, fails to account for all redevelopment costs; and it often includes a public subsidy for the project. There is a tendency, then, in practice for the process to enable projects that will realize no net gain in aggregate wealth, and often enough a net loss. The second element of the doctrine is the all but extreme judicial deference to legislative and executive determinations of public benefit. Because a substantial portion of cost, the economically correct land acquisition cost, cannot actually be measured, these determinations cannot actually be made. Strong judicial deference to these determinations is therefore misplaced. The third element of the doctrine is the fair market value measure for the *just compensation* criterion. This measure is entirely inadequate, which results in perverse effects on the spread of the distribution of wealth, with consequent perverse effects on aggregate economic welfare.

Thus the question: when should eminent domain be used to assist assemblage for private redevelopment? It is not possible to demonstrate that doing so will lead to a net gain in aggregate societal wealth. And doing so will tend to exacerbate the spread in the distribution of wealth. Thus, the answer in terms of aggregate economic welfare is: never.

The Outlines of a Solution

There is, and there will continue to be, a strong demand for the redevelopment of land, redevelopment that will advance the aggregate economic welfare. This redevelopment will, in most cases, require the assemblage of substantial development tracts. And, because this exchange will unavoidably involve a single buyer and a number of sellers, assemblage will inevitably be bedeviled by holdout, a substantial mode of market breakdown.

The exercise of the public power of eminent domain in aid of assemblage for private redevelopment will eliminate holdout. As we have seen, however, it will do so at a substantial cost: exercised in this context, eminent domain will lead to a systematic erosion of the aggregate economic welfare. It will do so because the decision to exercise the eminent domain power is inevitably based on the assumption that market breakdown is occurring, when in fact holdout might well be a symptom of the market working well.

Thus, the solution to the occurrence of holdout is not to seek to correct the consequences of an assumed market failure but instead to correct the potential market failure itself. If this can be done, then the market can efficaciously test, in the individual case, whether the assemblage will lead to a redevelopment that will advance the aggregate economic welfare. This will occur because, in fact, the well-functioning market is the best means available for determining the relative utility positions in the land to be assembled of the relevant parties—the current owners and the assembling developer.

In the burgeoning market for land redevelopment in the northern Virginia suburbs of the District of Columbia, two instances of another phenomenon occurred: the landowners of land targeted for redevelopment, one near a newly established mass transit station[131] and the other near the rapidly growing edge city of Tyson's Corner,[132] each formed themselves into a consortium that functioned as a single bargaining unit to deal with the developer. In each case, a successful assemblage took place without the intervention of the exercise of eminent domain.

In concept, this approach functions much like the single bargaining unit of a labor union negotiating with a single employer. The special district form of government provides an appropriate vehicle for forming a sellers' consortium for the assemblage of redevelopment tracts. In detail, different from the typical special district, which is initiated by the landowners in the proposed district themselves, this special district would be initiated in the particular instance by the developer seeking to assemble the redevelopment tract. The consortium would then be governed internally by a supermajority voting rule, which, if set at an appropriate level, will tend to eliminate strategic action holdout while accommodating the utility positions of most of the consortium members.

Such a vehicle is not likely to work perfectly in practice, in terms of arriving at the economically correct utility-based price for the assembled redevelopment tract. It will, however, serve to eliminate, better than any other means, strategic action holdout and allow only welfare-increasing redevelopment to proceed. In consequence, land targeted for private redevelopment will be retained in the market rather than being taken out of the market by the exercise of the eminent domain power. The market, after all, is the best—indeed, the only—means by which interpersonal comparisons of utility can be approached.

Conclusion

Hernando de Soto's principal point is that non-Western, non-First World economies fail because considerable portions of productive resources are not capital. These resources, that is, are not subject to allocationally efficient market exchange. Eminent domain assemblage for private development takes important productive

131 Nancy Scannell, *Courtlands Neighbors Complete Package Deal: Arlington Homeowner Consortium Holds Out for High Price*, The Washington Post, Dec. 20, 1986, at A1.

132 Robert A. Watts, *After Delays and Deals, Subdivision Is Sold*, The Washington Post, Jan. 15, 1987, at Va.-1.

resources out of the market, thereby keeping them from being capital. Thus, for a crucially important resource, the Western, First-World economy of the United States commits the same error that has prevented Third World countries from forming well-functioning markets that advance the aggregate economic welfare of society.

Bibliography

Adler, Jonathan. *When Is Two a Crowd? The Impact of Federal Action on State Environmental Regulation*, 31 Harv. Envtl. L. Rev. 67 (2007).

Alchian, Armen A. and Harold Demsetz. *Production, Information Costs, and Economic Organization*, 62 Am. Econ. Rev. 777 (1972).

Alexander, Gregory S. COMMODITY AND PROPRIETY: COMPETING VISIONS OF PROPERTY IN AMERICAN LEGAL THOUGHT (1997).

Alexander, Gregory S. *The Social-Obligation Norm in American Property Law*, 94 Cornell L. Rev. 745 (2009).

Alhadeff, David A. MICROECONOMICS AND HUMAN BEHAVIOR: TOWARD A NEW SYNTHESIS OF ECONOMICS AND PSYCHOLOGY (1982).

Allen, Mike. *Giuliani to Bar Food Vendors on 144 Blocks*, N.Y. Times, May 24, 1998a, §1, at 27.

Allen, Mike. *Sidewalk Vendors Face a New Set of Critics*, N.Y. Times, May 31, 1998b, at A27.

Allen, Mike. *Sidewalk Vendors Rally to Protest Street Restrictions*, N.Y. Times, June 4, 1998c at B3.

Allen, Mike. *City Pursuing Negotiations with Street Food Vendors*, N.Y. Times, June 15, 1998d.

Alston, Lee J., Gary D. Libecap, and Bernardo Mueller. TITLES, CONFLICT AND LAND USE: THE DEVELOPMENT OF PROPERTY RIGHTS AND LAND REFORM ON THE BRAZILIAN AMAZON FRONTIER (1999).

And Now, the Hot-Dog War. Editorial, N.Y. Times, June 4, 1998.

Anderson, Elizabeth S. *What is the Point of Equality?*, 109 Ethics 287 (1999).

Anderson, Robert T., Bethany Berger, Philip P. Frickey, and Sarah Krakoff. AMERICAN INDIAN LAW (2008).

Anderson, Terry L. SOVEREIGN NATIONS OR RESERVATIONS? AN ECONOMIC HISTORY OF AMERICAN INDIANS (1995).

Anderson, Terry L., Bruce L. Benson, and Thomas E. Flanagan. SELF-DETERMINATION: THE OTHER PATH FOR NATIVE AMERICANS (2006).

Arruñada, Benito and Nuno Garoupa. *The Choice of Titling System in Land*, 48 J.L. & Econ. 709 (2005).

Atuahene, Bernadette. *Legal Title to Land as an Intervention Against Urban Poverty in Developing Nations*, 36 G.W. Int'l L. Rev. 1109 (2004).

Atuahene, Bernadette. *Land Titling: A Mode of Privatization With the Potential to Deepen Democracy*, 50 St. Louis U. L.J. 761 (2006).

Banner, Stuart. *Two Properties, One Land: Law and Space in Nineteenth-Century New Zealand*, 24 Law & Soc. Inquiry 807 (1999).

Becker, Jo, et al. *White House Philosophy Stoked Mortgage Bonfire*, N.Y. Times, Dec. 20, 2008.

Becker, Lawrence. *The Moral Basis of Property Rights*, in NOMOS XXII: PROPERTY (J. Roland Pennock and John W. Chapman, eds, 1980).

Been, Vicki. Lucas v. The Green Machine*: Using the Takings Clause to Promote More Efficient Regulation?*, in PROPERTY STORIES (2nd ed., 2009).

Bell, Abraham and Gideon Parchomovsky. *Givings*, 111 Yale L.J. 547 (2001).

Bell, Abraham and Gideon Parchomovsky. *Of Property and Antiproperty*, 102 Mich L. Rev. 1 (2003).

Benedict, Jeff. LITTLE PINK HOUSE: A TRUE STORY OF DEFIANCE AND COURAGE (2009).

Binford, Henry C. THE FIRST SUBURBS: RESIDENTIAL COMMUNITIES ON THE BOSTON PERIPHERY (1988).

Birdsall, Nancy. *Rising Inequality in the New Global Economy*, 2 Wider Angle 1 (2005).

Bluestone, Daniel M. *"The Pushcart Evil": Peddlers, Merchants, and New York City's Streets, 1890–1940*, 18 J. Urb. Hist. 68 (1991).

Boardway, Robin W. *The Welfare Foundations of Cost-Benefit Analysis*, 84 Econ. J. 926 (1974).

Bobroff, Kenneth H. *Retelling Allotment: Indian Property Rights and the Myth of Common Ownership*, 54 Vand. L. Rev. 1559 (2001).

Bohlen, Celestine. *Moscow Journal: It's a Kiosk! It's a Mall! No, It's Slavyansky Ryad!*, N.Y. Times, Dec. 23, 1992, at A4.

Boudreaux, Karol C. *The Legal Empowerment of the Poor: Titling and Poverty Alleviation in Post-Apartheid South Africa*, 5 Hastings Race & Poverty L. J. 309 (2008).

Braudel, Fernand. CIVILIZATION AND CAPITALISM: THE WHEELS OF COMMERCE (Sian Reynolds, trans., 1982).

Breckenfeld, Gurney. COLUMBIA AND THE NEW CITIES (1971).

Breyer, Stephen. "Commencement Address of Justice Stephen Breyer," University of Pennsylvania Law School (May 19, 2003a).

Breyer, Stephen. "Commencement Address of Justice Stephen Breyer," Boston College Law School (May 23, 2003b).

Brion, Denis J. *An Essay on LULU, NIMBY, and the Problem of Distributive Justice*, 15 B.C. Envtl. Aff. L. Rev. 437 (1988).

Bromley, Ray. *A New Path to Development? The Significance and Impact of Hernando de Soto's Ideas on Underdevelopment, Production, and Reproduction*, 66 Econ. Geography 328 (1990).

Brophy, Alfred L. "Ingenium est Fateri per quos profeceris:" *Francis Daniel Pastorius' Young Country Clerks Collection and Anglo-American Legal Literature, 1680–1716*, 3 U. Chi. L. Sch. Roundtable 619 (1996).

Brophy, Alfred L. *"Necessity Knows No Law": Vested Rights and the Styles of Reasoning in the Confederate Conscription Cases*, 69 Miss. L.J. 1123 (2000).

Brophy, Alfred L. *Property and Progress: Antebellum Landscape Art and Property Law*, 40 McGeorge L. Rev. 602 (2009).

Bruegmann, Robert. SPRAWL (2005).

Buchanan, James M. and Yong J. Yoon. *Symmetric Tragedies: Commons and Anticommons*, 43 J.L. & Econ. 1 (2000).

Carman, Tim. *New Freedoms to Go: D.C. Street Vendors Try Out Laxer Rules*, Washington Post, Oct. 1, 2008, at F1.

Carney, Brian M. *The Weekend Interview with Anna Schwartz*, Wall St. Journal, October 18–19, 2008, at A11.

Carrier, James C. *Marine Tenure and Conservation in Papua New Guinea: Problems in Interpretation*, in THE QUESTION OF THE COMMONS: THE CULTURE AND ECOLOGY OF COMMUNAL RESOURCES (Bonnie J. McCay and James M. Acheson, eds, 1990).

Carstensen, Vernon Rosco. INTRODUCTION TO THE PUBLIC LANDS: STUDIES IN THE HISTORY OF THE PUBLIC DOMAIN (1963).

Casalbé, Jim. PURO GUANACO: DICCIONARIO DE SALVADOREÑISMOS (2002).

Cashin, Sheryll. THE FAILURES OF INTEGRATION: HOW RACE AND CLASS ARE UNDERMINING THE AMERICAN DREAM (2004).

Charles Faulkner Speech, Richmond Enquirer, Feb. 2, 1832.

Clift, Jeremy. *Hearing the Dogs Bark*, Finance & Development (December 2003).

Clinton, Robert N., Carole E. Goldberg, and Rebecca Tsosie. AMERICAN INDIAN LAW: NATIVE NATIONS AND THE FEDERAL SYSTEM (5th ed., 2007).

Clowney, Stephen. *Invisible Businessmen: Undermining Black Enterprise with Land Use Rules*, 2009 ILL. L. REV. 1061.

Clune, Margaret H. *Government Could Hardly Go On: Oregon's Measure 37, Implications for Land Use Planning, and a More Rational Means of Compensation*, 38 Urb. Law. 275 (2006).

Cohen, Felix S. HANDBOOK OF FEDERAL INDIAN LAW (1945).

Cohen, Felix. *The Erosion of Indian Rights, 1950–1953: A Case Study in Bureaucracy*, 62 Yale L.J. 348 (1953).

Commission on Legal Empowerment of the Poor. Report of the Commission, vol. 1, *Making the Law Work for Everyone* (2008).

Commuter Van Service Policy Study (N.Y. City Department of City Planning, 1997).

Condit, Carl W. THE PORT OF NEW YORK: A HISTORY OF THE RAIL AND TERMINAL SYSTEM FROM THE BEGINNINGS TO PENNSYLVANIA STATION (1980).

Conning, Jonathan and Partha Deb. "Impact Evaluation for Land Property Rights Reforms" (unpublished manuscript).

Coogan, Peter F., William E. Hogan, Detlev F. Vagts, and Julian B. McDonnell. 1 SECURED TRANSACTIONS UNDER THE UNIFORM COMMERCIAL CODE (2008).

Cooper, James Fenimore. THE CHAINBEARER (1845a).

Cooper, James Fenimore. SATANSTOE (1845b).

Cooper, James Fenimore. THE REDSKINS (1846).

Corcoran, Irma and Thomas Holme. SURVEYOR GENERAL OF PENNSYLVANIA (1992).

Council on Road to Vandalism. Editorial, N.Y. Daily News, Aug. 4, 1997, at 26.

Cross, Raymond. *Sovereign Bargains, Indian Takings, and the Preservation of Indian Country in the Twenty-first Century*, 40 Ariz. L. Rev. 425 (1998).

Cross, Raymond. *Tribes as Rich Nations*, 79 Or. L. Rev. 893 (2000).

Cypher, James M. and James L. Dietz. THE PROCESS OF ECONOMIC DEVELOPMENT 29 (2nd ed., 2004).

Dagan, Hanoch. *The Craft of Property*, 91 Cal. L. Rev. 1517 (2003).

Daley, Elizabeth and Mary Hobley. *Land: Changing Contexts, Changing Relationships, Changing Rights* (U.K. Dept. for Int'l Development, 2005).

Danforth, Sandra C. *Repaying Historical Debts: The Indian Claims Commission*, 49 N.D.L. Rev. 359 (1973).

Davidson, Nestor M. *Standardization and Pluralism in Property Law*, 61 Vand. L. Rev. 1597 (2008).

Davidson, Nestor M. *Property and Relative Status*, 107 Mich. L. Rev. 757 (2009).

Davidson, Nestor and Rashmi Dyal-Chand. *Property in Crisis*, 78 Fordham L. Rev. (forthcoming 2010).

Davies, James B., Susanna Sandström, Anthony Shorrocks, and Edward N. Wolff. *The Level and Distribution of Global Household Wealth* (Univ. of W. Ontario, RBC Fin. Group Econ. Policy Research Inst. Working Papers, Paper No. 20075, April 2008).

Davis, Kevin E. and Michael J. Trebilcock. *The Relationship Between Law and Development: Optimists versus Skeptics*, 56 Am. J. Comp. L. 895 (2008).

Davis, Mike. PLANET OF SLUMS (2006).

Davis, Otto A. and Andrew B. Whinston. *The Economics of Urban Renewal*, 26 Law & Contemp. Probs. 105 (1961).

De Scitovsky Tibor. *A Note on Welfare Propositions in Economics*, 9 Rev. Econ. Stud. 77 (1941).

De Soto, Hernando. THE MYSTERY OF CAPITAL: WHY CAPITALISM TRIUMPHS IN THE WEST AND FAILS EVERYWHERE ELSE (2000).

De Soto, Hernando. THE OTHER PATH: THE ECONOMIC ANSWER TO TERRORISM (2002), originally published as THE OTHER PATH: THE INVISIBLE REVOLUTION IN THE THIRD WORLD (1989).

Deech, Baroness Ruth. "Modernising Reproduction" (public lecture, Dec. 11, 2008).

Deininger, Klaus. *Land Policies for Growth and Poverty Reduction*, A World Bank Policy Research Report (2003).

Delgado, Richard. *Rodrigo's Twelfth Chronicle: The Problem of the Shanty*, 85 Geo. L.J. 667 (1997).

Deloria, Vine, Jr. *Reserving to Themselves: Treaties and the Powers of Indian Tribes*, 38 Ariz. L. Rev. 963 (1996).

Dew, Thomas Roderick. *Professor Dew on Slavery*, in THE PRO-SLAVERY ARGUMENT, AS MAINTAINED BY THE MOST DISTINGUISHED WRITERS OF THE SOUTHERN STATES—CONTAINING THE SEVERAL ESSAYS ON THE SUBJECT OF CHANCELLOR HARPER, GOVERNOR HAMMOND, DR. SIMMS, AND PROFESSOR DEW (Charleston, Walker, Richards & Co., 1852).

Diamond, Jared M. GUNS, GERMS, AND STEEL: THE FATES OF HUMAN SOCIETIES (1998).

DiMartino, Danielle and John V. Duca. *The Rise and Fall of Subprime Mortgages* (Fed. Reserve Bank of Dallas, 2007).

Dream On. Editorial, Wall St. Journal, July 21, 1997, at A22.

Dukeminier, Jesse, et al. PROPERTY (6th ed., 2006).

Duneier, Mitchell. SIDEWALK (2001).

Durand-Lasserve, Alain and Geoffrey Payne. *Evaluating Impacts of Urban Land Titling: Results and Implications: Preliminary Findings* (World Bank, 2006).

Durand-Lasserve, Alain. *Market-Driven Eviction Processes in Developing Country Cities: The Cases of Kigali in Rwanda and Phnom Penh in Cambodia*, 3 Global Urban Dev. 1 (2007).

Dussias, Allison M. *Squaw Drudges, Farm Wives, and Dann Sisters' Last Stand: American Indian Women's Resistance to Domestication and the Denial of Their Property Rights*, 77 N.C.L. Rev. 637 (1999).

Duthu, N. Bruce. *Crow Dog and Oliphant Fistfight at the Tribal Casino: Political Power, Storytelling, and Games of Chance*, 29 Ariz. L. Rev. 171, 194–195 (1997).

Dyal-Chand, Rashmi. *Exporting the Ownership Society: A Case Study on the Economic Impact of Property Rights*, 39 Rutgers L.J. 59 (2007).

EagleWoman, Angelique A. *The Philosophy of Colonization Underlying Taxation Imposed Upon Tribal Nations Within the United States*, 43 Tulsa L. Rev. 43 (2007).

Easterly, William. *Inequality does Cause Underdevelopment* (Center for Global Dev., Working Paper No. 1, Jan. 2002).

Eckert, Ross D. and George W. Hilton. *The Jitneys*, 15 J.L. & Econ. 293 (1972).

Elkin-Koren, Niva. *Making Technology Visible: Liability of Internet Service Providers for Peer-to-Peer Traffic*, 9 N.Y.U. J. Legis. & Pub. Pol'y 15 (2005–2006).

Eller, Ronald D. MINERS, MILLHANDS, AND MOUNTAINEERS: INDUSTRIALIZATION OF THE APPALACHIAN SOUTH, 1880–1930 (1982).

Ellickson, Robert C. *Suburban Growth Controls: An Economic and Legal Analysis*, 86 Yale L.J. 385 (1977).

Ellickson, Robert C. ORDER WITHOUT LAW: HOW NEIGHBORS SETTLE DISPUTES (1991).

Ellickson, Robert C. *Property in Land*, 102 Yale L.J. 1315 (1993).

Ellickson, Robert C. and Vicky L. Been. LAND USE CONTROLS: CASES AND MATERIALS (3rd ed., 2005).

Ely, James W. THE GUARDIAN OF EVERY OTHER RIGHT: A CONSTITUTIONAL HISTORY OF PROPERTY RIGHTS (3rd ed., 2008).

Engel, Kathleen C. and Patricia A. McCoy. *A Tale of Three Markets: The Law and Economics of Predatory Lending*, 80 Tex. L. Rev. 1255 (2002).

Engel, Kathleen C. and Patricia A. McCoy. *Turning a Blind Eye: Wall Street Finance of Predatory Lending*, 75 Fordham L. Rev. 2039 (2007).

Engerman, Stanley L. and Kenneth L. Sokoloff. *Factor Endowments, Institutions, and Differential Paths of Growth Among New World Economies: A View from Economic Historians of the United States*, in How Latin America Fell Behind (Stephen Haber, ed., 1997).

Epstein, Richard A. *Holdouts, Externalities, and the Single Owner: One More Salute to Ronald Coase*, 36 J.L. & Econ. 553 (1993).

Fairfax, Sally K., et al. *The Federal Forests Are Not What They Seem: Formal and Informal Claims to Federal Lands*, 25 Ecology L. Q. 630 (1999).

Fennell, Lee Anne. *Common Interest Tragedies*, 98 Nw. U. L. Rev. 907 (2004).

Fennell, Lee Anne. *Efficient Trespass: The Case for 'Bad Faith' Adverse Possession*, 100 Nw. L. Rev. 1037 (2006).

Fennell, Lee Anne. *Commons, Anticommons, Semicommons*, in Research Handbook on the Economics of Property Law (Kenneth Ayotte and Henry E. Smith, eds, 2009).

Ferguson, Niall. The Ascent of Money (2008).

"Field of Dreams" (motion picture, Universal Studios, 1989).

Field, Erica and Maximo Torero. *Do Property Titles Increase Credit Access Among the Urban Poor? Evidence from a Nationwide Titling Program*, paper, Harvard University (2006).

Field, Erica. *Entitled to Work: Urban Property Rights and Labor Supply in Peru*, 122 Q. J. of Econ. 1561 (2007).

Fischel, William A. The Homevoter Hypothesis (2001).

Fisher, William W. The Law of the Land: An Intellectual History of American Property Law (1991).

Fitzpatrick, Daniel. *Evolution and Chaos in Property Rights Systems: The Third World Tragedy of Contested Access*, 115 Yale L.J. 996 (2006).

Florida, Richard. *How the Crash Will Reshape America*, The Atlantic, March 2009, at 44.

Foote, Christopher L., et al. *Subprime Facts: What (We Think) We Know about the Subprime Crisis and What We Don't* (Fed. Res. Bank of Boston Pub. Pol'y Discussion Paper No. 08-2, 2008).

Frankena, Mark W. and Paul A. Paulter. An Economic Analysis of Taxicab Regulation (Federal Trade Commission, 1984).

Frederick, Missy. *Taking it to the Street: D.C. Struggles to Breathe New Life Into a Stale Outdoor Food Cart Scene*, Wash. Business J. (Sept. 12, 2008).

Galiani, Sebastian and Ernesto Schargrodsky. "Property Rights for the Poor: Effects of Land Titling" (paper, Universidad Torcuato Di Tella, 2005).

Garnett, Nicole Stelle. *The Road from Welfare to Work: Informal Transportation and the Urban Poor*, 173 Harv. J. on Legis. 173 (2001).

Garnett, Nicole Stelle. *Save the Cities, Stop the Suburbs?*, 116 Yale L.J. 598 (2006).

Garnett, Nicole Stelle. *Property In-Laws*, 156 U. Pa. L. Rev. Pennumbra 279 (2007).

Garreau, Joel. Edge City: Life on the New Frontier (1988).

Getches, David H., Charles F. Wilkinson, and Robert A. Williams, Jr. Federal Indian Law (5th ed., 2005).

Gilmore, Grant. *The Secured Transactions Article of the Commercial Code*, 16 Law & Contemp. Probs. 27 (1951).

Gilmore, Grant. *The Assignee of Contract Rights and his Precarious Security*, 74 Yale L.J. 217 (1964).

Gilmore, Grant. SECURITY INTERESTS IN PERSONAL PROPERTY (1965).

Gilmore, Grant. *Article 9: What it Does for the Past*, 26 La. L. Rev. 285 (1966).

Giuliani Says a New Plan Will Not Please Vendors. Editorial, N.Y. Times, June 19, 1998, at B8.

Glaeser, Edward L. and Joshua D. Gottlieb. *Urban Resurgence and the Consumer City*, 43 Urb. Stud. 1275 (2006).

Goldstein, Brandt J. *Panhandlers at Yale: A Case Study in the Limits of Law*, 27 Ind. L. Rev. 295 (1993).

Gómez-Ibáñez, José A. and John R. Meyer. GOING PRIVATE: THE INTERNATIONAL EXPERIENCE WITH TRANSPORT PRIVATIZATION (1993).

Gorton, Gary. "The Panic of 2007" (Nat'l Bureau of Econ. Research, Working Paper No. 14358, 2008).

Gould, L. Scott. *The Consent Paradigm: Tribal Sovereignty at the Millennium*, 96 Colum. L. Rev. 809 (1996).

Grava, Sigurd. *We're Not Yellow, We Go Anywhere*, 42 Transp. Q. 349 (1988).

Gravois, John. *The De Soto Delusion*, Slate, Jan. 25, 2005.

Green, Leah. *The Erie Canal and the American Imagination: The Erie Canal's Effects on American Legal Development, 1817-1869*, 56 Ala. L. Rev. 1167 (2005).

Grey, Thomas C. THE DISINTEGRATION OF PROPERTY, IN MODERN UNDERSTANDINGS OF LIBERTY AND PROPERTY (Richard Epstein, ed., 2000).

Guzman, Katheleen R. *Give or Take an Acre: Property Norms and the Indian Land Consolidation Act*, 85 Iowa L. Rev. 595 (2000).

Haber, Stephen. *Introduction: Economic Growth and Latin American Economic Historiography*, to HOW LATIN AMERICA FELL BEHIND (Stephen Haber, ed., 1999).

Haddock, David D. and Robert J. Miller. *Can a Sovereign Protect Investors from Itself? Tribal Institutions to Spur Reservation Investment*, 8 J. Small & Emerging Bus. L. 173 (2004).

Hagman, Donald G. and Dean J. Misczynski, eds WINDFALLS FOR WIPEOUTS (1978).

Hall, Ford P. *Certificates of Convenience and Necessity*, 28 Mich. L. Rev. 107 (1929).

Hand, John Oliver, Catherine Metzger, and Ron Spronk. PRAYERS AND PORTRAITS: UNFOLDING THE NETHERLANDISH DIPTYCH (2006).

Hansmann, Henry and Reiner Kraakman. *Property, Contract and Verification: The Numerus Clausus Problem and the Divisibility of Rights*, 31 J. Legal Stud. 373 (2002).

Harris, Hamil R. and Victoria Benning. *D.C. Cabbies to Suspend Service Today: 12-Hour Protest Aimed at New Regulations*, Washington Post, April 22, 1997, at B1.

Harris, J.W. PROPERTY AND JUSTICE (1996).

Harrison, Lawrence E. *Introduction: Why Culture Matters*, to CULTURE MATTERS: HOW VALUES SHAPE HUMAN PROGRESS (Lawrence E. Harrison and Samuel P. Huntington, eds, 2000a).

Harrison, Lawrence E. *Promoting Progressive Cultural Change*, in CULTURE MATTERS: HOW VALUES SHAPE HUMAN PROGRESS (Lawrence E. Harrison and Samuel P. Huntington, eds, 2000b).

Harrod, R.F. *Scope and Method of Economics*, 48 Econ. J. 389 (1938).

Heller, Michael A. *Property Rights: A View from the Trenches*, 19 Yale J. Int'l. L. 203 (1994).

Heller, Michael A. *The Tragedy of the Anticommons: Property in the Transition from Marx to Markets*, 111 Harv. L. Rev. 621 (1998).

Heller, Michael A. *The Boundaries of Private Property*, 108 Yale L.J. 1163 (1999).

Heller, Michael A. *Three Faces of Private Property*, 79 Or. L. Rev. 417 (2000).

Heller, Michael A. THE GRIDLOCK ECONOMY: HOW TOO MUCH OWNERSHIP WRECKS MARKETS, STOPS INNOVATION, AND COSTS LIVES (2008).

Heller, Michael A. and Rebecca S. Eisenberg. *Can Patents Deter Innovation? The Anticommons in Biomedical Research*, 280 Sci. 698 (1998).

Hernandez, Raymond. *City's Right to Bar Vendors from Streets is Upheld*, N.Y. Times, June 18, 1997, at B1.

Hicks, J.R. *The Foundations of Welfare Economics*, 49 Econ. J. 696 (1939).

Hicks, Jonathan P. *Many 125th Street Vendors Say They Will Resist Move*, N.Y. Times, Oct. 17, 1994a, at B3.

Hicks, Jonathan P. *Vendors Ouster and Boycott Divide Harlem*, N.Y. Times, Oct. 23, 1994b, at A1.

Horwitz, Morton J. THE TRANSFORMATION OF AMERICAN LAW (1977).

Hotelling, Harold. *The General Welfare in Relation to Problems of Taxation and of Railway and Utility Rates*, 6 Econometrica 242 (1938).

Hunter, Louis. A HISTORY OF INDUSTRIAL POWER IN THE UNITED STATES, 1780–1930, VOL. I: WATER POWER IN THE CENTURY OF THE STEAM ENGINE (1979).

Hurst, Willard. LAW AND THE CONDITIONS OF FREEDOM IN THE NINETEENTH-CENTURY UNITED STATES (1956).

Husock, Howard. *Enterprising Van Drivers Collide with Regulation*, City J., Winter 1996, at 60.

Illy, Hans. *Regulation and Evasion: Street Vendors in Manila*, 19 Policy Sciences 61 (2005).

Institute for Government Administration. THE PROBLEM OF INDIAN ADMINISTRATION (Lewis Meriam et al., 1928).

Jacobs, Jane. CITIES AND THE WEALTH OF NATIONS: PRINCIPLES OF ECONOMIC LIFE (1984).

Jewel, Anthony. *Free Enterprise: Indianapolis Mayor Calls on Private Sector to Get the Job Done*, Nat'l Cities Weekly, Jan. 22, 1996, at 8.

Jimu, I.M. *An Exploration of Street Vending's Contribution Towards Botswana's Vision of Prosperity for All by 2016*, 18 Botswana J. of African Stud. 19 (2004).

Jones, William K. *Origins of the Certificate of Public Convenience and Necessity: Developments in the State, 1876–1920*, 79 Colum. L. Rev. 426 (1979).

Kades, Eric. *Windfalls*, 108 Yale L.J. 1489 (1999).

Kades, Eric. *History and Interpretation of the Great Case of* Johnson v. M'Intosh, 19 Law & Hist. Rev. 67 (2001).

Kaldor, Nicholas. *Welfare Propositions of Economics and Inter-Personal Comparisons of Utility*, 49 Econ. J. 549 (1939).

Kaplow, Louis and Steven Shavell. *Why the Legal System is Less Efficient than Income Tax in Redistributing Income*, 23 J. Legal. Stud. 667 (1994).

Katz, Larissa. "Governing Through Owners" (unpublished manuscript, on file with author).

Katz, Larissa. *Exclusion and Exclusivity in Property Law*, 58 U. Toronto L.J. 275 (2008).

Katz, Larissa. "A Jurisdictional Principle of Abuse of Right" (research paper, 2009).

Kelley, Thomas. *Unintended Consequences of Legal Westernization in Niger: Harming Contemporary Slaves by Reconceptualizing Property*, 56 Am J. Comp. L. 999 (2008).

Kettles, Gregg W. *Regulating Vending in the Sidewalk Commons*, 77 Temple L. Rev. 1 (2004).

Kettles, Gregg W. *Formal Versus Informal Allocation of Land in a Commons: The Case of the MacArthur Park Sidewalk Vendors*, 16 S. Cal. Interdisc. L.J. 49 (2006).

King, Winter. *Illegal Settlements and the Impact of Titling Programs*, 44 Harv. Int'l L.J. 433 (2003).

Kozolchyk, Boris. *Secured Lending and its Poverty Reduction Effect*, 42 Tex. Int'l L.J. 727 (2007).

Krakoff, Sarah. City of Sherrill v. Oneida Indian Nation of New York*: A Regretful Postscript to the Taxation Chapter in Cohen's Handbook of Federal Indian Law*, 41 Tulsa L. Rev. 5 (2005).

Krinsman, Allan N. *Subprime Mortgage Meltdown: How Did it Happen and How Will it End?*, 13 J. Structured Fin., Summer 2007, at 13.

Krueckeberg, Donald E. *The Lessons of John Locke or Hernando de Soto: What If Your Dreams Come True?*, 15 Hous. Policy Debate 1 (2004).

Krugman Paul. *The Great Wealth Transfer*, Rolling Stone, Nov. 30, 2006.

La Forest, Anne Warner. ANGER & HONSBERGER LAW OF REAL PROPERTY (3rd ed., 2006).

Laitos, Jan. *The Problem with Wilderness*, 32 Harv. Envtl. L. Rev. 503 (2008).

Landes, David. *Culture Makes Almost All the Difference*, in CULTURE MATTERS: HOW VALUES SHAPE HUMAN PROGRESS (Lawrence E. Harrison and Samuel P. Huntington, eds, 2000).

Lanjouw, Jean O. and Philip I. Levy. *Untitled: A Study of Formal and Informal Property Rights in Urban Ecuador*, 112 Econ. J. 986 (2002).

Lanjouw, Jean O. and Philip I. Levy. *A Difficult Question in Deed: A Cost-Benefit Framework for Titling Programs*, 45 Wm. & Mary L. Rev. 889 (2004).

Larson, Jane E. *Free Markets Deep in the Heart of Texas*, 84 Geo. L.J. 179 (1995).

Laurence, Robert. *Learning to Live with the Plenary Power of Congress over the Indian Nations: An Essay in Reaction to Professor Williams' Algebra*, 30 Ariz. L. Rev. 413 (1988a).

Laurence, Robert. *On Eurocentric Myopia, the Designated Hitter Rule and "The Actual State of Things,"* 30 Ariz. L. Rev. 459 (1988b).

Leeds, Stacy L. *The Burning of Blackacre: A Step Toward Reclaiming Tribal Property Law*, 10 Kan. J.L. & Pub. Pol'y 491 (2000).

Leigh, Karen. *In D.C. Street-Food Wars, Hot Dogs Face Competition from Hummus*, Bloomberg News, June 11, 2008.

Lemann, Nicholas. The Promised Land: The Great Black Migration and How It Changed America (1991).

Letter to Jean Baptiste Le Roy, Nov. 13, 1789, in Oxford Dictionary of Quotations 293 (Angela Partington, ed., rev. 4th ed., 1996).

Libecap, Gary D. Contracting for Property Rights (1989).

Lindsay, Stace. Culture, Mental Models, and National Prosperity, in Culture Matters: How Values Shape Human Progress (Lawrence E. Harrison and Samuel P. Huntington, eds, 2000).

Little, I.M.D. A Critique of Welfare Economics (1950).

Llosa, Mario Vargas. *Foreword* to Hernando de Soto, The Other Path: The Invisible Revolution in the Third World (Alfred J. McAdam, trans., 1989).

Main, Carla T. *Bulldozed: "Kelo," Eminent Domain, and the American Lust for Land* (2007).

Malloy, Robin Paul. Law in a Market Context: An Introduction to Market Concepts in Legal Reasoning (2004).

Manaster, Kenneth A. *The Problem of Urban Squatters in Developing Countries: Peru*, 1968 Wis. L. Rev. 23.

Manders, Jonathan. *Sequencing Property Rights in the Context of Development*, 37 Cornell Int'l L.J. 177 (2004).

Maragia, Bosire. *The Indigenous Sustainability Paradox and the Quest for Sustainability in Post-Colonial Societies: Is Indigenous Knowledge All That Is Needed?*, 18 Geo. Int'l Envtl L. Rev. 197 (2006).

Marcuse, Peter. Comment on *The Lessons of John Locke or Hernando de Soto: What If Your Dreams Come True?*, 15 Hous. Policy Debate 39 (2004).

Martin, Douglas. *City Begins Enforcement of Food Cart Restrictions*, N.Y. Times, Apr. 21, 1994, at B3.

Mayer, Harold M. and Richard C. Wade. Chicago: Growth of a Metropolis (1969).

McDonnell, Julian. *Stripping Payment Streams from Chattel Paper* (Lexis Nexis Commentaries, 2007).

McGray, Douglas. *Check Cashers, Redeemed*, N.Y. Times Magazine, Nov. 9, 2008.

McKnight, Claire E. *Transportation with Women in Mind*, J. Urb. Tech. 1 (Fall 1994).

McNatt, Robert. *Council Peddles Plans to Limit Vendors*, Crain's New York Business, Feb. 1, 1993, at 12.

Megarry, Rt. Hon. Sir Robert and Sir William Wade. THE LAW OF REAL PROPERTY (Charles Harpum et al., eds, 7th ed., 2008).

Merrill, Thomas W. *Explaining Market Mechanisms*, 2000 U. Ill. L. Rev. 275.

Merrill, Thomas W. and Henry E. Smith. *Optimal Standardization in the Law of Property: The Numerus Clausus Principle*, 110 Yale L.J. 1 (2000).

Merrill, Thomas and Henry Smith. *What Happened to Property in Law and Economics*, 111 Yale L.J. 357 (2001).

Michelman, Frank I. *Ethics, Economics, and the Law of Property*, in NOMOS XXIV: ETHICS, ECONOMICS, AND THE LAW (J. Roland Pennock and John W. Chapman, eds, 1982).

Michelman, Frank. "Remarks at Property Panel, American Association of Law Schools, Is the Tragedy of the Common Inevitable?" (unpublished manuscript, Jan. 1985).

Miller, Geoffrey P. Comment, *Economic Efficiency and the Lockean Proviso*, 10 Harv. J.L. & Pub. Pol'y 401 (1987).

Miller, Matthew. *The Poor Man's Capitalist*, N.Y. Times, July 1, 2001.

Miller, Robert J. *Economic Development in Indian Country: Will Capitalism or Socialism Succeed?*, 80 Or. L. Rev. 757 (2001).

Mishan, E.J. WELFARE ECONOMICS: AN ASSESSMENT (1969).

Mitchell, Thomas W. *From Reconstruction to Deconstruction: Undermining Black Landownership, Political Independence, and Community Through Partition Sales of Tenancies in Common*, 95 Nw. U.L. Rev. 505 (2001).

Mitullah, Winnie V. and Kivutha Kibwana. THE TALE OF TWO CITIES: POLICY, LAW AND ILLEGAL SETTLEMENTS IN KENYA, IN ILLEGAL CITIES: LAW AND URBAN CHANGE IN DEVELOPING COUNTRIES (Edesio Fernandes and Ann Varley, eds, 1998).

Moringiello, Juliet M. *False Categories in Commercial Law: The (Ir)relevance of (In)tangibility*, 35 Fla. St. U. L. Rev. 119 (2007).

Mumford, Lewis. *The Fourth Migration*, 7 Survey Graphic 130 (May 1925).

Munzer, Stephen R. *The Commons and the Anticommons in the Law and Theory of Property*, in THE BLACKWELL GUIDE TO THE PHILOSOPHY OF LAW AND LEGAL THEORY (Martin P. Golding and William A. Edmundson, eds, 2005).

New Taxi Rules Too Taxing?. Editorial, Washington Post, April 24, 1997, at A24.

Newton, Nell Jessup. *Compensation, Reparations, & Restitution: Indian Property Claims in the United States*, 28 Ga. L. Rev. 453 (1994).

Ngugi, Joel M. "Re-Examining the Role of Private Property" in *Market Democracies: Problematic Ideological Issues Raised By Land Registration*, 25 Mich. J. Int'l L. 467 (2004).

Nozick, Robert. ANARCHY, STATE, AND UTOPIA (1974).

Obama Calls for New Regulations, BOSTON GLOBE, Feb. 26, 2009.

Ostrom, Elinor. GOVERNING THE COMMONS: THE EVOLUTION OF INSTITUTIONS FOR COLLECTIVE ACTION (1990; rev. 2007).

Otis, D.S. THE DAWES ACT AND THE ALLOTMENT OF INDIAN LANDS (Francis Paul Prucha, ed., photo. reprint 1973) (1898).

Painter, Charles C. THE INDIAN AND HIS PROPERTY, IN AMERICANIZING THE AMERICAN INDIANS: WRITINGS BY THE "FRIENDS OF THE INDIAN" 1880–1900 (Francis Paul Prucha, ed., 1973).

Paley, William. THE PRINCIPLES OF MORAL AND POLITICAL PHILOSOPHY (1821).

Pareto, Vilfredo. MANUAL OF POLITICAL ECONOMY (Ann S. Schwier, trans., A.M. Kelley 1971) (1906).

Payne, Geoffrey, et al. "Social and Economic Impacts of Land Titling Programmes in Urban and Peri-Urban Areas: International Experience and Case Studies of Senegal and South Africa" (report, March 2008).

Peñalver, Eduardo M. *Land Virtues*, 94 Cornell L. Rev. 821 (2009).

Peñalver, Eduardo M. and Sonia Katyal. *Property Outlaws*, 155 U. Pa. L. Rev. 1095 (2007).

Penn, William. THE EXCELLENT PRIVILEGE OF LIBERTY AND PROPERTY (1687).

Penner, J.E. *The "Bundle of Rights" Picture of Property*, 43 UCLA L. Rev. 711 (1996).

Penner, J.E. THE IDEA OF PROPERTY IN LAW (1997).

Pigou, A.C. WEALTH AND WELFARE (1912).

Pigou, A.C. THE ECONOMICS OF WELFARE (4th ed., 1932).

Pipes, Richard. PROPERTY AND FREEDOM (1999).

Pisani, Donald J. *The Squatter and Natural Law in Nineteenth-Century America*, 81 Agric. Hist. 443 (2007).

Plank, Thomas E. *Assignment of Receivables Under Article 9: Structural Incoherence and Wasteful Filing*, 68 Ohio St. L.J. 231 (2007).

Platteau, Jean-Philippe. INSTITUTIONS, SOCIAL NORMS, AND ECONOMIC DEVELOPMENT (2000).

Pommersheim, Frank. *The Reservation as Place: A South Dakota Essay*, 34 S.D. L. Rev. 246 (1989).

Porter, Michael E. *Attitudes, Values, Beliefs, and the Microeconomics of Prosperity*, in CULTURE MATTERS: HOW VALUES SHAPE HUMAN PROGRESS (Lawrence E. Harrison and Samuel P. Huntington, eds, 2000).

Posner, Richard A. ECONOMIC ANALYSIS OF LAW (5th ed., 1998).

Posner, Richard A. ECONOMIC ANALYSIS OF LAW (7th ed., 2007).

Priest, Claire. *Creating an American Property Law: Alienability and its Limitations in American History*, 120 Harv. L. Rev. 385 (2006).

Priest, George L. *The Ambiguous Moral Foundations of the Underground Economy*, 103 Yale L.J. 2259 (1994).

Prucha, Francis Paul. AMERICAN INDIAN POLICY IN CRISIS: CHRISTIAN REFORMERS AND THE INDIAN (1976).

Purdy, Jedediah. *A Freedom-Promoting Approach to Property: A Renewed Tradition for New Debates*, 72 U. Chi. L. Rev. 1237 (2005).

Purdy, Jedediah. *The American Transformation of Waste Doctrine: A Pluralist Interpretation*, 91 Cornell L. Rev. 653 (2006).

Putnam, Robert. MAKING DEMOCRACY WORK: CIVIC TRADITIONS IN MODERN ITALY (1993).

Reich, Robert B. THE WORK OF NATIONS: PREPARING OURSELVES FOR 21ST CENTURY CAPITALISM (1991).

Renuart, Elizabeth. *Stop Predatory Lending*, National Consumer Law Center (2002).

Riley, Angela R. *Good (Native) Governance*, 107 Colum. L. Rev. 1049 (2007).

Ripstein, Arthur. *Beyond the Harm Principle*, 34 Phil. & Pub. Aff. 215 (2006).

Robert McNatt. *Harlem On My Mind: Black America's Cultural Capital Is Thriving Again*, Business Week, Sept. 20, 2004, at 109.

Rogers, James Steven. *Policy Perspectives on Revised Article 8*, 43 UCLA. L. Rev. 1431 (1996).

Roe, Mark J. *Backlash*, 98 Colum. L. Rev. 217 (1998).

Rose, Carol M. *Possession as the Origin of Property*, 52 U. Chi. L. Rev. 73 (1985).

Rose, Carol M. *The Comedy of the Commons: Commerce, Custom and Inherently Public Property*, 53 U. Chi. L. Rev. 711 (1986).

Rose, Carol M. *"Enough and as Good" of What?* 81 Nw. U. L. Rev. 417 (1987).

Rose, Carol M. PROPERTY AND PERSUASION: ESSAYS ON THE HISTORY, THEORY, AND RHETORIC OF OWNERSHIP (1994).

Rose, Carol M. PROPERTY RIGHTS AND RESPONSIBILITIES, IN THINKING ECOLOGICALLY: THE NEXT GENERATION OF ENVIRONMENTAL POLICY (1997).

Rose, Carol M. *The Several Futures of Property: Of Cyberspace and Folk Tales, Emission Trades and Ecosystems*, 83 Minn. L. Rev. 129 (1998).

Rose, Carol M. *What Government Can Do for Property (and Vice Versa)*, in THE FUNDAMENTAL INTERRELATIONSHIPS BETWEEN GOVERNMENT AND PROPERTY (Nicholas Mercuro and Warren J. Samuels, eds, 1999).

Rose, Carol M. *Introduction: Property and Language, or the Ghost of the Fifth Panel*, 18 Yale J.L. & Human 1, 3 (2006).

Rose, Carol M. *Big Roads, Big Rights: Varieties of Public Infrastructure and Their Impact on Environmental Resources*, 50 Ariz. L. Rev. 409 (2008).

Rose, Carol M. *The Story of* Shelley v. Kraemer, in PROPERTY STORIES (2nd ed., 2009).

Rosser, Ezra. *Immigrant Remittances*, 41 Conn. L. Rev. 1 (2008a).

Rosser, Ezra. *Protecting Non-Indians From Harm? The Property Consequences of Indians*, 87 Ore. L. Rev. 175 (2008b).

Rothchild, John A. *The Incredible Shrinking First-Sale Rule: Are Software Resale Limits Lawful?* 57 Rutgers L. Rev. 1 (2004).

Royster, Judith V. *The Legacy of Allotment*, 27 Ariz. St. L.J. 1, 10 (1995).

Royster, Judith V. *Of Surplus Lands and Landfills: The Case of the Yankton Sioux*, 43 S.D. L. Rev. 283 (1998).

Royster, Judith V. *Foreword: Look Back in Anger*, 38 Tulsa L. Rev. 1 (2002).

Ruger, Theodore W. *A Question Which Convulses the Nation: The Early Republic's Greatest Debate About the Judicial Review Power*, 117 Harv. L. Rev. 826 (2004).

Sachs, Jeffrey. NOTES ON A NEW SOCIOLOGY OF ECONOMIC DEVELOPMENT, IN CULTURE MATTERS: HOW VALUES SHAPE HUMAN PROGRESS (Lawrence E. Harrison and Samuel P. Huntington, eds, 2000).

Sam Bass Warner. STREETCAR SUBURBS: THE PROCESS OF GROWTH IN BOSTON, 1870–1900 (2nd ed., 1978).

Samuelson, Paul A. ECONOMICS (10th ed., 1976).

Scannell, Nancy. *Courtlands Neighbors Complete Package Deal: Arlington Homeowner Consortium Holds Out for High Price*, The Washington Post, Dec. 20, 1986, at A1.

Schlatter, Richard. PRIVATE PROPERTY: THE HISTORY OF AN IDEA (1951).

Schultz, Theodore W. INVESTING IN PEOPLE: THE ECONOMICS OF POPULATION QUALITY (1981).

Schwantes, Carlos A. *The West Adapts to the Automobile: Technology, Unemployment, and the Jitney Phenomenon of 1914–1971*, 16 W. Hist. Q. 307 (1985).

Schwarcz, Steven L. *Systemic Risk*, 97 Geo. L.J. 193 (2008).

Schwarcz, Steven L. *Automatic Perfection of Sales of Payment Intangibles: A Trap for the Unwary*, 68 Ohio St. L.J. 273 (2007).

Sen, Amartya K. COLLECTIVE CHOICE AND SOCIAL WELFARE (1970).

Shagen, Paul W. Comment, *Indian Country: The Dependent Indian Community Concept and Tribal/Tribal Member Immunity from State Taxation*, 27 N.M. L. Rev. 421 (1997).

Shleifer, Andrei. *Establishing Property Rights*, in PROCEEDINGS OF THE WORLD BANK ANNUAL CONFERENCE ON DEVELOPMENT ECONOMICS (1994).

Shoemaker, Jessica A. *Like Snow in the Spring Time: Allotment, Fractionation, and the Indian Land Tenure Problem*, 2003 Wis. L. Rev. 729.

Shupack, Paul M. *Making Revised Article 9 Safe for Securitizations: A Brief History*, 73 Am. Bankr. L.J. 167 (1999).

Singer, Joseph William. ENTITLEMENT: THE PARADOXES OF PROPERTY (2000).

Singer, Joseph William. *Lone Wolf, or How to Take Property by Calling It a "Mere Change in the Form of Investment,"* 38 Tulsa L. Rev. 37 (2002a).

Singer, Joseph William. PROPERTY (3rd ed., 2002b).

Singer, Joseph William. *Double Bind: Indian Nations v. The Supreme Court*, 119 Harv. L. Rev. F. 1 (2005a).

Singer, Joseph William, INTRODUCTION TO PROPERTY (2nd ed., 2005b).

Smith, Henry E. *Semicommon Property Rights and Scattering in the Open Fields*, 29 J. Legal Stud. 131 (2000).

Smith, Henry. *Exclusion versus Governance: Two Strategies for Delineating Property Rights*, 31 J. Legal Stud. 453 (2002).

Smith, Henry E. *The Language of Property: Form, Context, and Audience*, 55 Stan. L. Rev. 1105 (2003).

Smith, Henry E. *Property and Property Rules*, 79 NYU L. Rev. 1719 (2004).

Soderlund, Jean R., ed. WILLIAM PENN AND THE FOUNDING OF PENNSYLVANIA, 1680–1684 (1983).

Solimano, Andrés. "The International Mobility of Talent: Determinants and Development Impact," lecture, Wider Angle (2005).

Spiegel, Henry William. THE GROWTH OF ECONOMIC THOUGHT (1983).

Steinbeck, John. THE GRAPES OF WRATH (1939).

Stewart, Richard B. *Regulation in a Liberal State: The Role of Non-Commodity Values*, 92 Yale L.J. 1537 (1983).

Stoebuck, William B. and Dale A. Whitman. THE LAW OF PROPERTY (3rd ed., 2000).

Street Peddlers in New York. Editorial, N.Y. Times, May 28, 1994, §1, at 18.

Takyi, Isaac K. *An Evaluation of Jitney Systems in Developing Countries*, 44 Transp. Q. 163 (1990).

Taylor, Alan. LIBERTY MEN AND GREAT PROPRIETORS (1990).

Tierney, John. *A Tale of Two Fisheries*, N.Y. Times Magazine, Aug. 27, 2000, § 6 (Magazine), at 38.

Transit Union Roadblock. Editorial, N.Y. Post, July 27, 1997.

Trebilcock, Michael and Paul-Erik Veel. *Property Rights and Development: The Contingent Case for Formalization*, 30 U. Pa. J. Int'l L. 397 (2008).

Trosper, Ronald. *Who is Subsidizing Whom?*, in AMERICAN INDIAN POLICY: SELF-GOVERNANCE AND ECONOMIC DEVELOPMENT (Lyman H. Legters and Fremont J. Lyden, eds, 1994).

Turner, Frederick Jackson. THE FRONTIER IN AMERICAN HISTORY (1920).

Tye, William B. *The Economics of Public Convenience and Necessity for Regulated Industries*, 60 Transp. Pract. J. 143 (1992).

U.S. Census Bureau. Residential Finance Survey, 2001.

Van and Car Service Issues Affecting NYCTA Surface Operations (N.Y. City Metropolitan Transportation Authority, 1992).

Venkatesh, Sudhir Alladi. OFF THE BOOKS: THE UNDERGROUND ECONOMY OF THE URBAN POOR (2006).

Villazor, Rose Cuison. *Blood Quantum Land Laws and the Race Versus Political Identity Dilemma*, 96 Calif. L. Rev. 801 (2008).

Waldron, Jeremy. *The Rule of Law in Contemporary Liberal Theory*, 2 Ratio Juris 79 (1989).

Walter, E.V. PLACEWAYS: A THEORY OF THE HUMAN ENVIRONMENT (1988).

Warner, Sam Bass. STREETCAR SUBURBS: THE PROCESS OF GROWTH IN BOSTON, 1870–1900 (2nd ed., 1978).

Washburn, Wilcomb E. THE ASSAULT ON INDIAN TRIBALISM: THE GENERAL ALLOTMENT LAW (DAWES ACT) OF 1887 (1975).

Watson, Donald Stevenson. PRICE THEORY AND ITS USES (1963).

Watts, Robert A. *After Delays and Deals, Subdivision Is Sold*, The Washington Post, Jan. 15, 1987, at Va.-1.

Weber, Max. THE PROTESTANT ETHIC AND THE SPIRIT OF CAPITALISM (1904).

Webster, Daniel. A DISCOURSE DELIVERED AT PLYMOUTH, DECEMBER 22, 1820, IN COMMEMORATION OF THE FIRST SETTLEMENT OF NEW ENGLAND (3rd ed., 1825).

White, G. Edward. THE MARSHALL COURT AND CULTURAL CHANGE (1988).

Wilkinson, Charles F. AMERICAN INDIANS, TIME, AND THE LAW: NATIVE SOCIETIES IN A MODERN CONSTITUTIONAL DEMOCRACY (1987).

Monte Williams. *Neighborhood Report: Lower Manhattan; Crackdown on Ave. C Peddlers*, N.Y. Times, March 12, 1995.

Williams, Robert A., Jr. *The Algebra of Federal Indian Law: The Hard Trail of Decolonizing and Americanizing the White Man's Indian Jurisprudence*, 1986 Wis. L. Rev. 219.

Williams, Robert A., Jr. *Learning Not to Live with Eurocentric Myopia: A Reply to Professor Laurence's Learning to Live with the Plenary Power of Congress over the Indian Nations*, 30 Ariz. L. Rev. 439 (1988).

Williams, Robert A., Jr. THE AMERICAN INDIAN IN WESTERN LEGAL THOUGHT: THE DISCOURSES OF CONQUEST (1990).

Williams, Robert A., Jr. LIKE A LOADED WEAPON: THE REHNQUIST COURT, INDIAN RIGHTS, AND THE LEGAL HISTORY OF RACISM IN AMERICA (2005).

Williams, Monte. *Neighborhood Report: Lower Manhattan; Crackdown on Ave. C Peddlers*, N.Y. Times, March 12, 1995, §16, at 6.

Williams, Stephen F. LIBERAL REFORM IN AN ILLIBERAL REGIME: THE CREATION OF PRIVATE PROPERTY IN RUSSIA (2006).

Williamson, Oliver E. *The New Institutional Economics: Taking Stock, Looking Ahead*, 38 J. of Econ. Lit. 595 (2000).

Wilson, Charles. MERCANTILISM (1963).

Wilson, Christine L. *Urban Homesteading: A Compromise Between Squatters and the Law*, 35 N.Y.L. Sch. L. Rev. 709 (1990).

Winston, Elizabeth I. *Why Sell What You Can License: Contracting Around Statutory Protection of Intellectual Property*, 14 Geo. Mason L. Rev. 93 (2006).

Wolff, Edward N. TOP HEAVY: THE INCREASING INEQUALITY OF WEALTH IN AMERICA AND WHAT CAN BE DONE ABOUT IT (expanded ed., 2002).

Wood, Gordon S. *Inventing American Capitalism*, N.Y. Rev. Books (June 9, 1994).

Woodruff, Christopher. *Review of de Soto's* The Mystery of Capital, 39 J. Econ. Lit. 1215 (2001).

World Bank. World Development Report 2006: "Equity and Development" (2005).

World Economic Forum. "Global Competitiveness Report 2008–2009."

Wray, L. Randall. "Lessons from the Subprime Meltdown" (The Levy Econ. Inst. of Bard College, Working Paper No. 522, 2007).

Wylie, Jeanie. POLETOWN: COMMUNITY BETRAYED (1989).

Wyman, Katrina Miriam. *From Fur to Fish: Reconsidering the Evolution of Private Property*, 80 N.Y.U. L. Rev. 117 (2005).

Zachary, G. Pascale. *Amsterdam Finds Booming Business in Anti-Squatters*, The Globe and Mail (Canada), March 26, 1999, at A4.

Ziff, Bruce H. PRINCIPLES OF PROPERTY LAW (4th ed., 2006).

Legislative Acts and Statutes

Conn. Gen. Stat. Ann. §§8-124–8-139, 48-1–48-25 (West 2006).
Fair Housing Act, 42 U.S.C. §3604(d) (1988).
N.Y., N.Y., Admin. Code §19-504.2(e)(3) (1993).
U.S. Constitution, amendment V.
U.S. Constitution, preamble.
Uniform Commerical Code §9.
Uniform Fraudulent Transfer Act §4(b).
Uniform Motor Vehicle Certificate of Title and Anti-Theft Act §21.
Uniform Motor Vehicle Certificate of Title and Anti-Theft Act §9.

Table of Cases

A&M Records, Inc., v. Napster, Inc.
Alaska v. Native Village of Venetie Tribal Government
Benedict v. Ratner
Berman v. Parker
Charles River Bridge v. Warren Bridge
City of Sherrill v. Oneida Indian Nation of New York
Coke & Reardon v. Ikard
County of Wayne v. Hathcock
Fallbrook Irrigation Dist. v. Bradley
Hagan v. Utah
Harrison v. Carswell
Hawaii Housing Auth. v. Midkiff
Hodel v. Irving
In re Commercial Money Center
In re Foreclosure Cases
J.A. Pye (Oxford) Ltd. v. United Kingdom
Jacque v. Steenburg Homes, Inc.
Johnson v. M'Intosh
Kelo v. City of New London
Kimball Laundry Co. v. United States
London County Council v. Allen et al.
N.J. Div. of Taxation v. United Trust Bank
National Peregrine, Inc. v. Capitol Federal Savings & Loan Ass'n (In re Peregrine Entertainment, Ltd.)
NetBank, FSB v. Kipperman (In re Commercial Money Center)
Network Solutions, Inc. v. Umbro Int'l, Inc.
Penarth Dock Engineering Co. v. Pounds
Poletown Neighborhood Council v. City of Detroit
PruneYard Shopping Center v. Robins

Qwik Payday Inc. v. Stork
Ruckleshaus v. Monsanto Co.
Schneider v. District of Columbia
Strickley v. Highland Boy Gold Mining Co.
Tee-Hit-Ton Indians v. United States
United States v. 50 Acres of Land
United States v. Lara
United States v. Miller
United States v. Navajo Nation
United States v. Sandoval
United States v. Sioux Nation of Indians

Index